HUMAN SECURITY REPORT 2012

SEXUAL VIOLENCE, EDUCATION, AND WAR:
BEYOND THE MAINSTREAM NARRATIVE

PUBLISHED FOR THE

HUMAN SECURITY REPORT PROJECT

SIMON FRASER UNIVERSITY, CANADA

VANCOUVER • HUMAN SECURITY RESEARCH GROUP
HUMAN SECURITY PRESS
2012

Human Security Press

Copyright © 2012 by Human Security Research Group.

Human Security Research Group
School for International Studies
Simon Fraser University
Suite 7200
515 West Hastings Street
Vancouver BC V6B 5K3
Canada
www.hsrgroup.org

ISSN 1557-914X

ISBN 978-0-9917111-0-9

Cover design: Susan Turner, Zuke Creative
Cover photo: Brent Stirton/IRIN news report: "The Shame of War," Sierra Leone

In-House Team for the Preparation of the *Human Security Report 2012*

Andrew Mack, director and editor-in-chief

Sebastian Merz, associate director

Mai Bui, research officer

Tara Cooper, researcher

Gwen Echlin, senior research assistant

John Laidlaw Gray, research assistant, e-resources

Kala Harris, senior program manager

Lindsey Ridgway, research assistant, e-resources

Former Members of the In-House Team: Jon Baskin, research assistant, e-resources; Tracey Carmichael, senior manager, e-resources; Emina Dervisevic, research officer, e-resources; Wendy Fehr, development director; Nancy Graham, program manager; Shawna Korosi, human resources manager; Zoe Nielsen, executive director; Marko Pajalic, research officer, e-resources.

Copy-editing: Kirsten Craven, Craven Editorial
Proofreading: Ruth Wilson, West Coast Editorial Associates
Design and Layout: Susan Turner, Zuke Creative

ACKNOWLEDGEMENTS

This publication was made possible by the generous support given by the Department for International Development (United Kingdom); the Norwegian Agency for Development Cooperation; the Norwegian Royal Ministry of Foreign Affairs; the Swedish International Development Cooperation Agency; the Swiss Federal Department of Foreign Affairs; and the UBS Optimus Foundation.

We would also like to thank Erin Baines, Susan Bartles, Sheena Bell, Michael Bimmler, Ania Chaluda, Geetanjali (Joey) Chopra, Dara Cohen, Josip Dasovic, Kendra Dupuy, Kailey Fuller-Jackson, Rebecca Furst-Nichols, Joshua Goldstein, Claudia García-Moreno, Amelia Hoover Green, Valerie Hudson, Friedrich Huebler, Lisa Inks, Karen Jacobsen, Lynn Lawry, Teresa Lawson, Dyan Mazurana, Håvard Mokleiv Nygård, Christina C. Pallitto, Amber Peterman, Wynne Russell, Mila Shah, Martha Snodgrass, Beth Stewart, Aisling Swaine, Shana Swiss, and Henrik Urdal for their input and valuable comments. Responsibility for the views expressed in this report remains solely that of the HSRP, however.

CONTENTS

List of Boxes

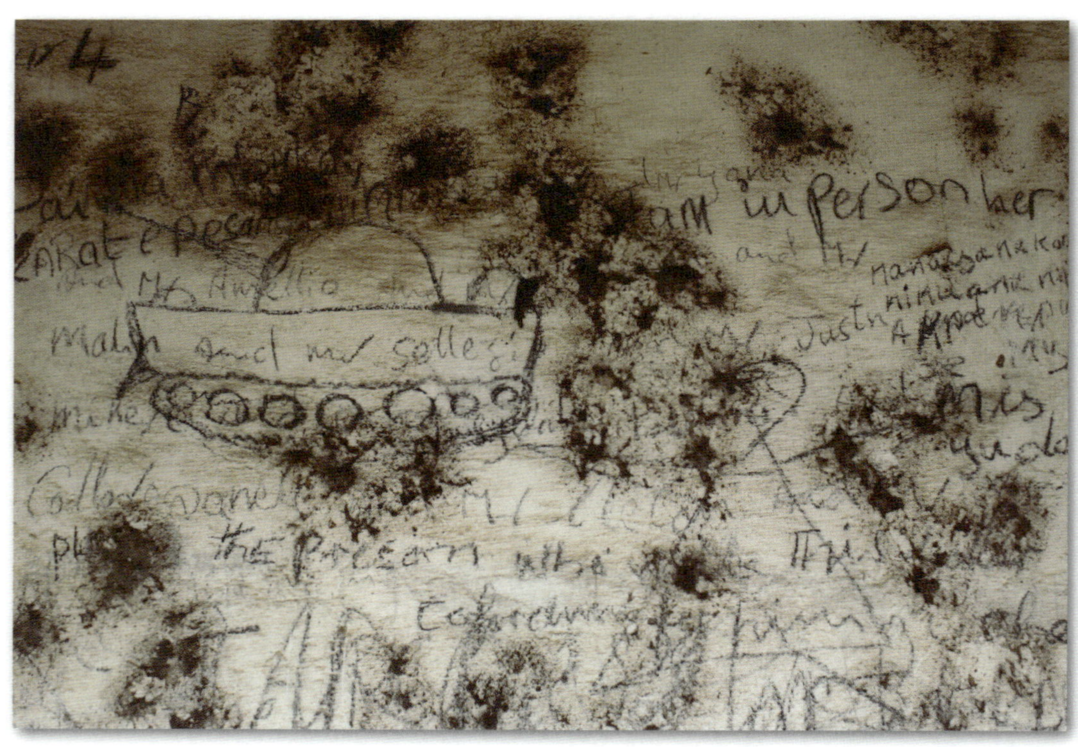

Veronique de Viguerie / UNICEF Photo of the Week (12 September 2011). SUDAN.

SEXUAL VIOLENCE, EDUCATION, AND WAR: BEYOND THE MAINSTREAM NARRATIVE

The *Human Security Report 2012* continues the examination of the human costs of war that started with the previous *Report* and our analysis of the apparent paradox of child mortality rates that improved in more than 90 percent of the years in which countries have been embroiled in war since 1970.[1]

Part I of the new *Report* examines the impact of wartime sexual violence on adults as well as children, and details some surprising revelations about the impact of war on educational systems.

As was the case with the previous *Report*, this year's counterintuitive findings pose a major challenge to a number of widely held assumptions about the human costs of war.

The focus of the first three chapters of Part I is sexual violence in wartime.

Rape and other sexual violations in wartime continue to pose a grave threat to human security in today's wars. They create massive suffering, and inflict psychological trauma, disease, unwanted pregnancies, stigmatization, rejection, grievous injury, and sometimes death on their victims—who are overwhelmingly female.

Long ignored, wartime sexual violence has become increasingly politically salient in the policy agendas of the international community over the past two decades. These changes are due in large part to the tireless investigations and increasingly effective advocacy campaigns of human rights and humanitarian organizations.

At the UN (United Nations) and other international agencies, and in the donor governments that provide assistance to war-affected communities, the issue of wartime sexual violence is now being addressed with a level of commitment that has long been needed, but too rarely provided in the past.

The mainstream narrative on wartime sexual violence that has emerged over the past two decades has been greatly influenced by a series of prominent UN reports and innovative initiatives—in particular, those associated with the Security Council's Women, Peace and Security policy agenda.

But while highly effective in drawing attention to wartime sexual violence and building support to prevent it, the mainstream narrative rests on a set of assumptions that are partial, misleading, and sometimes flat wrong. Some of the assumptions also have unfortunate implications for policy.

Chapter 1 examines some of the misunderstandings that underpin the mainstream narrative on sexual violence in wartime. It argues that this narrative is biased in two important ways.

First, it tends to treat the sexual violence perpetrated in the worst affected countries as if it were typical of all conflict-affected countries. In fact, in the majority of countries in conflict the reported levels of sexual violence are far less than the mainstream narrative suggests. Moreover, the evidence suggests that the level of sexual violence worldwide is likely declining, not increasing as claimed by senior UN officials.

Second, the mainstream narrative systematically neglects domestic sexual violence in war-affected countries, even though it is far more pervasive than the conflict-related sexual violence that is perpetrated by rebels, militias, and government forces, which receives the overwhelming majority of media and official attention.

Chapter 2 examines the incentive structures that drive not only media reporting of wartime sexual violence but also the analysis and policies of the UN and other international agencies, as well as major NGOs (nongovernmental organization). It argues that these incentive structures have created a one-sided narrative that distorts our understanding of sexual violence in war-affected countries and severely hinders the widely endorsed goal of creating policies that are "evidence-based."

> **In the majority of conflict countries, reported levels of sexual violence are far lower than the mainstream narrative suggests.**

Chapter 3 focuses on the impact of wartime sexual violence on children. Here the data are so bad that few conclusions can be drawn with confidence. But the limited data that do exist suggest that in the large majority of cases, sexual violence against children in wartime is perpetrated by family members and acquaintances—not strangers or combatants. The prevalence of sexual violence directed against children also appears to be significantly lower than among adults. Children seem to be partially protected from sexual violence simply because they are children.

Chapter 4 examines the impact of war on education. Here there is a wealth of reasonably robust data on educational enrolments and attainments around the world. Most official and NGO reporting on the impact of war on educational systems does, however, not rely on the cross-national statistical trend data, but rather on detailed descriptions of the effects of war on enrolments or attainments in individual countries. These descriptions are often complemented by selected single-country statistics—on the number of schools destroyed during conflict, for example—which rarely provide a globally representative picture.

The overall assessments that are drawn from these country case studies provide rich contextualized pictures of the impact of war on educational outcomes. But they are subject to selection bias—that is, they draw information disproportionately from the worst affected countries that are—understandably—the focus of most media and political attention. The mainstream narrative tends to treat the impact of war on the worst affected countries as if it were representative of all countries in conflict. It is not.

> **Part II finds that civil wars with external military intervention are twice as deadly as civil wars in which there is no external military intervention.**

Data from multi-country studies and some econometric analyses reveal a quite different story. Here the evidence indicates that during many conflict periods, educational outcomes—counterintuitively—improve.

Part II of the *Report* updates the trend data on organized violence published in previous *Reports* and *Human Security Briefs* and exam-ines the topical issue of persistent conflicts where it finds fewer causes for concern than do other analysts.

Perhaps the most encouraging finding is that peace agreements save lives even when the violence recurs. In fact, the data show that annual battle-death tolls drop by 80 percent in conflicts that restart after peace agreements have broken down. This represents a greater reduction in death tolls than for any other type of conflict termination.

Part II also finds that civil wars that are internationalized are twice as deadly as those in which there is no military intervention by an outside power.

We furthermore investigate trends in other types of organized violence and find that *non-state armed conflicts*—those that do not involve a state as one of the warring parties—have not been increasing as some have claimed. What is more, we find that the number of campaigns of deadly violence against defenceless civilians was lower in 2009 than at any time since 1989.

War and Sexual Violence: Myths and Realities

The advocacy of the UN, other international agencies, and major humanitarian and human rights NGOs on behalf of the victims of wartime sexual violence has made a major contribution to raising public awareness about the horrific nature of sexual violence in today's conflict zones and in bringing pressure to bear to implement policies to combat it.

But the lack of reliable and accessible cross-national data on sexual violence in wartime remains a major factor limiting our understanding of its scope and intensity. And, absent robust data, a series of myths about wartime sexual violence has flourished, largely unchallenged. The mainstream narrative that results is partial, misleading, and has negative implications for policy.

A Misleading Global Narrative

Chapter 1 of the *Report* argues that the mainstream narrative on wartime sexual violence is based in part on mistaken assumptions that have perpetuated a number of misunderstandings about sexual violence in wartime. We present five challenges to this narrative:

- *Conflicts with Extreme Sexual Violence Are the Exception Rather Than the Rule*

  In the absence of reliable cross-national survey data, accounts of wartime sexual violence tend to draw heavily on data from the worst affected countries, buttressed by shocking victim narratives, unsupported generalizations, and statistical "urban myths." The impression created is that the extreme sexual violence suffered in a relatively small number of war-affected countries is the norm. But recent research has revealed that in more than half of the years in which countries are in conflict, levels of reported conflict-related sexual violence are low to negligible. The Democratic Republic of the Congo (DRC), Rwanda, Sudan (Darfur), Sierra Leone, Liberia, and Bosnia—the countries that have received most media and advocacy attention—are the exceptions, not the rule.

- *Claims That Sexual Violence in Wartime Is Increasing Are Not Based on Evidence*

  There is no doubt that the *reporting* of conflict-related sexual violence in war zones has increased dramatically over the past two decades as the political salience of the issue has increased. But there is no compelling evidence to support assertions made by senior UN officials and in high-level UN and other official reports that wartime sexual violence has been increasing.

  Moreover, although there are no reliable cross-national trend data on sexual violence in wartime, *indirect* evidence suggests that its incidence has *declined* worldwide over the past two decades. It is likely that conflict-related sexual violence decreased along with the decline in the number and deadliness of armed conflicts. The *Report* assumes that when conflicts end, conflict-related sexual violence generally also stops, or at the very least declines appreciably.[2]

- *Strategic Rape Is Less Common Than Claimed*

  The mainstream narrative claims that *strategic rape*—the use of rape as a weapon of war— is a pervasive and a growing threat. While there are certainly cases where rape has been deliberately used as a weapon of war, no credible evidence has been produced to support claims that strategic rape is pervasive in most conflicts, nor that its incidence has been growing. It is certainly true that *reporting* of strategic rape has increased, but this is not the same as an actual increase.

- *The Most Prevalent Form of Sexual Violence in Wartime Is Ignored*

  The mainstream narrative on sexual violence in wartime focuses one-sidedly on sexual violence perpetrated by rebels, militias, and government forces and ignores almost completely *domestic sexual violence*—that perpetrated by intimate partners, relatives, and acquaintances. Yet, the latter claims far more victims in war-affected countries than does conflict-related sexual violence. This narrow focus has greatly limited our comprehension of the extent of sexual violence in war-affected countries, while high-level political attention and humanitarian assistance has been directed primarily at the survivors of conflict-related rape.

- *Male Victims and Female Perpetrators*

It is clear that the majority of perpetrators of wartime sexual violence are men, and women and girls make up the overwhelming majority of victims. But many males are also victimized by sexual violence in wartime, and some females are perpetrators. Indeed, recent survey data indicate that both male victims and female perpetrators may be far more numerous than generally believed. Yet, both are largely ignored in the mainstream narrative.

We do not, of course, dispute the fact that sexual violence in today's armed conflicts can cause immense suffering. But media reporting too often portrays wartime sexual violence in the worst affected countries in a way that suggests that the extreme abuses that generate news headlines are the norm. They are not—not even in the worst affected countries.

Consider the case of Liberia, a country notorious for the gross levels of wartime sexual violence perpetrated in the civil wars of the 1990s and early 2000s. Indeed, one much-cited *New York Times* article in 2009 claimed that three out of every four women in Liberia had been raped during these wars.

That appalling sexual atrocities were committed in Liberia's wars is indisputable, but while the media horror stories were mostly true, they were not the whole truth. The best nationwide data on sexual violence in wartime Liberia reveal a very different, but largely unreported, story.

In 2007 a nationwide population survey undertaken by the Demographic and Health Survey found that the lifetime prevalence rate of sexual violence for females aged 15 to 49 in war-affected Liberia was 18 percent. This is very high, but only a small fraction of the three out of four women in Liberia that the *New York Times* alleged were raped during the fighting. (We examine this much-cited, but quite wrong, assertion in detail in Chapter 1.)

To put the lifetime prevalence rate in Liberia in perspective, consider the situation in the United States. According to a major survey undertaken in 2010 for the Centers for Disease Control (CDC), the lifetime prevalence rate of sexual violence in the US is some 18 percent— *the same rate as in Liberia.*[3]

> Media portrayal of sexual violence in war often suggests that the extreme abuses generating news headlines are the norm.

The Incentives That Drive the Mainstream Narrative on Wartime Sexual Violence

Chapter 2 of the *Report* argues that the biases evident in the mainstream narrative on wartime sexual violence are determined in large part by the incentive structures that underpin both media coverage of today's wars and the work of international humanitarian and human rights agencies and NGOs, whose mission includes advocacy as well as service delivery.

Media reporting on wartime sexual violence is driven in large part by the "if it bleeds it leads" news imperative. Violence is news. Hence, the media focus on horrific victim narratives of conflict-related sexual violence—stories of mass rapes, mutilations, shocking sexual assaults on young children, etc.

The domestic sexual violence that takes place behind closed doors in war-affected countries—much of which is not even illegal in the countries where it happens—is ignored by the media almost completely. And domestic sexual violence in wartime is notably absent from the UN Security Council's high-profile wartime sexual violence agenda—despite the fact that it is far more pervasive than conflict-related sexual violence.

The strong media bias towards covering countries worst affected by wartime rape also ensures that news that is far less bad receives minimal coverage. As pointed out, a majority of war-affected countries have low to negligible levels of reported sexual violence.

The incentives that partially drive the official and NGO narratives on sexual violence in war-affected countries are rather different, but they have a similar effect. Here the critical issue is that the demand for humanitarian assistance in these countries, including for the survivors of sexual violence, invariably exceeds the resources available to meet it.

This has created a dilemma for donors, service providers, and advocates, one that lies at the very heart of the humanitarian enterprise. As Ian Smillie and Larry Minear put it:

> In a highly competitive environment—made competitive by great needs and inadequate funding—exaggeration not only pays, it is sometimes the only thing that will dislodge funding from donors who themselves have too few resources and too many supplicants.

With funding rarely sufficient to meet humanitarian needs, UN agencies and NGOs have a clear interest in disseminating information that will highlight the dire plight of those in need and attract the media coverage that helps persuade public and private donors into opening their wallets.

These complementary media and advocacy incentives explain in large part why the mainstream narrative on sexual violence in wartime is both partial and misleading.

Policy Implications

Few doubt that the provision of humanitarian assistance for the victims of sexual violence in wartime is often inadequate. Given this, why should it matter if NGOs and international agencies overstate the scope and intensity of conflict-related sexual violence in order to access adequate levels of humanitarian funding for the survivors of that violence? The beneficiaries will surely not complain.

The short answer is that without data, there can be no evidence-based policy. Without reliable data for needs assessments, for example, the effective and equitable allocation of humanitarian assistance to rape survivors becomes impossible. Without reliable data, policy-makers cannot know whether sexual violence in war-affected countries is increasing or decreasing. And, absent this most basic information, they can have little idea whether policies directed at deterring or stopping sexual violence are having any effect.

But these are only the most obvious challenges. Consider some of the negative policy responses that may result from the sources of bias in the mainstream narrative noted previously and the ensuing urban myths.

> Of the more than 4,000 NGOs that address the issue of wartime sexual violence, only 3 percent mentioned males in their informational materials.

First, the fact that many war-affected countries experience low or negligible levels of reported sexual violence has generated almost no interest in the policy community. And with a handful of important exceptions, it has received very little attention in the research community either. Yet, understanding why some countries suffer much lower rates of sexual violence than others could provide important insights for improving sexual violence prevention programs.

Second, as long as policy-makers in the UN and elsewhere erroneously believe that wartime sexual violence is increasing worldwide, they will have few incentives to seek to understand why it might be *decreasing*. In fact, the indirect evidence suggests that conflict-related sexual violence is declining. Since the end of the Cold War, the number and deadliness of armed conflicts has decreased substantially, and with it—we assume—the incidence of conflict-related sexual violence.

The decline in conflict numbers has been driven in part by the success of *peacemaking* initiatives—using diplomatic means to stop ongoing conflicts. Since there is considerable evidence that peacemaking is effective, the *Report* suggests that it may constitute a more viable indirect strategy for reducing conflict-related rape than the UN's direct prevention efforts for which there is little evidence of success.

Third, the omission of male victims from the mainstream narrative on wartime sexual violence—and from most official and NGO reports—has clear and inequitable policy consequences, the most obvious being that the needs of male survivors of wartime rape are largely ignored. The extent of this neglect is remarkable. One recent study found that of the more than 4,000 NGOs around the world that address the issue of wartime sexual violence, only 3 percent even mentioned males in their informational materials.

Finally, the mainstream narrative's one-sided focus on conflict-related sexual violence perpetrated by rebels, militias, and government troops has meant that the more pervasive threats that domestic sexual violence poses to the rights and integrity of women in wartime have been rendered largely invisible, not least on the agenda of the UN Security Council.

Moreover, the policy prescriptions being pursued by the UN in seeking to prevent conflict-related sexual violence have virtually no relevance for the more pervasive threat of domestic sexual violence in wartime. And because domestic sexual violence in war-affected countries is a continuation of the largely invisible domestic sexual violence that persists in peacetime, it does not constitute an "emergency" issue. As a consequence, its survivors, unlike the victims of conflict-related sexual violence, rarely receive humanitarian assistance.

Children and Wartime Sexual Violence

Chapter 3 of this *Report* addresses sexual violence against children in wartime. Yet, the fragmentary and unreliable nature of the data means that determining how, and to what true extent, children in conflict-affected countries are affected by wartime sexual violence is currently impossible.

The best data we have on the prevalence of sexual violence in poor countries comes from nationwide population surveys. But the few such surveys that are undertaken in wartime mostly ignore children, while the surveys that do ask questions about children's experience of sexual violence are mostly undertaken in peacetime.

The UN's Monitoring and Reporting Mechanism (MRM) collects data on a range of human rights violations against children in armed conflict, including sexual violence. But, as Chapter 3 demonstrates, the methodology of the MRM grossly underestimates the prevalence of sexual violence against children in conflict-affected countries—although it is useful in many other ways.

> Estimates of wartime sexual violence against children based on face-to-face interviews rather than anonymous responses are likely too low.

Without referring to its own inadequate MRM data, the UN has claimed that wartime violence against children—including sexual violence—is *increasing*. There is *no* evidence to support such an assertion. Indeed, as with adults, the worldwide incidence of sexual violence against children perpetrated by combatants has likely decreased as the number and deadliness of wars have declined.

The very limited evidence that we have suggests that the patterns of sexual violence against children in wartime are very similar to those against adults. In both cases, the large majority of sexual violence is *domestic* in origin—perpetrated by family members or close acquaintances, not by rebels, militias, or government troops. In both cases, sexual violence rates vary substantially from region to region and country to country.

The evidence also suggests that estimates of the prevalence of wartime sexual violence against children that are based solely on face-to-face interviews rather than anonymous responses are likely too low. This was demonstrated in the World Health Organization's multi-country surveys in the early 2000s. Women respondents were asked, both directly and anonymously, if they had been sexually violated as children. The anonymous responses indicated substantially higher rates of assault than the face-to-face responses. It is likely that similar degrees of under-reporting characterize survey-based estimates of sexual violence against adults, although this possibility has not been tested cross-nationally.

The one clear difference between children and adults with respect to sexual violence—in both war-affected countries and those at peace—is that children, especially young children, suffer lower levels of victimization than adults. This suggests that they receive a degree of normative protection simply because they are children.

Bridging the Knowledge Gaps

The absence of reliable cross-national data on the extent and severity of sexual violence against children, as well as adults, means that the aspirations of donor governments and international agencies for policy in this area to be evidence-based cannot be realized.

In poor countries where most wars take place, only well-run nationwide population surveys can generate reliable data that are robust enough to determine whether wartime sexual violence is increasing or decreasing—and to inform policy formulation, needs assessment, and impact evaluation.

The Impact of War on Children's Education

Chapter 4 examines the impact of war on education. Here access to reliable information is far better than is the case with wartime sexual violence. This is in large part because a major international effort has gone into collecting and collating cross-national educational data for the Millennium Development Goals (MDGs). The MDG target for education calls for all children to have the opportunity to complete primary school by 2015.

Mainstream accounts of the effect of war on educational outcomes, however, rarely draw on these cross-national statistical data. They typically review narrative descriptions, including disturbing victim accounts, of how particular impacts of war—the destruction of schools, or the rape of schoolchildren, for example—affect the educational system. Not surprisingly, these accounts tend to draw on findings from countries where the impact of armed violence has been substantial and where the need for assistance is greatest.

The mainstream narrative sometimes draws on sophisticated statistical analyses from *individual* countries—many of them undertaken by the Households in Conflict Network—on the impact of conflict on national educational systems. But findings from these studies, while valuable, are unlikely to be a reliable guide to the impact of war on educational systems *in general* because they tend to focus on countries most affected by conflict.

Taken together, these accounts paint a bleak picture. Indeed, reports from UNESCO (United Nations Educational, Scientific and Cultural Organization), the World Bank, and major NGOs have described the impact of conflict on education as "devastating," "disastrous," and destroying educational opportunities on an "epic scale."

But, as Chapter 4 points out, descriptive statistics from two major multi-country studies— one by the UNESCO Institute for Statistics and the other by the Education Policy and Data Center—make it clear that these are not accurate descriptions of the impact of warfare on education in most conflict-affected countries. The mainstream narrative draws inappropriate general conclusions from a limited number of unrepresentative case studies.

Data from the multi-country background study by the UNESCO Institute for Statistics' flagship 2011 *Global Monitoring Report* reveal, for example, that in only 11 percent of conflict periods was there a clear decline in educational attainment indicators. In more than 40 percent of cases, however, attainment indicators at the end of a conflict period were *higher* than at the beginning—sometimes even in the areas worst affected by warfare. Data from another multi-country study, undertaken by the Washington-based Education Policy and Data Center in 2010, also show that educational outcomes improved in a surprising number of cases in areas that were worst affected by conflict.

The most remarkable finding, however, came from a major econometric study undertaken by the Peace Research Institute Oslo (PRIO) for the World Bank's 2011 *World Development Report,* which revealed that, on average, there was "no discernible effect of conflict on education levels."[4] This finding stands in stark contrast to the assumptions of the mainstream narrative on the impact of conflict on educational outcomes.

> In low-intensity conflicts, the violence tends to be concentrated in small geographical areas, with most areas of the country not being directly affected.

The PRIO study also indicated that the average country in conflict improved its educational outcomes at approximately the same rate as the average nonconflict country—though from a lower baseline. If both conflict and nonconflict countries improve their educational outcomes at the same rate, this suggests that conflict has, on average, little net impact.

How can such deeply counterintuitive findings be explained? First, in many cases the impact of conflict on the educational system is too small to have a discernible *nationwide* effect on this rate of improvement. The average conflict in the new millennium has experienced fewer than 1,000 reported battle deaths a year, meaning the annual death toll from armed conflict in a given country is usually far smaller than the number of homicides. We do not expect countries with 1,000-plus homicides a year to have poor educational outcomes as a consequence.

And low war death tolls are likely to be associated with low levels of societal disruption and physical destruction. Moreover, in low-intensity conflicts the violence tends to be concentrated in relatively small geographical areas—with most areas of the country not being directly affected by the fighting.

Second, the negative effect of conflict on educational systems may manifest itself in a *slowing* of the pre-war rate of improvement, rather than a complete halt or reversal.

Third, armed conflict may cause educational outcomes to deteriorate briefly, so briefly that it will not be picked up by the data. Again, this would indicate the robustness of the positive long-term trends.

Fourth, rising educational outcomes in war do not *necessarily* mean that the disruptions and destruction of warfare have no effect. A negative effect may be present, but not discernible, in the outcome trend data because it is offset by other factors that *improve* outcomes.

If average incomes rise during wartime, which happens in a surprising number of cases, the positive impact of this change on educational outcomes may outweigh the negative impact of the conflict. But in other cases, international assistance can boost school attendance even in periods of conflict. In Afghanistan, for example, fewer than a million children went to school under the Taliban. Since the overthrow of the Taliban regime in 2001, a new government and massive inflows of foreign assistance have meant that more than six million children are now going to school, despite the ongoing political violence.[5]

In both these examples, educational outcomes improve despite the negative impact of conflict.

In other words, the statistical data on educational outcomes in conflict-affected countries do *not* support claims that war is "development in reverse," to use Paul Collier's memorable phrase. The impact of conflict on educational outcomes nationwide rarely causes them to decline absolutely. Where there is a discernible effect, it usually involves a reduction in the rate at which outcomes improve.

This means that educational systems in war-affected poor countries appear to be considerably more resilient than is generally assumed. But this fact tends to go unnoticed because the mainstream narrative, which draws primarily on case-study research, is heavily influenced by what happens in the worst affected countries. The data from the multi-country and econometric studies drawn on in this *Report*, which reveal a much less bleak picture of what happens to educational systems in wartime, are relatively recent, not easily accessible to nonspecialists, and remain largely unknown.

This is not all. There is a clear *association* between periods of conflict in a country and low educational attainments—i.e., in conflict countries educational outcomes are consistently lower than they are nonconflict countries. But it is far from obvious that it is the conflict that *causes* the lower outcomes.

The mainstream narrative draws attention to the reality that educational outcomes in war-affected countries are consistently lower than those in nonconflict countries, and assumes—plausibly enough—that it is the conflict that causes the difference. But the cross-national data suggest that this is not the case.

Chapter 4 reviews a series of case studies by the UNESCO Institute for Statistics that indicate that in a majority of cases the low educational outcomes that exist during periods of conflict were also present in the pre-conflict period. This suggests that the low educational outcomes in the conflict period are not primarily caused by the conflict but by factors that preceded it.

Even during periods of warfare there are plausible explanations for poor educational outcomes, other than the deaths, disruption, and destruction caused by the war itself. The background study undertaken for the World Bank's 2011 *World Development Report* by PRIO researchers found that state fragility—the weakness of institutions, governance, and state capacity in a given country—is more strongly associated with poor educational attainments than is conflict.[6]

There is a clear policy message here, namely that the most effective path to improving educational outcomes in wartime may be to reduce state fragility in peacetime.

Understanding state fragility in peacetime may help explain why educational outcomes in countries during wartime are lower than those in nonconflict countries. But is this explanation compatible with the fact that educational outcomes *improve*, on average, in wartime?

A complete answer to this question is beyond the scope of this *Report*. Here we simply note that, overall, states appear to have become less fragile over time. Indeed, the global level of fragility declined worldwide by some 20 percent between 1995 and 2010 according to the State Fragility Index.

If state fragility is an important part of the explanation for low educational outcomes, both in times of war and peace, we would expect that as fragility declines, then—other things being equal—overall educational attainments and other development indicators will improve. This is, in fact, what the data from the PRIO and other studies suggest.

Trends in Human Insecurity

Part II of this *Report* examines changes in the incidence and severity of organized violence around the world and finds little change in the post-Cold War trend towards fewer and less-deadly wars reported in previous editions of the *Human Security Report*.

Chapter 5 shows that the deadliness of warfare has declined over the last 50 to 60 years, and there are now significantly fewer armed conflicts around the world than during the peak of the early 1990s. The average number of *high-intensity conflicts* per year—defined as conflicts that reach 1,000 or more battle deaths in a calendar year—dropped by half from the 1980s to the new millennium.

A new analysis of military intervention in civil wars finds that conflicts that involve the military forces of external powers are, on average, twice as deadly as civil wars in which there are no such interventions. Given that foreign military interventions introduce new combatants and weapons systems into countries in conflict, this is not surprising.

The fact that military interventions are associated with greatly increased battle-death numbers is not necessarily an argument against military intervention for humanitarian—or indeed other—purposes. But in considering the pros and cons of such interventions, it is clearly a factor that should be weighed in the decision-making process.

Chapter 6 of this *Report* presents the first systematic analysis of post-World War II trends in conflict persistence, which has received increasing attention from academics and policy-makers. *Persistence* has two related meanings here. The first refers to the length of wars, and the second to the rate at which they start again after having stopped. The average duration of conflicts appears to have increased. And the trend data indicate that, in recent years, conflicts that stopped were increasingly likely to recur within a relatively short period.

A closer examination of the data, however, reveals a more encouraging picture. Most of today's conflict episodes are relatively short, and long-lasting conflicts are the exception rather than the rule. Moreover, persistent conflicts are often very small in scale. Finally, the rate of conflict recurrence has increased in large part because conflicts have become more difficult to win—but not necessarily more difficult to resolve through peacemaking and peacebuilding.

It is true that the *average* length of conflicts in progress has been increasing. This is in part because conflict numbers have been shrinking overall, while a number of intractable long-running conflicts have persisted. But it is not true that there is any tendency for *recent* conflicts to last a long time—most conflict episodes that have started during the last two decades have been short-lived and small in scale.

It is also a fact that in the new millennium, wars that end have been more likely to restart than in the past. This is not, however, because today's peace agreements are failing more frequently than those in the past.

Most of the conflicts that restart soon after they have stopped are very small. As the fighting in these small conflicts waxes and wanes from year to year, the death toll may change enough to cross the conflict threshold of 25 battle deaths in a calendar year. Conflict may thus stop, only to start a couple of years later as the violence increases slightly. It is this in-and-out pattern of low-intensity conflicts that has been the major cause of the recent increase in conflict recurrences.

> Conflicts that restart in the wake of collapsed peace agreements still see a reduction in annual battle-death tolls of more than 80 percent.

Because most of these recurring conflicts are small, and often geographically isolated, they almost never threaten governments and pose relatively few threats to citizens. As a result, there is no great incentive for governments to expend major resources in an effort to stop them.

Peace agreements have been highly prone to break down in the past, and some critics have argued in favour of "giving war a chance," by pursuing victory on the battlefield rather than peace agreements at the bargaining table. The rationale here is that conflicts that end in victory are less likely to recur, and thus will save more lives in the long run than those that end in peace agreements.

The critics are wrong. Peace agreements today are more stable than is usually assumed. And conflicts that restart in the wake of peace agreements that break down still see a dramatic reduction—some 80 percent, on average—in annual battle-death tolls. Peace agreements, in other words, succeed in saving lives even when they "fail."

The final chapters of this *Report* cover trends in those forms of organized violence that do not fit the traditional definition of conflict. Chapter 7 discusses new research on *non-state conflicts*—those that do not involve a government as one of the warring parties. It finds no evidence that these somewhat volatile and generally low-intensity struggles are becoming either more frequent or deadly, as some have claimed.

Similarly, Chapter 8 finds that the number of campaigns of *one-sided violence*—deadly attacks against defenceless civilians—was lower in 2009 than at any time since 1989, the first year for which data are available.

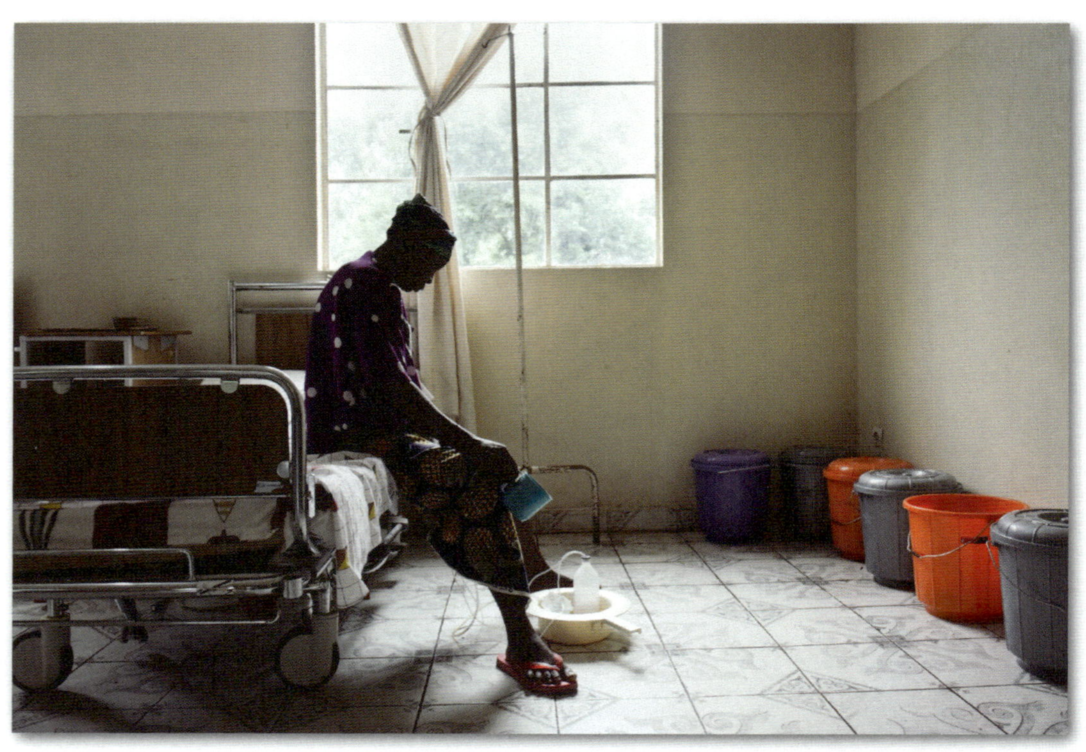

Sven Torfinn / Panos Pictures. DEMOCRATIC REPUBLIC OF THE CONGO.

SEXUAL VIOLENCE, EDUCATION, AND WAR

Part I of this *Report* continues the Human Security Report Project's analysis of the human costs of war. It challenges a number of myths about wartime sexual violence, and argues that the impact of war on education is considerably less than claimed.

SEXUAL VIOLENCE, EDUCATION, AND WAR

Introduction

The mainstream narrative on war and sexual violence is often compelling, but also partial and misleading in significant ways. Most importantly, it presents the worst affected countries as the norm, while ignoring wartime domestic sexual violence.

The pervasive biases in the mainstream narrative described in Chapter 1 are determined in large part by the incentive structures that drive media coverage of wartime sexual violence, and the advocacy efforts of international agencies and NGOs.

The available evidence suggests that patterns of sexual violence against children are similar to those against adult women, except that the rate of victimization is substantially lower. Children appear to have a degree of protection simply by being children.

The impact of conflict on education is often described as disastrous. Yet, the data indicate that it is much less devastating than claimed. Indeed recent statistical studies show that educational outcomes actually improve during most periods of warfare.

Eric Kanalstein / UN Photo. AFGHANISTAN.

INTRODUCTION

Part I of this *Report* examines the impact of war on the incidence of sexual violence perpetrated against children as well as adults, and analyzes the effects of war on educational outcomes. Its counterintuitive findings present a major challenge to prevailing assumptions about the human costs of war.

During the past decade, international advocacy campaigns have pushed the long-neglected issue of wartime sexual violence high on the agenda of the international community. But Chapter 1 argues that, while often compelling, the mainstream narrative associated with this advocacy exaggerates the prevalence of conflict-related rape. At the same time, it ignores the far more pervasive wartime domestic sexual violence almost completely.

The mainstream narrative presents the prevalence of sexual violence in the worst affected countries. But the best available data we have indicate that in most years of active conflict, reported levels of conflict-related sexual violence are low to very low. The far more common domestic sexual violence, which takes place behind closed doors in private, gets almost no attention.

The incentive structures that shape the reporting and analysis of the media and international agencies and NGOs (nongovernmental organizations) help explain the one-sided nature of the mainstream narrative, as we discuss in Chapter 2. Media coverage is driven by news that sells—hence the focus on headline-grabbing stories of horrific, often public, wartime rape campaigns perpetrated by vicious rebel or militia groups and government forces.

NGOs and humanitarian agency reporting is driven in large part by the need to secure resources for underfunded humanitarian operations in war zones. Given this reality, it is not surprising that humanitarian advocacy focuses on issues that are most likely to help generate much-needed funding.

However well intentioned, the one-sided nature of the mainstream narrative—and other misunderstandings—risk distorting our understanding of wartime sexual violence and make the creation of informed, evidenced-based policy difficult, if not impossible.

Chapter 3 focuses on the impact of sexual violence against children in wartime and finds that here too the mainstream narrative is misleading. For example, high-level UN (United Nations) reports claim that wartime sexual violence against children has been increasing, despite the fact that there is no evidence to support such a claim. In fact, the only available—indirect—evidence suggests that wartime sexual violence against children, as is the case with adults, is decreasing.

The data also indicate that by far the most common perpetrators of sexual violence against children in wartime are not armed combatants, but family members and acquaintances. The prevalence of sexual violence against children, especially young children, is substantially lower than that against adult women, despite the fact that children are less capable of defending themselves from assault than adults. This suggests that some form of normative constraints appear to be providing children with a measure of protection from sexual predation.

In Chapter 4 we continue our analysis of the human costs of war by turning to the effect of conflict on educational outcomes. Our findings here are again at odds with the mainstream narrative—in this case the widely held belief that war generally has a "disastrous" effect on educational outcomes.

In fact, the results of a major econometric study commissioned for the *World Development Report 2011* reveal that educational outcomes in countries in conflict improve on average. This is not to suggest that war is good for education—far from it—it indicates rather that most contemporary wars are not deadly enough to reverse the long-term improvement in educational outcomes.

The data clearly show that, on average, educational outcomes in war-affected countries are lower than those for countries at peace. Yet—contrary to prevailing assumptions—the lower educational outcomes experienced by conflict-affected countries are often not caused by war itself. The fact that the educational outcomes in countries experiencing war were already lower *prior* to the period of war indicates that their primary determinants are also likely to have existed prior to the war.

Marie Frechon / UN Photo. DEMOCRATIC REPUBLIC OF THE CONGO.

CHAPTER 1

Sexual Violence in War-Affected Countries

In 2002 Elisabeth Rehn and Ellen Johnson Sirleaf, the latter now president of Liberia, delivered a major report to the UN (United Nations) that examined the impact of sexual violence against women and girls in war-affected countries.

Although well aware of the available literature on this issue, Rehn and Johnson Sirleaf reported that they had been quite unprepared for what they learned from their on-the-ground investigations of sexual violence in the world's war zones.

The stories were horrific:

Wombs punctured with guns. Women raped and tortured in front of their husbands and children. Rifles forced into vaginas. Pregnant women beaten to induce miscarriages. Foetuses ripped from wombs. Women kidnapped, blindfolded and beaten on their way to work or school. We saw the scars, the pain and the humiliation. We heard accounts of gang rapes, rape camps and mutilation. Of murder and sexual slavery. We saw the scars of brutality so extreme that survival seemed for some a worse fate than death.[7]

This and other official reports, plus the tireless investigations of human rights and humanitarian advocacy groups, have drawn international attention to the long-neglected issue of wartime sexual violence against women, helped galvanize action against the perpetrators, and increased assistance to its survivors.

But these same reports are problematic—not because shocking violations like those described by Rehn, Johnson Sirleaf, and many others are untrue—but because the accounts in which they are embedded are misleading.

The mainstream narrative informed by reports from the UN human rights organizations, and media-propagated "urban myths," presents a picture of wartime sexual violence that is, with some exceptions, both partial and often deeply misrepresentative.

In particular:

- It focuses disproportionate attention on the relatively small number of countries that are deeply affected by conflict-related sexual violence—by which we mean sexual violence perpetrated by combatants. This has created the impression that the extraordinarily high levels of rape reported in war-affected Bosnia, Rwanda, the Democratic Republic of the Congo (DRC), Sierra Leone, Liberia, and Sudan are characteristic of all war-affected countries. They are not.

- It depicts wartime sexual violence as increasing, but provides little evidence to support such a claim. All we can say with certainty is that reporting of sexual violence has increased significantly. Indirect evidence suggests that the overall level of wartime sexual violence may have *decreased* worldwide.

- It argues that *strategic rape*—the use of rape as a weapon of war—is a pervasive and growing threat but presents no evidence to support this claim. Some evidence suggests that its incidence is less prevalent than claimed, and that it may have declined in recent years.

- It presents men—invariably combatants—as the perpetrators of sexual violence; women and girls as the victims. Little is said about sexual violence against males, while female perpetration is ignored almost completely despite recent evidence indicating that it may be far more prevalent in wartime than is generally understood.

- It concentrates on sexual violence perpetrated by combatants—i.e., rebels, militias, and government forces—while ignoring almost completely noncombatant sexual violence. Yet, the evidence indicates that the latter—most of it perpetrated within the household or extended family—is much more pervasive than the former.

Lacking useful data on sexual violence, official and NGO (nongovernmental organization) accounts of wartime rape and other forms of sexual violence tend to rely on statistics that are often of questionable reliability and on survivor accounts of individual atrocities, which—while true and deeply shocking—are not representative.

Focus and Scope

This chapter argues that the mainstream narrative on sexual violence in war-affected countries is biased in two important ways. We use the term *mainstream narrative* here to mean the manner in which people frame, perceive, and explain the social world.[8]

First, it exaggerates the worldwide prevalence and intensity of wartime sexual violence by inappropriately generalizing from shocking victim accounts and statistics drawn from a relatively small number of the worst affected countries.

Second, it systematically neglects domestic sexual violence in war-affected countries, despite the fact that its impact is far more pervasive than that of conflict-related sexual violence. It also largely ignores sexual violence against males in wartime.

In other words, wartime sexual violence is both overstated and understated. In Chapter 2 we argue that both forms of bias have unfortunate implications for policy.

This chapter relies heavily on a small number of population surveys—all undertaken over the past 10 years—that have examined the prevalence and drivers of sexual violence in conflict-affected countries. Notwithstanding the various ethical and methodological challenges confronted while conducting surveys in war-affected countries, these constitute the most reliable sources of data that currently exist on the prevalence, scope, and intensity of sexual violence in conflict-affected societies.

What Do We Mean by Sexual Violence?

The term sexual violence includes, but is not limited to, rape. As Anne Marie Goetz, Chief Advisor for Governance, Peace and Security for the UN's Development Fund for Women (UNIFEM), points out, international law further includes in its definition of sexual violence:

> forced prostitution; sexual slavery; forced impregnation; forced maternity; forced termination of pregnancy; enforced sterilization; indecent assault; trafficking; inappropriate medical examinations and strip searches.[9]

We do not seek to examine these types of sexual violence in this report, not because they are unimportant, but because no reliable data are available in most war-affected countries to estimate their scope or intensity. Nor, for essentially the same reason, do we include lesser forms of sexual abuse—such as unwanted sexual comments and unwanted sexual touching.

The most commonly studied form of sexual violence is rape. Yale scholar Elisabeth Wood's definition is a useful guide:

> By *rape*, I mean the penetration of the anus or vagina with any object or body part or of any body part of the victim or perpetrator's body with a sexual organ, by force or by threat of force or coercion, or by taking advantage of a coercive environment, or against a person incapable of giving genuine consent.[10]

Rape thus defined is the central focus of Part I of this report, but we also include some forms of sexual violence that do not fall within the rubric of rape as defined here, notably the use of *sexual torture*—castration or other intentional violence against male genitalia; or the mutilation of women's genitals[11] and breasts, both of which occur in some conflict situations.[12]

We make a distinction between the two major types of sexual violence that occur during wartime. First, there is *conflict-related sexual violence*, by which we mean that perpetrated by combatants—rebels, militia fighters, and government forces.[13] Second, there is *domestic sexual violence*, which includes not only that perpetrated by intimate partners but also by other household or family members. The evidence we have indicates that the large majority of noncombatant sexual violence in wartime is made up of domestic sexual violence. We discuss the different categories of sexual violence in war-affected countries in more detail in the box on page 23.

Finally, we note that throughout this chapter, where we discuss survey data on sexual violence, we are only using the *best estimate*—i.e., that which indicates the most probable rate of sexual violence. In reality, all survey-based estimates are subject to considerable uncertainty, usually expressed as *confidence intervals*.[14]

The Sources of Evidence

Developing evidence-based policies to combat wartime sexual violence requires reliable quantitative data on the rate and severity of sexual violence in addition to qualitative data. Robust quantitative data are, however, rarely available in conflict and post-conflict environments.

The most influential reporting comes from the investigations of international human rights organizations like Human Rights Watch (HRW) and Amnesty International. These and other human rights organizations provide timely information on violations of all forms of human rights—including wartime rape and other forms of sexual violence.

HRW, Amnesty, and other human rights organizations bear witness to rights violations and advocate for justice on behalf of victims. However, the detailed information they collect on particular incidents of sexual violence and survivor narratives is rarely suitable for making quantitative assessments of the *overall* prevalence and incidence of human rights violations in a country. For that purpose, population surveys are the most appropriate.

The most comprehensive cross-national data on the extent of conflict-related sexual violence in war-affected countries come from a new dataset compiled by Dara Cohen of the University of Minnesota. Using data from the US State Department's annual reports on human rights abuses, Cohen categorizes the severity of reported sexual violence in conflict-affected countries on a four-point scale, from "systematic" or "massive" to zero.[15] This is the only cross-national quantitative study that provides data on reported levels of conflict-related sexual violence. But determining whether what is being recorded by the State Department are actual changes in the level of sexual violence, or simply changes in the *reporting* of this sexual violence, can be very difficult.[16]

> Evidence-based policies against wartime sexual violence require qualitative data as well as reliable quantitative data, which are rarely available.

A critically important source of cross-national data on the prevalence of sexual violence in individual war-affected countries is provided by nationwide population surveys. These surveys provide estimates of domestic, as well as conflict-related, sexual violence and are a reflection of the more general international concern to map the worldwide incidence of sexual violence against women that has grown since the UN's landmark World Conference on Women in Beijing in 1995.[17] Most have been undertaken since the beginning of the new millennium.

Providing that the survey samples are selected to ensure that they are representative of the national population, the national rate of victimization will, in principle, be approximately the

SEXUAL VIOLENCE TERMINOLOGY

In the literature on sexual violence in war-affected countries two broad categories of sexual violence can be distinguished:

- *Conflict-related sexual violence* is that perpetrated by combatants—rebels, militias, and government forces. This is the sexual violence that most studies and reports focus on.
- *Domestic sexual violence* is that perpetrated by intimate partners[18] and by other family/household members. It also includes sexual assaults by noncombatant acquaintances, although these usually only constitute a very small minority of assaults.[19]

In practice, estimates of conflict-related sexual violence can include not only violence perpetrated by combatants but also cases of *stranger rape* perpetrated by civilians unknown to the victim. Many studies of sexual violence in war-affected countries do not specify whether perpetrators identified as "strangers" or "outside of the household" were combatants or noncombatants. But where they do, the data suggest that the overwhelming majority of sexual violence perpetrated *by strangers* during wartime is, in fact, attributable to combatants.

War-affected countries: the term "war-affected" describes both those countries in conflict and those during the immediate post-conflict years.[20] When wars end, the incidence of sexual violence perpetrated by combatants is usually sharply reduced, but it does not end.[21]

Lifetime prevalence of sexual violence: this is by far the most commonly used measure of sexual violence in the literature. It refers to the percentage of the population that have ever been victimized by sexual violence during their lifetime.[22] This measure has the virtue of simplicity—almost everyone who has been victimized by sexual violence remembers that this is the case.[23]

In WHO's (World Health Organization's) multi-country surveys on sexual violence that we discuss in Chapters 2 and 3, respondents were asked if they had been assaulted as a child.[24] The resulting data provided a rare insight into the prevalence of sexual violence against children, though not all of the 10 countries were war-affected.

Incidence of sexual violence: this, as the term suggests, is a measure of the number of incidents of sexual violence in a given population unit (e.g., incidents per 100 or 1,000 people) within a given time period. So, while *prevalence* data tell us what percentage of a population had experienced sexual violence at least once during a particular period, *incidence* data tell us the total number of incidents—some individuals are likely to be victimized more than once.[25]

Incidence data are very rarely collected in population surveys. If they were, they would likely reveal that the incidence, as well as the prevalence, of domestic sexual violence is much higher than conflict-related sexual violence. This is because individuals subjected to conflict-related sexual violence are rarely assaulted on an ongoing basis for months or years on end, as is often the case with respect to domestic sexual violence.[26]

same as that of the sample population. Where such surveys are professionally and sensitively administered, they can provide robust estimates of the national rates of both domestic and conflict-related sexual violence.

However, relatively few population surveys in this area are national in scope; most have been subregional, or have been undertaken solely in refugee or internally displaced persons (IDP) camps. As such, they cannot be assumed to be a reliable guide to national rates of sexual violence in war-affected countries.

Moreover, the extraordinarily sensitive nature of the questions that are asked in surveys on sexual violence confronts a range of challenging ethical issues[27] and a much higher probability of under-reporting than is likely with, for example, questions about maternal health or child mortality.[28]

A further challenge arises because surveys often rely on different definitions of sexual violence and different survey methodologies. This, plus the paucity of nationwide surveys, makes cross-national comparisons of survey findings on wartime sexual violence often difficult, and sometimes impossible.

The minimal amount of data collected on wartime sexual violence stands in sharp contrast with the huge data-collection efforts undertaken for the Millennium Development Goals (MDGs). In the latter case, large-scale population surveys, using common definitions and methodologies, have been undertaken at regular intervals across large numbers of developing countries. The data from the surveys undertaken for the MDGs enable policy-makers to track trends in poverty, health, education, gender equality, and other development issues and help determine the impact of their policies.

Yet, despite the huge increase in international attention being paid to wartime sexual violence, no remotely comparable data-collection effort has been devoted to gathering information on its prevalence and severity. We demonstrate in this chapter that as a consequence, highly misleading assumptions about the scope and intensity of sexual violence in war-affected countries have become widely accepted in the media, in the UN and other international agencies, and in the advocacy community.

Five Challenges to the Mainstream Narrative

It is in large part because there are so few reliable statistics on wartime sexual violence that myths about its incidence have flourished virtually unchallenged. In this section we examine in detail the five misleading characterizations of wartime sexual violence noted in the introduction to this chapter.

Reporting of Wartime Sexual Violence Is Biased towards the Extreme Cases

Most discussion on wartime sexual violence focuses on the worst affected countries. Influential high-level reports undertaken for, or by, the UN and leading human rights and humanitarian advocacy NGOs draw their examples and statistics overwhelmingly from a number of countries where rates of sexual violence are without a doubt very high. War-affected countries with far lower levels of reported sexual violence are not discussed.

This pervasive bias creates the misleading impression that the massive extent of conflict-related sexual violence in a relatively small number of conflicts is the norm for all of them. Mainly because there are no reliable cross-national statistics to provide a corrective, there have been virtually no challenges to this mistaken assumption.

As Dara Cohen puts it:

One of the central problems in the literature on wartime sexual violence is that the vast majority of existing research is case studies of what are thought to be particularly severe incidents … there is little exploration of cases where sexual violence is thought to be minimal.[29]

For example, in 2005, the Integrated Regional Information Networks (IRIN), the UN's highly regarded humanitarian news and analysis organization, published a much-cited report, *Broken Bodies, Broken Dreams: Violence against Women Exposed*, one chapter of which focuses exclusively on wartime sexual violence.[30] Drawing on information from 18 conflicts fought around the world between 1993 and 2005, the report describes the myriad ways in which women and girls are subjected to sexual violence in wartime.

> ## A pervasive bias creates the impression that most conflicts are associated with massive conflict-related sexual violence.

The report focuses on countries that were badly afflicted by both armed conflict and conflict-related sexual violence—those in which the need for humanitarian assistance was great. This is both understandable and wholly appropriate. But in concentrating on the horrific sexual violence in just 18 of the 53 conflict-affected countries during this period, the report creates the impression that the violations in these countries were the norm. This was not the case. The large majority of the conflict-affected countries that were completely ignored in the report suffered from minor conflicts and almost certainly had far lower levels of conflict-related sexual violence. IRIN's discussion of wartime rape is evocative and powerful, but it fails to point out anywhere that the sexual violence it is reporting on was atypical of most countries in conflict.

A much clearer idea of the variation in the severity of sexual violence in war-affected countries is now possible thanks to the new dataset compiled by Dara Cohen that we noted previously.[31]

Following a similar methodology to that used by the Political Terror Scale (PTS),[32] Cohen used data from the US State Department's annual reports on human rights issues to extract information on conflict-related sexual violence from 1980 to 2009. Each country is scored for each year that it was in conflict on a four-point scale providing an estimate of the extent of reported rape—from "systematic" or "massive" (Level 3) to "no reported rape" (Level 0).[33]

For the period 2000–2009, only 9 percent of the years of active conflict are characterized by the highest level of sexual violence. Thirty-five percent of the years of active conflict are associated with "widespread" reports of sexual violence (Level 2). Yet in most years of active conflict during the new millennium, the average level of reported sexual violence is at either Level 1 (very low incidence, 44 percent), or Level 0 (no reported conflict-related rape, 12 percent).[34]

In other words, the countries that experience extremely high levels of sexual violence, like the DRC, and receive most of the media attention are far from the norm.

Extraordinarily, little research has been undertaken to investigate why some countries at war have very low levels of conflict-related sexual violence—though notable exceptions are found in the pioneering work of Elisabeth Wood and Dara Cohen.[35]

The failure to recognize the huge variation in the incidence of sexual violence in war-affected countries, or to analyze its causes, has important, and unfortunate, policy implications. A comparison between countries with high levels of wartime sexual violence and the lack of attention on countries with low levels of wartime sexual violence may provide valuable insights into why sexual violence does or does *not* occur—knowledge that could help inform violence prevention policies.

> **Failure to analyze variation in the incidence of sexual violence has unfortunate policy implications.**

There Is No Compelling Evidence that Wartime Sexual Violence Is Increasing Worldwide

According to high-level UN reports and claims by senior UN officials during the past decade, sexual violence in armed conflicts around the world is increasing:

- In 2002 Elisabeth Rehn and Ellen Johnson Sirleaf claimed, "Violence against women during conflict has reached epidemic proportions."[36]

- In 2005 the above-cited UN-related report *Broken Bodies, Broken Dreams* claimed, "What is especially disturbing, however, about the statistics from the past ten years is how rife the phenomenon [of sexual violence in conflict-affected states] appears to have become."[37]

- In 2006 a major UNICEF (United Nations Children's Fund) report claimed, "Sexual violence has become an increasingly common aspect of contemporary warfare."[38]

- In 2007 Jan Egeland, former UN Under-Secretary-General for Humanitarian Affairs and Emergency Relief Coordinator, echoed Rehn and Johnson Sirleaf in asserting, "Rape in war has reached epidemic proportions."[39]

- In 2008 a high-level Wilton Park conference involving UN and other experts concluded that while existing data were "generally viewed as inadequate, available trend analysis suggests a marked increase in the scale and brutality of war-related sexual violence over the past two decades."[40]

Hardly any evidence has been produced to support the claim that sexual violence in wartime is increasing. However, some of the limited indirect evidence available suggests that the level of combatant-perpetrated sexual violence in war-affected countries has declined worldwide. But to the best of our knowledge, no UN report or senior official has ever hinted that this is even a possibility.

Indirect evidence suggests that the absolute level of conflict-related sexual violence has decreased, rather than increased, in recent years. This is primarily because there has been a global reduction in the number of large-scale armed conflicts. If the number and severity of conflicts decreases, we should—other things being equal—expect a decline in conflict-related sexual violence as well.

Over the past 20 years, *high-intensity* wars (i.e., those that generate 1,000 or more battle deaths a year) are down by more than 50 percent. Interstate wars, which typically have very high death tolls, have become extremely rare since the end of the Cold War.

This decline in the number of wars has helped drive down worldwide battle-death tolls: in the 1990s the worldwide toll of battle deaths was still well in excess of 400,000; in the new millennium, this figure has almost halved.[41]

Given this enormous decrease in conflict intensity, we believe that it is reasonable to assume that the overall level of conflict-related sexual violence has declined along with the number and deadliness of conflicts. When wars stop, rapes perpetrated by rebels, militias, and government forces may not stop completely, but their number surely declines. Some authors claim that "the nature of warfare is changing,"[42] resulting in increased targeting of civilians with sexual and other forms of violence. But there is little evidence to support this so-called new war thesis, which we critique in more detail in Chapter 3. We point out that the available data on deadly violence against civilians provide no support for claims that they are increasingly targeted in wartime.

Dara Cohen's new dataset indicates that *reported* sexual violence in the average civil conflict has increased over time.[43] But it is important to note that this finding does not necessarily mean that sexual violence itself has increased. The change may simply result from the increased reporting of sexual violence, rather than an increase in sexual violence itself.[44] As Amber Peterman, Cohen, and co-authors point out in a recent *Foreign Affairs* article, "no one knows what the relationship is between increased reports and increased rape."[45]

This is quite true. But we do know that the reporting of human rights violations, which of course includes cases of sexual violence, has grown dramatically since the mid-1980s. Between the mid-1980s and the late 1990s, for example, references to "human rights" in the *Economist* increased by some 300 percent.[46] And no one doubts that global interest in wartime sexual violence has increased substantially since the 1990s.

So, it is quite possible, indeed we believe likely, that *reporting* of sexual violence has increased sharply as interest and concern about it has grown. At the same time, the dramatic decline of conflict intensity makes it highly unlikely that the level of conflict-related sexual violence has increased globally.

Purdue University's Ann Marie Clark and Kathryn Sikkink of the University of Minnesota have provided a telling example of how increased human rights reporting can create a misleading impression that actual violations have increased.

In their 2011 study on how changes in human rights reporting may distort our understanding of human rights abuses, the authors examined what happened in Brazil as the

country slowly began transitioning from authoritarian military rule in the mid-1970s, democ-
ratized further during the 1980s, and became fully democratic in the 1990s.[47]

Despite this highly positive political change, data from the PTS, which provides annual country estimates of human rights abuses, indicated that the 1990s was a period in which the human rights situation in Brazil had *deteriorated* appreciably relative to the previous authoritarian and transition decades.[48]

The reason for the counterintuitive PTS finding is, however, not that the human rights situation was worse in the 1990s than previously—quite the contrary. As Clark and Sikkink point out, an authoritative study released in Brazil in 2007 showed that the worst period in Brazil for the state killing and disappearance of political opponents was in the 1970s, not the 1990s.[49] What happened was that over time "increased attentiveness to and awareness of a wider variety of abuses affected the level of coding."[50]

The sources used for coding—including the State Department—started collecting data on violations that had not been collected previously and likely more data on violations that had been collected previously. Human rights violations had *not* increased overall; *reporting* of abuses had.

> There has been an explosion of reporting on sexual violence since the beginning of the new millennium.

With respect to conflict-related sexual violence, increased attention and reporting almost certainly had a similar effect. There is no doubt that there has been an explosion of *reporting* on sexual violence since the beginning of the new millennium.

This is particularly true of the DRC, which has been the focus of extraordinary attention from the media, donor governments, international agencies, and NGOs. But as Severine Autesserre points out in a recent study:

> Sexual violence has not always dominated the discourse on the Congo. During the large-scale fighting that took place between 1994 and 2003, even though sexual violence existed at higher levels than today, few people discussed it.[51]

Indeed, the first major report drawing attention to wartime sexual violence in the Congo—a Human Rights Watch report—was not published until 2002.[52]

The difficulty in determining whether or not increases in reported sexual violence reflect actual increases in sexual violence is that there is no other source of cross-national data—*independent* from the level of reporting. To determine this would require the sort of data that only high-quality population surveys can provide. Such surveys, as we have pointed out, are notable mostly by their absence.

There is, in other words, no compelling evidence to support UN claims that the *absolute* level of wartime sexual violence worldwide is increasing. And there is no reliable direct evidence to support the claim that the level of sexual violence in an average conflict has increased.

"Strategic" Rape: Less Common Than Claimed

There is now a huge literature on strategic rape, or rape used intentionally as a weapon of war—i.e., deliberate policies, by governments as well as rebels, to use targeted rape campaigns to advance military and political goals.[53]

In 2002 an influential UN study, *Women, Peace and Security*, argued that "Gender-based and sexual violence have *increasingly become weapons of warfare* and are one of the defining characteristics of contemporary armed conflict."[54]

In 2005 a World Bank report on gender, conflict, and development claimed that gender-based violence in wartime is "consciously planned and targeted."[55]

In June 2011 Margot Wallstrom, the UN Secretary-General's Special Representative on Sexual Violence in Conflict, stated that "Sexual violence has become a tactic of choice for armed groups, being cheaper, more destructive and easier to get away with than other methods of warfare."[56]

But while strategic rape has become a subject of intense interest and debate in the policy, research, and advocacy communities, no evidence has been produced to support assertions that it has increased.

It is certainly possible to find examples of widespread sexual violence in wartime that has been perpetrated for a strategic purpose—perhaps the most notorious recent case being the Serbian rape campaign in Bosnia in the early 1990s.[57] Overall, however, the evidence suggests that strategic rape is the exception rather than the rule in most conflicts.

In 2011 a pilot study on the incidence of sexual violence in 20 African countries with recent or ongoing armed conflicts, undertaken by researchers at the Peace Research Institute Oslo (PRIO), found that the use of rape as a *weapon of war*, i.e., as a tactic that involves selective targeting of victims, is not as pervasive as the literature suggests. Indeed, contrary to the dominant narrative, the data from Africa suggest—and nothing more than suggest—that its prevalence may be declining:[58]

> In some African conflicts of the last decade, sexual violence has been characterized by selective targeting of victims. Yet, in most of the sample, we see fewer reports of selective targeting than during many of the wars of the 1990s. Governments, rebels and militias seemingly commit sexual violence without a clear purposeful selection of victims: the violence seems indiscriminate.[59]

In many cases claims that rape is being intentionally deployed as a 'weapon of war' are based on little more than assertion and anecdotes. On the other hand, researchers who have done extensive fieldwork and interviewed combatants in countries where "strategic rape" is reported to have occurred often have a very different understanding.[60]

In the DRC, for example, there have been frequent assertions, including some by high-ranking UN officials, that rape is strategically targeted. But a 2010 study by Sweden's Nordic Africa Institute, based on intensive interviews with government forces, notes that both soldiers and their officers had made it clear that sexual violence had not been used as part of any explicit military strategy.

Authors Maria Eriksson Baaz and Maria Stern note that in conducting their interviews:

Soldiers were always asked whether they had ever received orders to rape. Their answer was always no … While sexual violence is often used to humiliate and intimidate, this humiliation and intimidation is also much less strategic and far more complex than a combat strategy to further military gains.[61]

Sexual violence perpetrated by armed groups and government forces in the DRC does not appear to be directed at selected ethnic groups as was clearly the case in Bosnia and in Rwanda. Rather, as in the case of Liberia, rape is perpetrated "against any woman, regardless of political or ethnic affinity with the perpetrator."[62] This does not suggest intentional top-down strategically targeted rape campaigns.

In the absence of explicit orders, there may, of course, be the tacit approval from commanders. But the evidence suggests that it may also be the sheer inability to control the behaviour of troops that leads to sexual violence.

In the DRC, for example, a major part of the reason for the high levels of sexual violence appears to be that the military command system is too dysfunctional, disorganized, fragmented, and corrupt to prevent undisciplined, and often unpaid, troops from indulging in opportunistic looting and rape on a large scale. The fact that many government soldiers are heavy drug and alcohol users, and that their number includes poorly integrated members of former rebel groups, has meant that, even when attempted, discipline is difficult to enforce.[63]

Whether wartime rape is part of an organized top-down military strategy, or is rather driven by the opportunistic behaviour of undisciplined armed combatants, has obvious implications for policy that we discuss in Chapter 2.

Men as Victims and Women as Perpetrators

In the mainstream narrative on wartime sexual violence, males—usually rebels, militiamen, or government soldiers—are named the perpetrators; women are the victims. There is no doubt that women suffer disproportionately from sexual violence. But the evidence suggests that things are more complex than is generally assumed. Men are often victims and women are sometimes perpetrators.

A *gender perspective* on wartime sexual violence in practice usually means focusing on the incidence, causes, and consequences of sexual violence against women and girls. The experiences of men and boys have been mostly ignored, despite the fact that sexual violence against males in wartime has been reported in many countries around the world.[64]

The neglect of sexual violence against males is particularly evident in the case of the United Nations Security Council, whose 2008 Resolution 1820 that deals specifically with preventing wartime sexual violence fails to explicitly mention males at all.[65] The same is of course true of the landmark Security Council Resolution 1325 on Women, Peace and Security passed in 2000, which explicitly focuses on the effect of war on women and girls.[66]

Lara Stemple has pointed out that, in general, international human rights instruments dealing with sexual violence largely exclude males, "reflecting and embedding the assumption that sexual violence is a phenomenon relevant only to women and girls."[67]

There is extraordinarily little cross-national data on the extent of wartime sexual violence against men and boys, but what evidence there is suggests that it may be considerably greater than usually assumed.[68] Part of the problem is that even when sexual violence is recorded, it may not be described as such but may be labelled as "torture" with no reference to the sexual nature of the violations.[69]

Although understanding of the extent and variety of sexual violence directed against males in wartime is slowly growing,[70] relatively few of the small number of population surveys that ask questions about sexual violence against women in war-affected countries also ask about violations perpetrated against men and boys. And when such questions are asked, male victims may be even more reluctant than women to admit being violated. The paucity of reliable survey data contributes to, and reinforces, the general invisibility of males in the dominant "male perpetrator/female victim" narrative on wartime sexual violence.

> Little cross-national data exist on wartime sexual violence against men and boys, but what we have suggests that it may be greater than assumed.

Although data are too scarce to permit confident generalizations about the sexual violence that is perpetrated against males, the limited evidence we have suggests that it differs from that perpetrated against females.[71] There may be less forced sexual intercourse—although that certainly takes place—and more sexual torture, including castration and other forms of sexual mutilation, than is the case with wartime sexual violence against women.

In these cases, as with strategic rape, sexual violence is being used primarily to achieve nonsexual ends—to assert power over the victims, to coerce information, to prevent victims from procreating, or simply to terrify and humiliate them.[72]

The most comprehensive survey data on the extent of sexual violence against males in wartime come from major surveys carried out in Liberia and the DRC. In both cases the findings were published in the *Journal of the American Medical Association (JAMA)*. We have to keep in mind that, as pointed out above, these two countries had some of the worst records of wartime sexual violence, meaning that the findings cannot be generalized. But the studies provide information that most others have failed to collect. They are highly unusual not only because they ask detailed questions about men as victims of sexual violence but also because one of them inquires about women as perpetrators.

The Liberia survey, which was nationwide, was undertaken in May 2008. The sample size was substantial—1,666—and was composed of nearly equal numbers of men and women.[73]

A third of all respondents—representing one-third of the adult population—reported having served with fighting forces at some time.[74] The *JAMA* study used a very broad definition of who should be considered *combatants*. But a narrower definition would still result in a very high figure.[75] And fully one-third of the combatants were reportedly female—a remarkably high rate of female participation.[76]

Joining an armed group provided no protection against sexual violence—quite the contrary. Thirty-three percent of male combatants in Liberia were victims of sexual violence—although here the term *sexual violence* encompasses not only rape but also lesser violations.[77] Eighty-six percent of the perpetrators of sexual violence against male combatants were other combatants.

Forty-two percent of female combatants were victims of sexual violence, again mostly at the hands of other combatants.[78]

Noncombatant males suffered a much lower level of sexual violence (circa 7 percent) than combatant males (33 percent). The same applies to women. Nine percent of noncombatant females were victimized by sexual violence, compared with 42 percent of combatant females.[79]

> That women may be perpetrators of sexual violence is ignored almost completely in the mainstream narrative.

A 2010 survey of 998 adults aged 18 or older in three of the most war-affected regions in the DRC—North Kivu, South Kivu, and Ituri—also found rates of sexual violence for males that were far greater than normally assumed. Twenty-four percent of males reported that they had experienced sexual violence compared with 40 percent of females.[80] Both of these figures are extraordinarily high and reflect the pervasive violence and breakdown of authority in the Eastern Congo.

While the reality of sexual violence against males is slowly becoming acknowledged at the UN and occasionally in the media, the fact that women may be perpetrators of sexual violence, as well as victims, is ignored almost completely in the mainstream narrative. As a consequence, female perpetration has remained largely unexamined[81] and few attempts have been made to address it.

Only two major population surveys have asked questions about female perpetrators. The 2004 survey by Jana Asher and colleagues found that women in war-affected Sierra Leone participated in mixed gender groups of perpetrators in some 26 percent of the reported incidents of gang rape.[82]

The 2010 survey noted above, which was also published in *JAMA*, revealed that in the Eastern DRC female survivors of conflict-related sexual violence reported that a remarkable 41 percent of their perpetrators were also female. Male victims reported that 10 percent of their perpetrators were female. In both cases, an overwhelming proportion of the female perpetrators were combatants.[83]

It is unlikely that female perpetration of sexual violence is common in all conflicts. Indeed, the level of female perpetration indicated by the surveys in Sierra Leone and the DRC may be exceptionally high. But there is no doubt that it takes place elsewhere. There is evidence of female perpetration of sexual violence in the wars in Liberia and Haiti, and during the genocide in Rwanda.[84]

The reason we know so little about female perpetration is that the conventional view of wartime sexual violence has ignored its very possibility. This is why questions about the gender of the perpetrator are almost never asked in surveys.

The surveys in Liberia and the DRC on sexual violence against males, and in Sierra Leone and the DRC on women as perpetrators, have attracted little attention. Yet, they suggest that the exclusive focus on men as perpetrators/women as victims in the dominant narrative on wartime sexual violence is highly misleading.

The failure of the international community to take the issue of wartime sexual violence against men and boys seriously and the failure to acknowledge the role that women may play as perpetrators of sexual violence reinforce the oversimplified mainstream narrative and impoverish our understanding of the complexities of conflict-related sexual violence. This has important practical consequences for the creation of effective policy, which we discuss in more detail in the next chapter.

Armed Combatants Are *Not* the Major Perpetrators of Wartime Sexual Violence

The assumption that permeates the literature on sexual violence in war-affected countries is that it is directly related to the conflict, i.e., that it is perpetrated primarily by *combatants*—rebels, militias, and government forces. This is true of media reporting, human rights, and humanitarian advocacy reports, and major reports on wartime sexual violence undertaken by—or for—the UN and its agencies.

What is missing from this picture is domestic sexual violence. Yet, while gang rapes by combatants get the headlines, the survey data suggest that most sexual violence in war-affected countries is *domestic*—which means it takes place primarily in the family. The most frequent perpetrators are not combatants, but husbands, other partners, household members, and relatives.

Evidence for this is both compelling and largely ignored. For example, a series of survey-based studies using the neighbourhood method undertaken in war-affected countries found that:[85]

- In Sri Lanka a 2008 survey of sexual violence in two IDP camps and one resettlement village revealed that "in the vast majority of cases the perpetrators were known by victims and were overwhelmingly husbands."[86]
- In two Somali refugee camps and a nearby village in the Somali area of Ethiopia, more than 70 percent of rapes were perpetrated by husbands or other intimate partners. Strangers were responsible for less than 15 percent of the violations.[87]
- In a survey of sexual violence carried out in refugee camps in Northern Uganda, 5 percent of women reported being raped by someone outside of the household, while 30 percent experienced forced sex with intimate partners.[88]

WHY DOMESTIC SEXUAL VIOLENCE IS INVISIBLE IN WARTIME

In 2011 a major study on sexual violence in the Democratic Republic of the Congo (DRC) revealed that more than 400,000 women had been raped nationwide within a 12-month period between 2006 and 2007. In the worst affected region, Nord-Kivu, 20 percent of women of reproductive age reported to having been raped in their lifetime.[89]

Horrific accounts of savage sexual assaults by rebels, militias, and government forces, particularly in the war-affected eastern part of the DRC, have become the focus of intense media scrutiny, numerous advocacy reports by NGOs (nongovernmental organizations), investigations by international agencies, and resolutions of the UN (United Nations) Security Council.

Unsurprisingly, the DRC has been described by the UN as "the rape capital of the world."[90] But population surveys carried out over the past decade suggest that there are at least two other war-affected countries for which a more compelling claim to this title could be made. Thirty-nine percent of women in Uganda have been victims of sexual violence in their lifetime,[91] and in parts of Ethiopia, 44 percent of women report to having experienced sexual violence.[92]

This raises an obvious question. Why do high levels of sexual violence in the DRC receive so much attention from the international community, while what appear to be substantially higher levels of sexual violence in war-affected Uganda and Ethiopia receive so little?

Part of the answer is that the overwhelming majority of sexual violence in Uganda and Ethiopia takes place "in the family"; only a very small portion of the sexual violence appears to have been perpetrated by armed groups.

In Uganda, where 39 percent of women aged 15–49 were victims of sexual violence, 75 percent of them reported that the violence was perpetrated by current or former partners and boyfriends; another 11 percent by other relatives, friends, and acquaintances. Police and soldiers were perpetrators of less than 1 percent of the sexual violence.[93]

The major WHO (World Health Organization) survey undertaken in Ethiopia at the beginning of the new millennium was not nationwide but taken in a largely rural district south of the capital, Addis Ababa. It found that while 44 percent of women experienced intimate-partner sexual violence, less than 1 percent experienced sexual violence by nonpartners.[94]

None of these war-affected countries have been labelled a "rape capital," even though their rates of sexual violence are substantially higher than those in the DRC. This is in large part because domestic sexual violence is inherently unnewsworthy. It is part of an unchanging backdrop of quiet human suffering, mostly hidden from public view. It remains a taboo subject in many countries—one rarely discussed and even more rarely reported to the authorities. Its public invisibility helps explain the absence of media coverage.

Sexual violence perpetrated by intimate partners is also by far the most common type of sexual violence in the DRC.[95] Yet, unlike in Uganda or Ethiopia, sexual violence in the DRC has been associated in the media and by advocacy groups almost exclusively with armed conflict. The brutal rapes perpetrated, often in public by rebel, militia, and government forces, have been portrayed as the most common forms of sexual violence in the DRC.

Media coverage of "conflict rape" has been huge and this is not surprising: gang rapes have been numerous, victims have been mutilated and sometimes killed, and the world's biggest peacekeeping force has done little to prevent the assaults. Yet, the prevalence of domestic sexual violence, which is almost twice as high as that of conflict-related sexual violence, has received relatively little attention.

The shocking excesses are not the only reason that sexual violence in the DRC—similar to that in Sierra Leone, Liberia, Rwanda, the Sudan, and Bosnia—has received more attention than that in Uganda and Ethiopia. The former countries have all hosted major UN peace operations; the latter have not.

Peace operations typically include not only thousands of peacekeepers but large numbers of civilian personnel from a range of UN agencies, and from other international organizations, donor countries, and humanitarian NGOs. With them come the international media.

Staff in these agencies have been remarkably effective in advocating on behalf of the victims of conflict-related sexual violence—and other humanitarian causes. Advocacy reports from the field are often amplified by UN agencies, complemented by NGO advocacy efforts in donor government capitals, and given further momentum by sympathetic media coverage. Efforts on behalf of the victims of domestic sexual violence in war-affected countries have not had the same success.

While the UN addresses domestic sexual violence in its development programming, it also bears some responsibility for the relative invisibility of domestic sexual violence on the agenda of the international community in conflict-affected countries. Over the past five years, an effective campaign has been waged within the world body to persuade the Security Council that conflict-related sexual violence is a "threat to international peace and security."[96] But domestic sexual violence is conspicuously absent from this agenda.

Framing sexual violence as a military security issue calls for security policy responses, namely the provision of physical protection from combatant sexual assaults. While important, these measures do little for the victims of domestic sexual violence.

Getting conflict-related sexual violence recognized as an international security issue has helped raise its political salience on the Security Council's agenda and mobilize resources to combat it. But it has marginalized domestic sexual violence in war-affected countries still further.

Overall, the Learning Network reported that in the five countries surveyed using the neighbourhood method:

> rates of rape by a spouse or friend were far higher than rates of rape by a stranger. Such evidence contradicts common understanding of the kinds of GBV [gender-based violence] that are experienced by women in communities affected by crisis.[97]

Even in the war-affected countries that are the worst affected by combatant-perpetrated sexual violence, the evidence indicates that the nationwide incidence of domestic sexual violence is higher than rape by rebels, militias, government troops, or other strangers.

In the DRC, which is one of the countries worst affected by sexual violence, a new study, using data from the 2007 nationwide Demographic and Health Survey (DHS), was undertaken by Amber Peterman and colleagues. It found that the number of women who experienced *intimate partner sexual violence* (IPSV) in their lifetime was almost twice as high as the number of women who were raped by other individuals—the latter, of course, include the rebels, militias, and government troops whose sexual violence generates so much media coverage.[98]

Why should rape perpetrated by combatants in countries like the DRC be the source of so much attention from the international community, while domestic sexual violence, which appears to be far more prevalent, receive so little?

We examine this question in greater detail in Chapter 2. Here we simply note that the sexual violence perpetrated by rebels and other combatants is often horrifically brutal and frequently takes place in public. Gang rapes by multiple perpetrators are not uncommon, and victims are often mutilated and sometimes killed. Media coverage of the worst excesses, from Bosnia to the Congo, has understandably been extensive.

Domestic sexual violence, by contrast, remains a taboo subject—one very rarely discussed openly or reported to the authorities. It is largely hidden from public view and far fewer of its victims are killed or mutilated than is the case with conflict-related rape. It is, in other words, inherently less newsworthy.

No one doubts that the sexual violence associated *directly* with warfare—i.e., that perpetrated by combatants—is a huge challenge needing urgent attention. It certainly differs from domestic sexual violence in its nature and likely also in its causes,[99] but if the international community is serious about reducing sexual violence in war-affected countries, then far greater attention needs to be paid to the largely ignored problem of domestic sexual violence than has been the case to date.

Based on the available data, domestic sexual violence seems to be the most pervasive, though not normally the most extreme, threat to women and children—boys as well as girls—in war-affected countries. It is also by far the most common source of sexual danger in peacetime—far more so than stranger rape.[100]

Combatant-perpetrated sexual violence decreases substantially when wars come to an end. There is, however, little reason to expect that the incidence of domestic sexual violence will decline when the fighting stops—nor is there any evidence to suggest that it does. Indeed, in cases where male fighters are demobilized and return home—often to destroyed homes and the frustrations and privations of unemployment—domestic violence, sexual as well as physical, may increase.

This chapter has examined a number of pervasive biases in the mainstream narrative on sexual violence in war-affected countries. It has argued that these biases not only preclude a more comprehensive and nuanced understanding of what drives wartime sexual violence but that they also divert attention from important policy options.

In Chapter 2 we analyze what drives the biases that permeate so much of the literature on sexual violence in war-affected countries and examine the implications for policy.

Albert Gonzalez Farran / UN Photo. SUDAN.

CHAPTER 2

Getting It Wrong about Wartime Sexual Violence—and Why It Matters

In the previous chapter we argued that research findings on wartime sexual violence are often misunderstood and misreported, not only by the media and advocacy groups but also by the UN (United Nations) and its agencies. In this chapter we ask why this might be the case and look more closely at what implications this may have for policy.

No one doubts that the sexual violence experienced by countless individuals in countries is one of the grossest violations of human rights. It scars its survivors mentally, as well as physically; it rips families apart; and it inflicts humiliation, shame, enormous pain, psychological trauma, and frequently death on its victims.

And as LaShawn Jefferson points out, it is "the only crime for which the community's reaction is often to stigmatize the victim rather than prosecute the perpetrator."[101]

It is encouraging that the seriousness of these violations—which is not contested—is increasingly being recognized. What is less clear, however, is why the mainstream narrative should so persistently get it wrong about the sexual violence perpetrated by combatants. Moreover, why should the domestic sexual violence that takes place in wartime, which claims more victims than conflict-related sexual violence, be ignored almost completely?

Explaining the Biases

The pervasive biases that we described earlier are best understood in terms of the incentive structures that underpin both media coverage of wartime sexual violence, and the reporting, analysis, and advocacy of international agencies and NGOs (nongovernmental organizations), whose mission includes humanitarian advocacy and service delivery.[102]

Dramatically high rates of sexual violence, victim narratives that depict gang rapes by armed groups, the savage physical violence perpetrated against victims, and the rape and mutilation of children are newsworthy precisely because they are shocking. A core news imperative of the global media business remains:"If it bleeds, it leads."

The fact that there is little or no reported sexual violence perpetrated by armed groups in many armed conflicts should be good news, but these cases are not newsworthy—news-gatherers rarely focus on things that do not happen.

Similarly, domestic sexual violence in countries in conflict is of little interest to the media. It is not new, it takes place behind closed doors, and it is mostly invisible.

The Incentives That Drive Humanitarian Organizations

With respect to international agencies and NGOs whose mission includes humanitarian advocacy and service delivery, the misleading claims are driven by rather different incentives.

Those engaged in humanitarian advocacy and service delivery—including for victims of sexual violence—typically bring a strong, often passionate, commitment to providing assistance for those in need. But securing funding to address these needs is a continuing challenge. Humanitarian needs are great, but the demands on donors from UN agencies and international NGOs are always greater than the funds available to meet them.

This is so despite the fact that the absolute level of humanitarian assistance has risen significantly since the end of the Cold War, in part as a consequence of powerful advocacy campaigns waged by international humanitarian organizations. Between 2000 and 2010, humanitarian assistance almost doubled in value.[103] And between 2000 and 2009, the share of this aid concentrated in conflict-affected states had increased from about 40 percent to 65 percent.[104]

But despite the increase in overall funding, there remains a large gap between what is *requested* via mechanisms like the UN's Consolidated Appeals Process (CAP) and what is actually *allocated* by the donors.[105]

With demand for humanitarian funding greatly exceeding supply, it is not surprising that competition for funding among UN agencies that play a major humanitarian role (such as UNICEF [United Nations Children's Fund], UNHCR [United Nations High Commissioner for Refugees], and the World Food Program) between the agencies and NGOs, and between the NGOs themselves, is often rife.

In their critical 2004 analysis of contemporary humanitarian practice, *The Charity of Nations*, Ian Smillie and Larry Minear identify a dilemma that lies at the heart of today's humanitarian enterprise:

> In a highly competitive environment—made competitive by great needs and inadequate funding—exaggeration not only pays, it is sometimes the only thing that will dislodge funding from donors who themselves have too few resources and too many supplicants.[106]

With funding never sufficient to meet humanitarian needs, UN agencies and NGOs have a powerful incentive to seek the media headlines that most effectively highlight the plight of those in need.

In this context, the so-called CNN effect can play an important role. The term refers to the impact of the media in bringing home to those living in donor countries the extent of a humanitarian crisis, the desperate plight of the survivors, and the moral and political imperatives to assist them. The CNN effect can help pressure donors to respond to crises and private individuals to give to appeals from humanitarian agencies and NGOs.

Fundraisers in humanitarian organizations well understand that emotive appeals for assistance have a greater impact than the statistics—hence the frequency with which shocking victim narratives of conflict-related sexual violence feature in major UN and NGO reports on wartime sexual violence. The problem is that the affecting narrative accounts, while true, are presented in such a way as to suggest that they are the norm. This is rarely the case and in this sense they are misleading.

On the other hand, there is no incentive for humanitarian agencies to focus on domestic sexual violence in wartime, even though it appears to result in far more victims than conflict-related sexual violence. The fact that domestic sexual violence occurs both in times of peace as well as war means that it is not seen as an emergency issue. As such, it is not a compelling candidate for humanitarian assistance.

A further source of potential bias lies in the fact that assessments of humanitarian need are rarely independent. Most requests to donors for humanitarian assistance are based on assessments by the very organizations that will be beneficiaries of any funding that is granted. This inevitably causes conflicts of interest to arise. As a 2003 report from the Overseas Development Institute put it, it is difficult to believe that analyses of humanitarian need are objective if the organization making the assessment has a vested interest in the result.[107]

There is compelling evidence that many assessments of the gravity of humanitarian crises by NGOs and UN agencies are exaggerated.[108]

Does Getting It Wrong Really Matter?

Few deny that the demand for resources to combat wartime sexual violence and to assist its victims is far greater than the supply, so why should it matter if the scope and incidence of sexual violence are exaggerated in order to secure the resources that everyone agrees are needed?

After all, as Tufts University's Kelly M. Greenhill and co-author Peter Andreas note:

> large numbers often help stimulate and increase funding flows to agencies and organizations whose mission is dealing with the negative externalities of conflict (such as humanitarian crises).[109]

The beneficiaries of humanitarian assistance have no reason to be concerned about its provenance. And humanitarian fundraisers can well argue that if protecting the vulnerable and

"MAGICAL NUMBERS" AND WARTIME SEXUAL VIOLENCE

Prize-winning *New York Times* columnist Nicholas Kristof has played a critically important role in drawing international attention to wartime sexual violence. But some of his widely cited claims have also spread misinformation about the extent of sexual violence in the worst affected countries.

In a 2009 *New York Times* article, for example, Kristof claim that, "as many as three-fourths of women" had been raped in Liberia's civil war.[110] The provenance of this much-publicized claim is not clear from the article, but Kristof is likely referring to a 2004 WHO (World Health Organization) report.[111]

But even a cursory reading of the WHO survey report makes it clear that it could never support such an extraordinary claim.

The WHO figures do indeed show that 77 percent of women in the survey had been raped, but in fact all the respondents had been chosen precisely because they were *survivors of sexual violence*.[112] So the data reveal that three-quarters of survivors of sexual violence had been raped rather than having suffered other forms of sexual assault. This is hardly surprising. Yet the figure tells us absolutely nothing about the nationwide prevalence of rape.

The best estimate for the rate of sexual violence against females in Liberia in this period is very high, but nothing remotely like the figure cited by Kristof and endlessly recycled in the media by advocacy groups and even in UN (United Nations) publications.

In 2007, a major nationwide survey by the Demographic and Health Survey (DHS) organization found that the lifetime prevalence rate of sexual violence among Liberian women aged 15 to 49 was 18 percent.[113] As we pointed out earlier, this is the same as the prevalence rate for adult women in the United States.

While Kristof's misleading claim has been reiterated countless times, the lower, and far more accurate, estimate has largely been ignored by the media. It simply wasn't newsworthy.

If this type of error—and the media treatment of it—were exceptional, there would be little cause for concern. But it is far from exceptional. In fact, it is symptomatic of what Kelly M. Greenhill calls:

> the resilience of conflict-related magical numbers … that are deemed to be "true" simply because they are widely believed to be true.[114]

The problem of inflated "magical number" war statistics is also evident in claims about the global total of child soldiers, the number of children killed in modern wars, civilian deaths as a share of all violent war deaths, and the intense controversies over war death tolls in Darfur, Iraq, and the Democratic Republic of the Congo (DRC). We examine the incentive structures that drive such inflated claims—and why they matter for policy—in this chapter.

saving lives require an overemphasis on the extent and gravity of the problem, so be it—the ends justify the means.

This attitude is understandable. But while inflated claims about the extent of wartime sexual violence may help mobilize support for international action in the short term, they cannot form the basis for effective policy in the long term.

As Greenhill points out, bad data can have a decidedly negative impact on policy:

> at best, inaccurate numbers can lead to wasted resources and effort where such expenditures are unnecessary; at worst, they may result in too few supplies and personnel being deployed where they are required most acutely.[115]

Not only will funds be allocated inequitably—and not necessarily for the most pressing needs—but the competition for resources among advocacy organizations and service providers may generate a quest for ever more shocking statistics and victim narratives.[116] The resulting distortion of evidence will likely increase the already considerable skepticism with which donors regard many of the claims made by humanitarian agencies and NGOs about the gravity of humanitarian emergencies.[117] This "crying wolf" phenomenon may in turn affect donor willingness to respond to future crises.

Why "Getting It Right" Matters for Policy

In this section we consider the policy implications of accepting the five myths about wartime sexual violence identified in Chapter 1.

These myths, along with other misleading claims about wartime sexual violence, are driven by what Andreas and Greenhill refer to as the "politics of numbers." This, they warn, "can help to perpetuate failing and flawed policies, distort funding, generate and support misleading indicators of policy 'progress' and 'success,' manipulate media coverage and cloud public debate."[118]

The Bias towards the Extreme Cases of Conflict-Related Sexual Violence

In Chapter 1 we noted the disproportionate attention paid to those countries that are worst affected by conflict-related sexual violence. And we pointed out that a significant number of countries in conflict, which experience relatively little—or no—reported sexual violence, are largely ignored in the mainstream narrative.

This means that almost no attention is paid by policy-makers—and little by researchers—to the critical question of why some countries in conflict experience remarkably low levels of sexual violence, while others suffer greatly.

Yet, a better understanding of what causes the difference in wartime sexual violence rates could well help improve sexual violence prevention programs. Unfortunately, this issue is of almost no interest to policy communities and receives very little attention in the research community—the works of Elisabeth Wood, Dara Cohen, and Ragnhild Nordås being rare, but important, exceptions.[119]

The Policy Implications of the Unfounded Belief That Wartime Sexual Violence Is Increasing

The widely held conviction that conflict-related sexual violence around the world is increasing means that there has been little policy interest in determining why it might be decreasing. Little scholarly research has been devoted to this question either.

In fact, there are reasons for believing that conflict-related sexual violence has declined since the end of the Cold War.

In Chapter 1 we argued that it was reasonable to expect that, all else equal, conflict-related sexual violence will decline if the number and deadliness of armed conflicts decline substantially. Given that wars have become less deadly and frequent over the past two decades—and in the absence of independent trend data on sexual violence—we should therefore assume that conflict-related sexual violence would have declined as well.[120]

> Policy-makers are unlikely to show interest in determining why sexual violence may be decreasing if they are convinced it is increasing.

If ending wars reduces conflict-related sexual violence, then, as we explain below, strategies to end wars—including *peacemaking* (seeking to stop ongoing wars via negotiations) and post-conflict *peacebuilding* (seeking to prevent wars that have stopped from starting again)—also become indirect strategies for reducing conflict-related sexual violence.

Given that there is little evidence thus far that any of the international strategies for preventing wartime sexual violence in war-affected societies have had more than marginal success,[121] examining the potential for indirect strategies to achieve this end would make a lot of policy sense.

But policy-makers are unlikely to show any interest in determining why sexual violence might be decreasing if they are convinced that it is increasing, which is why seeking to "get it right" with respect to sexual violence trends is important for policy.

The Policy Implications of the Strategic Rape Thesis

If mass rape is strategic—e.g., if it has been initiated as part of a top-down policy intended to terrorize civilians, or as part of a campaign of ethnic cleansing—the international community may have some immediate leverage that can be used to pressure the leaders of the government or rebel forces to stop. These may include threats to withhold aid to governments, to impose sanctions,[122] or to push for indictments in the International Criminal Court.

If, as studies suggest, rape perpetrated by soldiers and rebels is not part of a top-down strategic plan, but is due to the fact that the military command system is simply too weak to stop the abuse, there is relatively little that the international community can do in the short term. In the longer term, however, bringing perpetrators of rape to justice may provide a measure of deterrence against sexual violence in future wars.[123]

We have argued that some of the claims that sexual violence is deployed as a "weapon of war" are based on little more than anecdotal accounts. Pushing for policy initiatives on the basis of false assumptions is clearly a recipe for bad policy. It underlines yet again the need for reliable data—the *sine qua non* of evidence-based policy.

The Failure to Address Sexual Violence against Males and Female Perpetration

In the mainstream narrative on wartime sexual violence, the overwhelming emphasis is on sexual violence directed against women and girls. The attention devoted to this issue is long overdue and wholly warranted—the impact of wartime sexual violence on women and girls has been ignored for centuries, and women are far more likely to be victimized than men.

Less understandable is the fact that sexual violence against men and boys has been largely ignored. While the UN continues to stress the importance of gender sensitivity, its policy prescriptions continue to treat wartime sexual violence as a phenomenon that affects only women or girls. Male victims are very rarely even mentioned in the reports related to the Security Council's 1325 agenda, and the issue of female perpetration of sexual violence remains completely invisible.

The UN's failure to address the issue of sexual violence against males in any meaningful manner has led to considerable criticism.[124] The Secretary-General's 2012 report on *Conflict-Related Sexual Violence* belatedly acknowledges that men may be victimized by sexual violence,[125] but then notes that:

> recent information underscores that the situation of male victims ... require[s] deeper examination. The issue must be understood from all perspectives and addressed at all levels as part of a *comprehensive approach to protecting civilians.*[126]

The second sentence in the above quote is far from clear, but it likely means that sexual violence against men and boys will be dealt with as part of the UN's broader Protection of Civilians agenda, and not the Security Council's agenda on conflict-related sexual violence.[127]

The omission of males from the mainstream analysis on conflict-related sexual violence not only distorts our understanding of the nature of wartime sexual violence, it also has negative policy consequences—namely that the needs of male victims are systematically ignored.

The lack of attention to the male survivors is remarkable:

> 4076 nongovernmental organizations (NGOs) around the world address rape during wartime and other forms of political sexual violence. Of these, only 3% mention the experience of males in their informational materials, typically as a passing reference.[128]

And, as Charli Carpenter has pointed out:

> while the humanitarian assistance community has taken strides in addressing the physical and psycho-social needs of female rape survivors ... services for male survivors of such violence in conflict situations are nearly non-existent.[129]

This is not to minimize the issue of sexual violence perpetrated by men against women—far from it. The point is simply that if the substantial amount of sexual violence against males is systematically neglected then policy responses are bound to be insufficient and inequitable.

While international agencies and NGOs are slowly beginning to address wartime sexual violence against males, the issue of female perpetration of sexual violence has attracted almost no attention. This is in spite of the fact that, as we noted in Chapter 1, findings from the few studies that ask about the gender of perpetrators indicate that conflict-related sexual violence perpetrated by women is more common than usually assumed.

> The point is simply that if the substantial amount of sexual violence against males is systematically neglected then policy is bound to be insufficient and inequitable.

Bringing female perpetrators to justice is unlikely to happen as long as national governments and the international community fail to recognize that female perpetration of conflict-related sexual violence is a reality.

Responding to Domestic Sexual Violence in Wartime

The focus on rape perpetrated by rebels, militias, and government troops has—understandably—been intensive, yet, as we pointed out in Chapter 1, the more pervasive threat to the rights and integrity of women posed by domestic sexual violence in wartime has been ignored almost completely.

Just how domestic sexual violence in wartime can be countered is a challenge that is both complex and lacking in any obvious short-term solutions. One thing is clear however: until the problem is taken more seriously, by both the international community and national governments, there will be little effective action to resolve it.

Lack of interest is not the only challenge in determining appropriate policy responses. Indeed, as we point out later in this chapter:

- The policy prescriptions that are advocated by the UN for preventing conflict-related rape have little relevance for domestic sexual violence.

- The fact that marital rape is neither a crime nor a priority for most governments in war-affected countries rules out many obvious domestic law and order responses to domestic sexual violence in war-affected states.

- The fact that domestic sexual violence is prevalent in peacetime as well as wartime means that it does not, by definition, qualify as an emergency issue. This may complicate the access that survivors of domestic violence have to medical and psychological support, since most assistance in conflict settings is *humanitarian*, i.e., it is specifically designed to bring assistance to those suffering as a consequence of emergencies—a term that includes wars as well as natural disasters.

The UN and Wartime Sexual Violence

The reason why the five myths outlined in Chapter 1 have had an impact on policy-making is that despite the increased attention that the issue of wartime sexual violence has received, little effort has gone into collecting reliable evidence. The systems in place to monitor patterns of sexual violence are clearly insufficient.

In October 2000 the UN Security Council passed the groundbreaking Resolution 1325 on Women, Peace and Security and took responsibility for, among other things, creating a policy framework and process for dealing with the manifold challenges of addressing conflict-related sexual violence.

The political and legal framework that has guided this process has been informed by a series of Security Council resolutions that included—and followed—Resolution 1325.[130]

But while the Council had set itself—and UN member states—a large number of challenging goals, it has taken only perfunctory and inadequate steps towards monitoring progress to meet those goals.

What this lack of reliable statistics has meant in practice is that almost 12 years after the passage of Resolution 1325, which had flagged the need to "consolidate data on the impact of armed conflict on women and girls,"[131] neither the UN nor any other international agency has any idea whether wartime sexual violence is increasing or decreasing, either worldwide or in individual war-affected countries.

The same lack of the most basic data means that policy-makers have little idea whether or not their sexual violence prevention policies are having any impact. And it has permitted the misleading claims about the extent of conflict-related sexual violence noted in Chapter 1 to go largely unchallenged.

Things are, however, slowly beginning to change. The UN is finally addressing the need to acquire data on wartime sexual violence. It is far from clear, however, that what will be provided will be adequate to monitor whether wartime sexual violence is increasing or decreasing, or to determine the impact of UN and other sexual violence prevention programs.

In April 2010 the UN Secretary-General submitted a report to the Security Council that called for data to be collected on, among other things, the "incidence of sexual violence in conflict-affected countries." The report stresses the importance of collecting data on quantitative indicators:

> Indicators are signposts of change; a means for determining the status quo and the progress towards the intended goal. They indicate trends and … are critical for effective monitoring and evaluation.[132]

The Secretary-General's report notes that indicator data on the incidence of sexual violence would be collected by population surveys.[133] But this, he cautions, would require "specialized and careful technical and conceptual development."[134] The pilot phase of data collection on the incidence of wartime sexual violence could take two to five years.[135]

How the implementation of such surveys would be funded was unclear, and the past reluctance of donor governments to pay for data collection in this area suggests that lack of sufficient funding may pose a significant barrier to progress.

In December 2010 the UN Security Council adopted Resolution 1960, which formally requested the UN Secretary-General to establish monitoring, analysis, and reporting arrangements on conflict-related sexual violence.[136] But it is clear from the cautious language of the Secretary-General's January 2012 report, *Conflict-Related Sexual Violence,* that data collection is seen as problematic:

> Common information bases and methodologies for data collection for cases of conflict-related sexual violence are under discussion *and continue to remain a challenge owing to the varying mandates and responsibilities of partner institutions.*[137]

It is extraordinary, though perhaps not surprising given political sensitivities among member states, that almost 12 years since the passage of Resolution 1325 on Women, Peace and Security, the collection of the most basic data on conflict-related sexual violence should still be "under discussion."

The Secretary-General's 2012 report notes that a "technical-level working group" was being established to "review information, monitor and verify incidents of sexual violence, analyse data, trends and patterns, [and] prepare reports."[138]

How this would be accomplished, or when the technical working group might start reporting on its findings, is not spelled out. Perhaps significantly, there is not a single reference in the Secretary-General's 2012 report to the use of population surveys, which had been stressed as the primary means of gathering sexual violence data in the 2010 report.

In fact, the 2012 report makes clear that the UN's primary mode of collecting data will be based, not on surveys, but on the "monitoring and verification of incidents."[139] The model here is the Monitoring and Reporting Mechanism (MRM) that the UN uses to collect data that is relevant to its mandate on children and armed conflict, and which is discussed in detail in Chapter 3. In collecting sexual violence incident data, the 2012 report emphasizes the need for coordination with the MRM's data collection exercises.

Almost 12 years since the passage of Resolution 1325, the collection of the most basic data on conflict-related sexual violence is still "under discussion."

MRM-type data are useful for a variety of purposes, from identifying the perpetrators of conflict-related sexual violence, to providing information on particular incidents, and recording government and UN efforts to stop and prevent rape. But they are not useful for measuring overall trends in rates of sexual violence.

The MRM relies on counts of incidents of sexual violence that are reported to the UN. But this grossly understates the extent of wartime sexual violence, compared with the data derived from high-quality population surveys.

In other words, the methodology now being used by the UN to report on sexual violence in wartime cannot provide the reliable, objective, and comprehensive data that the Secretary-General's report claims is the goal of the new monitoring and reporting arrangements.

> Population surveys are the only way to access accurate and robust data on wartime sexual violence.

Some idea of the extent to which the UN's methodology undercounts the incidence of sexual violence is evident in a recent article by Tia Palermo and Amber Peterman in the *Bulletin of the World Health Organization*:

> More than 15,000 rapes were reported each year to the United Nations mission in the DRC in both 2008 and 2009 … The major limitation of this figure is that it is based only on cases reported to the United Nations mission. In contrast, a recent study using population estimates and data from the nationally representative Demographic and Health Survey (DHS) conducted from 2006–2007 showed that *the rate of rape among women aged 15 to 49 years in a 12-month period was 26 times higher than the estimates based on reports to United Nations authorities.*[140]

The only way to access reasonably accurate and robust data on the nationwide incidence and prevalence of wartime sexual violence is via high-quality population surveys—like those used in the major international effort to track progress towards the Millennium Development Goals (MDGs). Nothing remotely like this effort currently exists for tracking trends in wartime sexual violence, and the January 2012 Secretary-General's report, *Conflict-Related Sexual Violence*, suggests that little progress is likely on this front any time soon.

Combatting Wartime Sexual Violence: The Key Challenges

Since the end of the 1990s, the protection of civilians in war-affected countries from "imminent threats of physical violence" (including sexual violence) has become an increasingly important policy focus within the UN—and a source of considerable debate. In 1999 a landmark report by then Secretary-General Kofi Annan noted that the protection of civilians "is fundamental to the central mandate of the Organization. The responsibility for the protection of civilians cannot be transferred to others."[141]

The UN, the report argues, was the only international organization that could undertake this role. But in 2009 a major independent study commissioned by the UN's Department of Peacekeeping Operations and the Office for the Coordination of Humanitarian Affairs noted that, a decade after the first peacekeeping mission was mandated to protect civilians, there was still considerable confusion within the UN as to what this meant:

the UN Secretariat, troop- and police-contributing countries, host states, humanitarian actors, human rights professionals, and the missions themselves continue to struggle over what it means for a peacekeeping operation to protect civilians, in definition and in practice.[142]

> Stopping sexual violence in today's civil wars is perhaps the greatest challenge confronting the UN's protection of civilians agenda.

The report highlighted the shortcomings of the UN's current approach to protecting civilians, pointing to gaps in policy guidance, planning, and preparedness; lack of mission-wide strategy; inconsistent civilian and military leadership; resource constraints; and a lack of capacity to collect and analyze information on day-to-day threats and potential crises.[143]

Given these challenges, it is not surprising that one of the report's authors subsequently wondered publicly whether the protection of civilians in volatile war-affected countries might not be an "impossible mandate."[144]

Stopping sexual violence in today's civil wars is perhaps the greatest challenge confronting the UN's protection of civilians agenda. Indeed, Anne Marie Goetz of UN Women (or the United Nations Entity for Gender Equality and the Empowerment of Women, UNIFEM) has suggested that stopping wartime sexual violence amounts to a *"doubly impossible"* mandate for UN peacekeepers.[145]

Providing effective protection against conflict-related sexual violence is extraordinarily challenging. The taboos and sensitivities that relate to rape are associated with massive under-reporting, and the government security forces, including police and military, that have primary responsibility for protecting civilians from sexual attacks are often major perpetrators.[146] In most cases, UN peacekeepers are simply too few in number to provide adequate protection for civilians at risk.

At the UN there have been increasingly insistent calls to end the pervasive and enduring culture of impunity that continues to protect perpetrators—government forces as well as rebels—from prosecution. Bringing perpetrators to trial and punishing them would not only serve the cause of justice, but would also, so it is claimed, act as a deterrent to future violations.

> There have been increasingly insistent calls to end the culture of impunity that protects perpetrators from prosecution.

There has been real progress at the normative level over the past decade. Specific acts of sexual violence have been designated as both war crimes and crimes against humanity under the Rome Statute of the International Criminal Court (ICC), and a number of high-level officials have been indicted for crimes involving sexual violence.

But while few doubt that these international legal developments are important, particularly for the long term, there is little evidence that they have—thus far—had a major impact in terms of deterring sexual violence in countries.

This is not surprising. Those ultimately responsible for acts of sexual violence are unlikely to be deterred from sanctioning rape or other forms of sexual violence unless they believe that there is a finite possibility that they may be arrested, tried, and punished.

There is some statistical evidence that the deterrent effect of national human rights trials can be effective over time in reducing violations, but that evidence does not yet include deterrence of crimes of sexual violence.[147]

> ## The UN often has too few resources to provide adequate security for all civilians who are at risk.

A second approach to preventing conflict-related sexual violence, one that has a more immediate impact and that has been adopted by the UN in its peace operations, focuses on the direct physical protection of women and girls in war-affected countries. Here a range of tactics are already being used to a greater or lesser extent in peacekeeping missions. These include:

- Using peacekeepers to escort women who are attending markets, looking after crops or livestock, or collecting water, firewood, or animal fodder away from home.
- Creating mobile stand-by Rapid Reaction Force units that can be deployed to deal with threats to the peace—including rape.
- Establishing protected safe havens.
- Designing and managing gender-sensitive internally displaced persons (IDPs) and refugee camps.[148]

These and other physical protection measures can make an important difference in particular situations, but no one in the UN believes that they are sufficient. As the UN's Department of Peacekeeping Operations (DPKO) points out:

- We often protect civilians in harsh conditions, with limited or insufficient resources, and with partners who sometimes lack the will or capacity to do their part.
- Peacekeeping operations often deploy amid the unrealistic expectation that they will be able to protect all civilians at all times.

The problem is that in the countries worst affected by conflict-related sexual violence the UN simply has too few resources for its physical protection measures to provide adequate security for all civilians who are at risk.[149]

Although there is currently little evidence that either deterrence or physical protection measures are having an impact on the incidence of conflict-related sexual violence, this does not mean that there are no other prospects for improvement.

Currently, the most effective strategies for substantially reducing the worldwide incidence of conflict-related sexual violence appear to be international action to end the wars in which it flourishes—and to prevent wars that have ended from starting again. There is now considerable evidence that what the UN calls *peacemaking*—the use of mediation to negotiate peace agreements between the warring parties—has played an important role in stopping conflicts since the end of the Cold War.[150] And the evidence suggests that post-conflict peacebuilding programs that seek to stabilize post-conflict settings and prevent wars from recurring also have a positive effect.[151]

And as we have noted previously, we have good reason to assume that when conflicts end, the incidence of sexual violence perpetrated by soldiers and rebels will also decline, though it may not cease entirely.

Domestic Sexual Violence in War-Affected Countries

The UN's policies for addressing wartime sexual violence focus almost entirely on abuses that are conflict related. The domestic sexual violence in war-affected countries, which the evidence suggests claims far more victims than that perpetrated by combatants, is ignored completely in the mainstream narrative.

Note that we are not arguing that domestic sexual violence *in general* is ignored by the international community. It is, in fact, the central focus of numerous programs around the world undertaken by the UN and its agencies, as well as countless NGOs, all of which seek to prevent all forms of violence against women and bring assistance to its victims.[152] The majority of these efforts take place in peacetime, but because today's conflicts rarely encompass all of the national territory of war-affected countries, some programs will likely continue during periods of conflict in parts of the country not directly affected by the fighting.

However, the fact that the mainstream narrative on wartime sexual violence ignores domestic sexual violence completely, while the UN has excluded it from its Women, Peace and Security agenda, means that it has become invisible politically in wartime. This in turn means that it receives little or no high-level political attention and few of the resources that are devoted to addressing the far more highly publicized challenges of conflict-related sexual violence.

Key officials have, however, made it explicit that the UN's focus lies elsewhere. In her opening address to the much-cited 2008 Wilton Park conference on the role of peacekeepers in dealing with conflict-related sexual violence, the UN's Anne Marie Goetz described three types of sexual violence that occur in today's war-affected countries. They are:

- *Widespread and systematic rape*—i.e., organized campaigns of sexual violence during wartime.
- *Widespread and opportunistic rape*—i.e., large-scale unorganized sexual violence in war-affected countries.
- *Isolated and random rape*—"rape that occurs at all times, in all societies and that is unrelated to political strategy (*widespread and systematic sexual violence*) or the chaos of armed conflict (*widespread and opportunistic sexual violence*)."[153]

Goetz does not mention domestic sexual violence per se, but it is likely included in the last category. Domestic political violence in wartime is, however, far from being "isolated and random." Indeed, as we have pointed out, the limited evidence we have indicates that it is far more pervasive than conflict-related sexual violence, even in cases like the DRC where the level of conflict-related rape rates are extremely high.

It is clear that domestic sexual violence is *not* an issue that the UN believes that the Women, Peace and Security agenda should address. It follows that, like isolated and random rape, it should be treated as "a domestic criminal matter warranting a *domestic law and order response*, quite distinct from sexual violence as a matter of international peace and security."[154]

But in many war-affected countries, domestic sexual violence *cannot* be dealt with via a national or international law and order response. First, as we flagged earlier, in the large majority of poor countries where most wars take place, marital rape is not illegal. Indeed, fewer than 60 countries in the world have legislation explicitly criminalizing marital rape.[155] And even in those countries where it is illegal, the perpetrators are often protected by a de facto culture of impunity.

Second, domestic sexual violence is neither a war crime nor a crime against humanity under international law, and cannot thus be prosecuted by the ICC under the terms of the Rome Statute.

This is not all. The physical measures intended by the UN to provide protection against conflict-related sexual violence—like firewood patrols and escorting women to markets—are wholly irrelevant when it comes to protecting women and girls from sexual violence within the home.

The neglect of domestic sexual violence is not restricted to the Security Council's agenda on wartime sexual violence. UN Action against Sexual Violence in Conflict, which was launched in March 2007, is a concerted effort by 13 UN entities to end sexual violence in war and its aftermath by:

> improving coordination and accountability, amplifying advocacy and supporting country efforts to prevent conflict-related sexual violence and respond more effectively to the needs of survivors.[156]

But there is no high-level multi-agency effort that is remotely comparable to UN Action that addresses the pervasive problem of domestic sexual violence in wartime.

The UN's reluctance to address domestic sexual violence in wartime under its Women, Peace and Security agenda is understandable. Peacekeepers lack the resources to tackle conflict-related sexual violence effectively, let alone the more pervasive problem of wartime domestic sexual violence. And, as noted earlier, because domestic sexual violence is a persistent and endemic problem, it is difficult to characterize it as an emergency issue requiring humanitarian assistance.

> Fewer than 60 countries have laws against marital rape. Even where it is illegal, perpetrators are often protected by a de facto culture of impunity.

There remains, however, a real inequity in the current situation. Domestic sexual violence may appear less serious than conflict-related rape—it certainly is not associated with the well-known savageries of mass gang rapes that have been common in some war zones. However, domestic sexual violence is not only more pervasive than conflict-related sexual violence but it also tends to be more persistent. Unlike conflict-related sexual violence, it can, and often does, continue over many years.

But whatever the relative seriousness of the two types of sexual violence, the reality is that conflict-related sexual violence is receiving long overdue attention from the UN, particularly the Security Council, and its survivors have been receiving greatly increased assistance from the international community. At the same time, however, the plight of the survivors of domestic sexual violence in wartime has been excluded from the Security Council's policy agenda on wartime sexual violence. And although more pervasive and persistent than conflict-related sexual violence, it has become virtually invisible in the mainstream narrative.

> Domestic sexual violence is both more pervasive and persistent than conflict-related sexual violence. It can, and often does, continue over many years.

There are legal and practical reasons for this exclusion—it is difficult, for example, to claim that domestic sexual violence in wartime is a threat to international peace and security. The result, however, is the same—the victims/survivors of domestic sexual violence in wartime are rendered effectively invisible at the highest level in the UN, and their plight is ignored.

Focusing on Normative Change

Preventing either conflict-related or wartime domestic sexual violence is extraordinarily difficult. It is true that growing numbers of states are introducing legislation to provide women with legal protection from domestic sexual abuse, but translating new laws into effective policy on the ground is likely to be a very lengthy process. Progress requires not just new legislation but major changes in popular and official attitudes.

A major impediment to reducing the level of sexual violence in many developing countries—in conflict situations as well as in peacetime—is that substantial percentages of women believe that their partners have the right to have sex with them, even if the women do not want to—and that it is acceptable for their male partners to punish them physically if they refuse. In Sierra Leone, for example, the 2002 Physicians for Human Rights survey found that:

> Despite 80 percent of women expressing that there should be legal protection for the rights of women, more than half of women reported that their husbands had the right to beat them and that it was a wife's duty to have sex with her husband even if she did not want to.[157]

As Figure 2.1 from a WHO (World Health Organization) multi-country study, shown below, makes clear, the attitudes of women in Sierra Leone are far from being exceptional. In many of the surveyed areas, especially those with rural populations, a significant proportion of the interviewed women—and sometimes the large majority—did not believe that refusing sex with a husband is acceptable if a woman does not want to have sex.

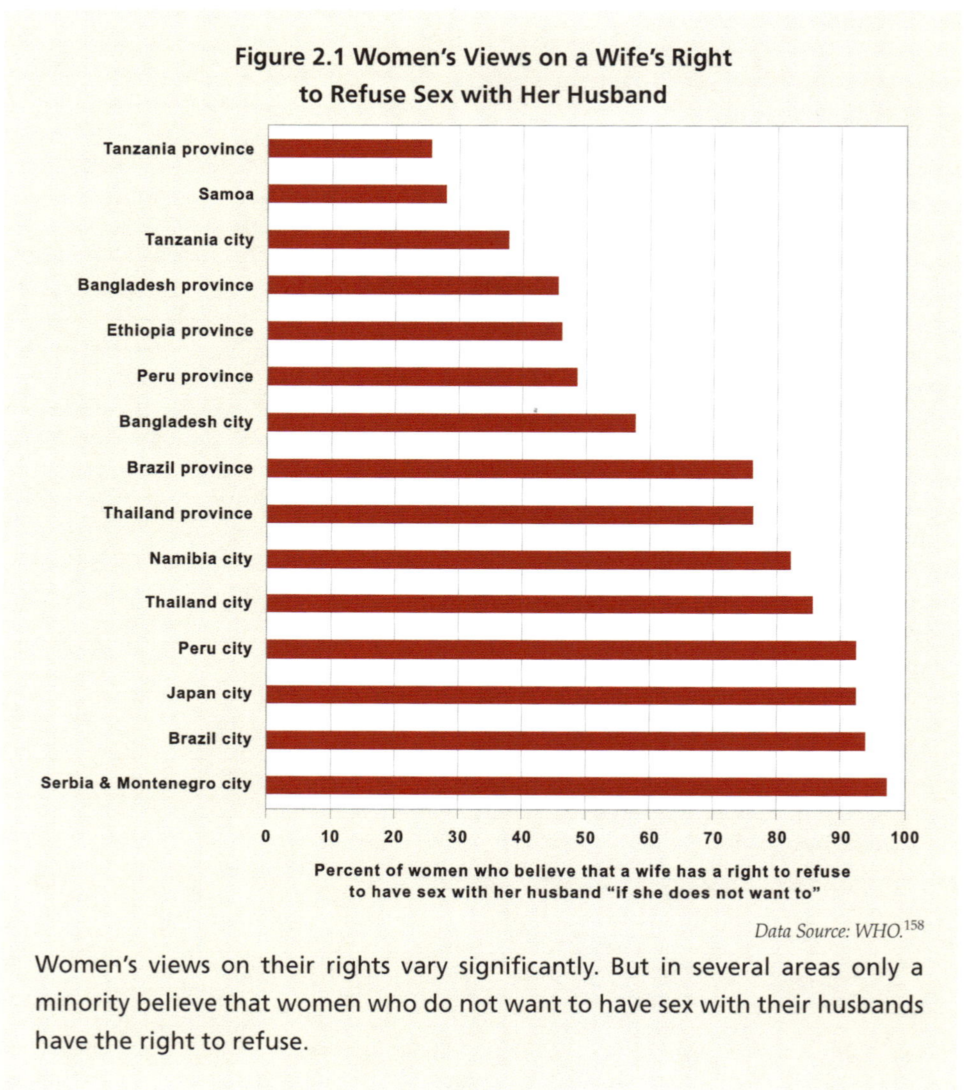

Data Source: WHO.[158]

Women's views on their rights vary significantly. But in several areas only a minority believe that women who do not want to have sex with their husbands have the right to refuse.

Since marital rape is not illegal in the large majority of poor countries where most wars take place, it is unlikely that the often dramatic cross-national variation in the rates of domestic sexual violence is a function of legislation and law and order policies—though these may make a difference in particular cases. The variation is, however, strongly associated with differences in popular norms and beliefs about the acceptability of sexual violence—beliefs that are held not only by perpetrators but sometimes by their victims as well.

It is probably no coincidence that the WHO study recorded low levels of domestic sexual violence in areas where women's rights norms are more entrenched. In the nine surveyed areas where a majority of women believe they have a right to refuse sex with their husbands, the prevalence of intimate-partner sexual violence was 19 percent on average, just over half the average for the remaining regions.[159]

WHO has pointed to other norms and beliefs that help perpetuate sexual violence:

- "Family responses to sexual violence that blame women without punishing men, and concentrate instead on restoring 'lost' family honour."[160]

- "Sexual violence committed by men is to a large extent rooted in ideologies of male sexual entitlement. These belief systems grant women extremely few legitimate options to refuse sexual advances."[161]

- Weak legal sanctions for sexual violence send the message that such violence is condoned, and may even exclude certain forms of sexual violence from the legal definition.[162]

The large degree of variation in levels of sexual violence, both within and between countries, demonstrates that such violence is not an immutable consequence of "human nature."[163] And the fact that widely held norms and attitudes about sexual behaviour have made domestic sexual violence appear "acceptable" in many countries makes changing such norms an obvious prevention strategy.

Changing norms via policy interventions has been successful in other contexts. In fact, there is a long history of national- and community-level public health education campaigns that have sought to change norms and attitudes that are associated with social behaviours that have a negative impact on health—notably those against smoking, drinking and driving, drinking while pregnant, not wearing seatbelts, and practicing unsafe sex. Some of these campaigns, which have often been undertaken in conjunction with legislative change and stress on penalties for noncompliance, have been notably successful.

> ## Low levels of domestic sexual violence occur where women's rights are more entrenched.

During the past two decades, there has also been increasing interest among public health professionals, as well as human rights advocacy groups, in initiatives that seek to change the social norms and attitudes that have normalized and legitimized sexual violence and other violations, even in countries where it is legally proscribed.[164] Few of these interventions have been rigorously evaluated,[165] but some community interventions to reverse long-established practices that put women at risk appear to have been remarkably successful. One such practice is female genital cutting, which is widely practiced in Muslim communities in parts of Africa.

In Senegal, for example, a movement to end the prevalent practice of female genital cutting has been spreading "through the very ties of family and ethnicity that used to entrench it."[166] In the past 15 years, the movement has gained such momentum that "a majority of Senegalese villages where genital cutting was commonplace have committed to stop it."[167]

This remarkable change was not achieved by legislation or domestic law enforcement—in fact, police had put little effort into enforcing the ban on female genital cutting imposed by the Senegalese parliament in 1999. Rather, the change in this previously widely accepted practice has been driven by relatively low-cost community-level activism directed at changing norms and attitudes.[168] Community activists stressed both the health risks of the practice and the fact that there is no religious requirement for genital cutting in Islam. In fact, the practice predates Islam's arrival by centuries.[169]

The Senegal case is far from unique. Findings from similar campaigns in Ethiopia, Egypt, Kenya, and the Sudan suggest that in all cases there have been "substantial reductions in FGC [female genital cutting] and accompanying shifts in the norms that undergird the practice."[170]

Included in the successful campaigns to reduce genital cutting were the following:

- Programs that encouraged "community deliberation, collective reflection and changes in social attitudes and norms."
- Appeals for change that were "value-centred" and involved, "some process of consciousness raising and deliberation on values, rights and gender-based discrimination."
- Approaches that built on local traditions and "introduced rights-based concepts, without necessarily using human rights language."[171]

Interestingly, a 2004 study of the Senegal campaign against genital cutting found that it also reduced the incidence of intimate-partner violence.[172]

While these campaigns are not necessarily blueprints for reducing domestic sexual violence, they demonstrate that it is possible to make major changes in norms that relate to highly sensitive sexual practices that harm women.

Gender Inequality and Wartime Sexual Violence

Underpinning much of current discussion in UN agencies and elsewhere about the causes of sexual violence is the widely held conviction that, as WHO puts it, "gender inequalities increase the risk of violence by men against women and inhibit the ability of those affected to seek protection."[173] This thesis applies to sexual, as well as physical, violence and should in principle apply to sexual violence in wartime.

There is some indirect statistical evidence to support the idea that gender inequality increases the probability of conflict-related sexual violence, notably econometric studies by Mary Caprioli of the University of Minnesota–Duluth and by Uppsala University's Erik Melander, both published in 2005.[174]

Caprioli found, "The higher the level of gender inequality within a state, the greater the likelihood that such a state will experience internal conflict."[175]

Melander, who examined the impact of gender equality on the deadliness of conflict, rather than on the risk of conflict onsets, found that more gender-equal societies "are associated with lower levels of intrastate armed conflict."[176]

In 2010 Stanford University's James Fearon reviewed both studies and found generally weaker associations when using additional data. But he also notes that "overall there is some indication that higher levels of gender equality associate with a lower propensity for conflict."[177]

If the findings are correct, this would mean that as the risk of conflict drops, greater gender equality should also be, indirectly, associated with less conflict-related sexual violence.

It is important, however, to note that none of these studies have particularly robust results. Moreover, there may not be a clear causal link between increasing gender equality and decreasing the risk and deadliness of armed conflict. Fearon argues that the finding may simply indicate that societies that endorse the idea of gender equality "are the sort of societies that are less likely to have civil wars."[178]

> Cross-national evidence shows that where women have higher levels of income and education, they tend to be at lower risk of sexual violence.

Increasing gender equality is, of course, important in its own right and during the past decade there has been a huge expansion in efforts to achieve change in this area. These have included legislative action, education programs in schools, media interventions—including media advertising and "edutainment" campaigns—and interventions at the community level.[179] Data collected to measure progress towards achieving MDGs indicate that there has been an overall improvement in gender equality during this period.[180]

WHO has reviewed a number of individual case studies of efforts to reduce domestic sexual violence by reducing gender inequality. A major WHO report points out that while some of these efforts have indeed been associated with reductions in sexual violence, few of the programs have been subject to any kind of scientific impact evaluation.[181] This is important because there is some cautionary evidence that campaigns intended to promote gender equality, and thus reduce sexual violence, can have perverse effects—i.e., they can lead to a backlash that can actually worsen domestic sexual violence.[182]

During one such campaign in Nicaragua, for example, the reported incidence of sexual violence doubled over a period of a year and a half.[183] Researchers evaluating the program noted that while some of the increase was simply a function of more reporting of sexual violence, it was also due to a violent male backlash against the growing resistance of women to male hegemony.

This and other cases serve as a reminder of the possible unintended consequences of policy initiatives in this field.[184] Just how great a threat such backlash reactions are to gender equality and empowerment programs is currently impossible to say.

There is cross-national evidence to support the thesis that where women have higher levels of income and education they tend to be at lower—not negligible—risk of sexual violence. But overall the evidence is inconclusive thus far and the very limited data that exists suggest that the process of achieving greater gender equality can threaten traditional male roles, which in turn may be associated with increased risks of intimate-partner violence.[185]

Conclusion

The first two chapters of this *Report* have presented a critical analysis of the assumptions that underpin the mainstream narrative on wartime sexual violence.

We have argued that this narrative—which has become increasingly prominent since the passage of Security Council Resolution 1325 on Women, Peace and Security in 2000—is misleading in two important ways. First, the level of conflict-related sexual violence is overstated in a number of different respects. Second, domestic sexual violence, sexual violence against males in wartime, and the role of women in perpetrating sexual violence have been largely ignored.

We also argued that these misleading assumptions have negative implications for policies aimed at preventing wartime sexual violence and bringing assistance to its survivors and justice to its perpetrators.

The mainstream narrative, we suggested, is driven in large part by the very different—but complementary—incentive structures that shape media reporting and the humanitarian advocacy and service delivery imperatives of international agencies and major NGOs. But it is also the case that the misleading claims we have identified have been able to flourish largely unchallenged because there are no reliable cross-national data that could be used as a corrective.

With respect to reducing wartime sexual violence, the challenges remain daunting.

In the long term, ending the culture of impunity that protects combatants who perpetrate sexual violence during periods of war should make a difference. But while impunity has become an issue of increased concern and debate, particularly among international lawyers, there has thus far been little concerted action on the ground where it counts the most. The number of perpetrators brought to justice remains extraordinarily small compared with the number of sexual violence crimes that are perpetrated in wartime.

> Misleading assumptions affect policies to prevent sexual violence and bring assistance to survivors and justice to perpetrators.

The UN's goal of providing women and children with physical protection from conflict-related sexual violence in peace operations continues to be an "impossible mandate," largely because peacekeeping forces lack the resources needed to undertake this hugely demanding task effectively.

The governments of countries in conflict have an important potential protection role to play here, but government forces and militias are often the major perpetrators of the very sexual violence they are supposed to prevent. Where this is the case they are part of the problem, not the solution.

These somewhat bleak realities do not mean that the prospects for reducing conflict-related sexual violence are minimal, however.

We argued previously that it was reasonable to assume that sexual violence perpetrated by soldiers and rebels will decline when conflicts come to an end. We further argued that given that there has been a substantial decline in the number and deadliness of wars since the end of the Cold War, there is good reason to believe that the worldwide incidence of conflict-related sexual violence will also have declined.

The evidence presented in the last *Human Security Report* indicates that this decline is due in considerable part to initiatives by the international community to end wars and prevent them from starting again—"peacemaking" and "post-conflict peacebuilding" in UN-speak.[186] Insofar as this is true, then such initiatives are also important indirect strategies for reducing conflict-related sexual violence.

Reducing domestic sexual violence in wartime presents an even greater challenge, not least because the problem remains largely unacknowledged in the many poor countries where marital rape is not a criminal offence, and in part because the UN Security Council ignores the problem completely in its high-profile Women, Peace and Security mandate.

But here, too, there are grounds for cautious optimism about the future. There is evidence from campaigns to reduce female genital cutting that indicates that carefully crafted policies engaging local communities can greatly reduce harmful practices.[187] Similar approaches could potentially yield success regarding domestic sexual violence in wartime.

In Chapter 3 we turn to examine the impact of conflict on the incidence of sexual violence against children. Here the challenge of policy analysis is even greater, because reliable cross-national data are almost nonexistent.

Robin Hammond / Panos Pictures. DEMOCRATIC REPUBLIC OF THE CONGO.

CHAPTER 3

Children and Wartime Sexual Violence

In 2006, in an analysis prepared for the United Nations Division for the Advancement of Women (UNDAW) and UNICEF (United Nations Children's Fund), Dyan Mazurana and Khristopher Carlson drew attention to sobering findings about the impact of war on children. The authors reported that some 2 million children had been killed in armed conflicts around the world over a 10-year period. An additional 6 million had been permanently disabled or injured, over 14 million had been displaced, and more than 1 million had been orphaned and separated from their parents. Over 250,000 children had been forced to serve in rebel, militia, or government forces.[188]

While often drawn from official sources, these and similar claims are questionable, in large part because reliable cross-national data on how conflict affects children are rarely available.[189] But notwithstanding important caveats about the reliability of some of these findings, few would dispute that huge numbers of children—those least able to protect themselves—are at grave personal risk in wartime.

One of the many dangers that children confront in war-affected countries is sexual assault. This includes not just the gang rapes by rebel forces and militias that capture the media headlines, but also the largely invisible assaults by family members and acquaintances. Yet, despite growing attention to the plight of children in armed conflict, despite many horrific accounts of individual cases of child rape, remarkably little is known about the incidence or prevalence of wartime sexual violence against children.

In this chapter we examine the fragmentary evidence that exists on the extent of wartime sexual violence against children. We locate our discussion within the broader context of the UN's (United Nations) Children and Armed Conflict policy agenda that has become increasingly politically salient in the new millennium and addresses sexual violence against children along with other "grave violations." We point out that the UN's own system for tracking the incidence of conflict-related sexual violence against children is incapable of estimating either the extent or severity of the problem. The system ignores domestic sexual violence in wartime completely, even though the evidence suggests that it is far more prevalent than conflict-related sexual violence.

In the final section we examine some of the policy implications of our findings and ask if it is possible to generate data on wartime sexual violence that is reliable enough to create an evidence base for policy where none currently exists.

Key Findings

Many of our findings are similar to those that relate to sexual violence against adults. They include:

- Claims made by high-level UN reports that wartime sexual violence against children has been increasing lack any supporting evidence. The indirect evidence suggests that such violations are *decreasing* worldwide. At the same time, the UN's own system for reporting violations against children in war-affected countries, the Monitoring and Reporting Mechanism (MRM), grossly undercounts the incidence of conflict-related sexual violence against children.

- Even though most sexual violence against children in wartime is perpetrated by family members and acquaintances, not combatants, this form of sexual violence receives only minimal attention in UN, NGO (nongovernmental organization), and media analyses, and is not counted in the UN's own reporting system.

- As is the case with adults, sexual violence rates against children vary substantially from region to region and from country to country around the world.

- Unless respondents in surveys are given the option of responding anonymously to questions about any sexual violations that occurred when they were children, their responses will underestimate the extent of the violations.

Determining the true global extent to which sexual violence affects children during wartime is currently impossible given the fragmentary and unreliable nature of the data. Not surprisingly, our knowledge of how war affects the incidence of sexual violence against children in wartime is even more limited than is the case for adults.[190]

But one finding does emerge from the very limited data. As we argue below, the prevalence of sexual violence against children appears to be quite different from that against adults. Because children are clearly more vulnerable than adults, we might expect that they would be more likely to become victimized by sexual violence. Not only are they less able to defend themselves, but in the case of domestic sexual violence, children often live in a dependent relationship with their abusers, making it extremely unlikely that they will seek help. In some cases they may not even be aware at the time that they are being victimized.[191]

In fact, the prevalence rates of sexual violence against children appear to be significantly lower than against adults. Rates of abuse differ to a greater degree than can be explained solely by the fact that sexual violence against children is under-reported. This suggests that normative constraints are providing children with protection from sexual predation—during wars as well as in peacetime.

The Children and Armed Conflict Narrative

What constitutes a child in today's world is contested, particularly with reference to armed conflicts. The UN and most humanitarian organizations hold that childhood does not end until the age of 18, a view that finds legal support in the 1989 UN Convention on the Rights of the Child, which states that "a child means every human being below the age of eighteen years unless under the law applicable to the child, majority is attained earlier."[192]

But outside of international treaties there is little consensus about the age at which adulthood begins. In many countries, individuals of 17 and younger see themselves as adults and are treated as such. They marry, hold jobs, often lead independent lives, and are sometimes held legally responsible for their actions.

The research literature on children and sexual violence reflects this divergence in views about what constitutes childhood. Some research focuses on *young children*—those under 15 years old—and excludes the 15- to 17-year-olds. Other research and much of the advocacy is guided by the UN definition—i.e., all individuals under 18 years of age are considered children. We discuss the findings of both types of studies in this chapter.

The Children and Armed Conflict agenda, which began to emerge from the UN in the second half of the 1990s, has played a critical role in framing the narrative on how war-affected children are perceived in the international community and much of the media. In this narrative, children are typically presented as "increasingly becoming the direct targets of violence."[193]

The UN agenda was heavily influenced by a powerfully written 1996 report undertaken for the UN on the *Impact of Armed Conflict on Children* by Graça Machel.[194] Machel had been a member of FRELIMO, Mozambique's liberation movement against Portuguese colonial rule, and was subsequently a minister in the post-independence government. Her hugely influential report argues that the crisis facing children in war-affected countries had to be understood in terms of new modes of armed violence that were emerging in the post-Cold War era that were quite different from traditional forms of warfare. These "new wars,"[195] as they were later dubbed, were flourishing in a security environment that, as Machel puts it, had become:

> devoid of the most basic human values; a space in which children are slaughtered, raped, and maimed; a space in which children are exploited as soldiers; a space in which children are starved and exposed to extreme brutality. Such unregulated terror and violence speak of deliberate victimization. There are few further depths to which humanity can sink.[196]

The atrocities to which this passage refers have certainly taken place in wartime, but the report presents a picture that is more than somewhat misleading. Similar to the reports on wartime sexual violence against women discussed in Chapters 1 and 2, Machel discusses particular—often extreme—cases as if they were representative of the situation for all children in all armed conflicts. They are not.

The mainstream narrative has remained largely the same since the publication of Machel's report in 1996. Although researchers and some officials are increasingly arguing the need to understand children as individuals with agency, not simply as passive victims, the website of the Office of the Special Representative of the Secretary-General for Children and Armed Conflict currently notes that children are:

> the primary victims of armed conflict … [They] are killed or maimed, made orphans, abducted, deprived of education and health care, and left with deep emotional scars and trauma. They are recruited and used as child soldiers, forced to give expression to the hatred of adults.[197]

But despite its partial and misleading nature, the depiction of the plight of children in armed conflict produced by Machel and in subsequent reports has been highly effective politically. Responding to pressure from advocacy organizations and the high-level official reports, the UN Security Council has become increasingly engaged over the past decade and a half with what has become a clearly defined Children and Armed Conflict policy agenda. Since 1999 it:

> has greatly elevated the relevance of child protection concerns within its international peace and security agenda and has allowed for opportunities to improve efforts and actions for the protection of children.[198]

Yet, despite the increased attention, and despite the fact that wartime sexual violence against children has become a major issue for the Security Council, some 16 years after the publication of the Machel report, the UN still has no real understanding of the scope or severity of the problem worldwide. Moreover, there is little evidence that UN policies to prevent sexual violence against children in wartime, or to bring its perpetrators to justice, are having any real impact.

The Knowledge Gaps

The remarkable absence of reliable information in this area is part of a much broader problem of inadequate data on almost all issues related to child protection in war-affected countries. As Alastair Ager and co-authors point out, without:

> coordinated and reliable data collection … humanitarian action in support of children's protection will continue to be planned in a manner that is critically ignorant of scale, circumstance and effectiveness of response.[199]

The authors focused on the situation in Darfur, but the problems they identified are common to most conflict- or crisis-affected countries.[200] Among other things this means that the international community lacks access to any reliable data that can determine whether the incidence of sexual violence against children around the world is increasing or decreasing.

Official concern about the huge knowledge gaps in this area has, however, been growing among donors and international agencies that are increasingly demanding that policy be evidence-based. These pressures have given impetus to efforts at the UN to collect data on children affected by armed conflict.

In 2005 the UN Security Council, responding to a series of reports and advocacy efforts that drew attention to the plight of children in conflict-affected countries, established the MRM to report on grave violations of children's rights in wartime, to inform policy, and to help bring perpetrators to justice.

In 2006, however, the UN's Office of Internal Oversight Services (OIOS) reported to the Security Council on the workings of the MRM. It noted major problems:

> There is no systematic picture—in a statistical, aggregate sense—available on whether the extent to which [the situation of] CAAC [Children Affected by Armed Conflict], on a country by country basis, or as a global phenomenon, has improved or deteriorated. The cited estimates of two million children killed and continued existence of 250,000 or 300,000 global child soldiers, for instance, are entirely informal calculations that have not been derived from MRM aggregation.[201]

> ### Donors and international agencies are increasingly demanding that policy on child protection in war-affected countries be evidence-based.

The claims about the "300,000 global child soldiers" and "two million children killed" in wars around the world that are noted in the OIOS review are suspiciously similar to the unsubstantiated, but widely circulated UNICEF figures cited at the beginning of this chapter. They are typical of the pervasive "urban myths" about the effects of war that get endlessly recycled by NGOs and UN agencies.[202] (We examine some other challenges the MRM confronts below.)

Although there are no reliable data that support these claims, they have become widely accepted. This is not surprising. The assertions made are in line with the mainstream official and media reporting and analyses that focus largely on the worst affected countries. They are rarely questioned, in part because people assume that claims made by international organizations and major NGOs are reliable, and in part because there are no alternative sources of accessible and reliable data with which to challenge them. Last but not least—as we noted in Chapter 2—focusing on the worst cases is useful for advocacy and for directing public and donor attention towards the need to protect those who are most vulnerable in war-affected countries.

Is Wartime Violence against Children Increasing?

In 2009 a high-level follow-up study to Graça Machel's influential 1996 report was released.[203] Published by the Office of the Special Representative of the Secretary-General for Children and Armed Conflict and UNICEF with funding from 12 governments and several other UN agencies, the new study proclaimed that wars were having an "even more horrific impact on children, and on civilians generally" than in the early 1990s.[204]

> There is no evidence to support claims that conflict-related violence, including sexual violence, is having an increasing impact on children.

In fact, there is *no* evidence to support claims that conflict-related violence, including sexual violence, was having a greater worldwide impact on children in the 2000s than during the 1990s.[205] But it is not difficult to understand why such claims should have gained credibility.

In the years that followed the 1996 Machel report, a so-called new wars thesis flourished in the UN, as well as in parts of the research community.[206] New wars theorists argued that the nature of armed conflict had changed since the end of the Cold War. "Old wars" were fought for political ends by disciplined armies and paid heed to the proscription of deliberate attacks on civilians. New wars are very different—more akin to the anomic savagery depicted in the Machel report and described previously.[207]

New wars, it was claimed, are fought by undisciplined armed groups that lack popular support and whose members are prone to extreme violence, including ethnic cleansing, strategic rape, genocide, and other gross violations of human rights. New wars both occur in failed or failing states, and also cause them to fail. They are motivated more by predation and/or ethnic hatred than by the political or ideological ends that drove old wars.

And whereas the intentional killing of civilians was proscribed in theory, if not always in practice, in most old wars, in new wars the same civilians have become prime targets. To support this contention, new war analysts pointed to the widely cited claim that there has been a dramatic shift in the ratio of civilian to military deaths over the past 100 years. At the beginning of the 20th century, just 10–15 percent of war fatalities were civilian; by the late 1990s, it was claimed, the figure had ballooned to approximately 80 percent.[208]

If 80 percent of war victims are now civilians and if children under the age of 15 make up between 30 and 40 percent of civilians in poor countries where most wars are fought,[209] then it follows logically that the threat to children must have increased considerably as a consequence of the emergence of new wars since the Cold War era.

Yet, as the 2005 *Human Security Report* noted, the claim that the percentage of civilian war deaths today is 80 or 90, while endlessly reiterated, including by the UN and its agencies, is yet another urban myth, one unsupported by any compelling empirical evidence.[210]

A 2009 study by Erik Melander and colleagues from Uppsala University points out that the best evidence from historians is that the claim that 10–15 percent of war deaths at the beginning of the 20th century were civilians is wrong—the figure is far too low. There are in fact no clear long-term trends in civilian to military fatality ratios over time, though the average ratio would appear to have decreased since the end of the Cold War.[211]

As for the post-Cold War era, there is no evidence that warfare has become either more deadly, or more barbarically fought. Nor is there evidence that civilians—and hence children—are being increasingly victimized.

> While post-conflict environments are far from risk-free for children, they are considerably less dangerous than war zones.

Critical assessments of the new wars thesis have pointed out that it greatly exaggerates the difference between Cold War and post-Cold War conflicts.[212] Its proponents also fail to note that wars had become less numerous and less deadly in the post-Cold War period, and that the number of genocides and politicides had declined by some 80 percent since the late 1980s.[213]

The best cross-national indicator that we have of the direct impact of war on noncombatants is the death toll from the targeted and unopposed killing of civilians by both non-state armed groups and government forces.

Here the data, which we review in Chapter 8 of this *Report*, is unequivocal: deadly violence against civilians, a large proportion of whom are children, did not increase after 1996 as the UN report claimed; indeed, the total death toll *declined by around half from the 1990s to the 2000s.*[214]

As we noted in Chapter 1, and as Part II of the *Report* demonstrates, the number and deadliness of armed conflicts have dropped substantially since the 1990s. Given this, we have reasonable grounds to expect that the worldwide level of wartime violence against children, including conflict-related sexual violence, will have declined as well. While post-conflict environments are far from risk-free for children, they are considerably less dangerous than war zones.

Notwithstanding the indirect evidence that suggests that sexual violence against children may have declined, UN officials have persisted in claiming that it has increased. For example, the Office of the Special Representative of the Secretary-General for Children and Armed Conflict asserts that "The rape and sexual violation of children and women is *increasingly a characteristic of conflict.*"[215]

Typically, no evidence was provided to support this assertion.

Why should international agencies and NGOs believe that conflict-related sexual violence has been increasing while conflict numbers and battle deaths have declined substantially, as have deaths of civilians?

Part of the reason is that the statistical data that reveal these declines are little known outside the research community. Reports by and for the UN are often based on extrapolations from individual case studies, plus horrendous victim narratives on sexual violence from countries that are worst affected by it. These narrative accounts are buttressed by statistical urban myths, like the false assertion discussed above that the vast majority of those killed in war since the end of the Cold War have been civilians, or the claim that three out of four women in Liberia were raped in the civil war noted in Chapter 2 of this *Report*.

But there is, as we suggested earlier, an additional factor. Since the end of the Cold War, the *reporting* of sexual violence by the media and advocacy organizations has greatly increased, which has created the impression that the violence itself has increased.[216] But, as Chapter 1 pointed out, increased reporting does not necessarily mean increased violations. The near-total lack of reliable reporting of wartime sexual violence in the Cold War period, contrasted with the explosion of reporting over the past decade, has made it *appear* that wartime rape has increased. Absent reliable and accessible data to check assumptions, appearances can indeed be deceptive.

The UN's Monitoring and Reporting Mechanism

As noted earlier, in 2005 the UN established its own system of monitoring rights violations against children. The MRM was intended to provide "timely, objective, accurate and reliable information"[217] on six major rights violations—including sexual violence—perpetrated against children affected by armed conflict.

> MRM task forces in the field underestimate the extent of sexual violence against children.

The MRM initiative was an indication of growing UN awareness of the importance of monitoring and evaluation, and MRM reports contain much useful information on specific violations. But, in its present form, it is incapable of providing reliable data on the extent, or nationwide severity, of rights violations.

The reality is that the reports from the MRM task forces in the field severely underestimate the extent of sexual violence against children in war-affected countries, as a number of MRM task force reports to the Security Council have pointed out. In addition, the MRM does not have task forces in all countries in conflict.

The main problem is that the MRM relies on reports of violations from UN agency and other staff in the field. This approach, while useful for many purposes, notoriously under-reports the nationwide incidence of sexual violence against children—and indeed the incidence of other severe violations.

A 2008 Watchlist review of the workings of the MRM noted that in one 14-month period in Nepal, the MRM country task force recorded just 11 cases of sexual violence. In Sri Lanka, zero cases had been reported. In the Democratic Republic of the Congo (DRC), the MRM task force "faced challenges verifying the hundreds of cases it received between June 2006 and May 2007."[218]

Nationwide population surveys are the only instruments that can provide approximate estimates of the nationwide incidence of sexual violence, but the MRM does not include data from such surveys.[219] Indeed, the 2010 MRM guidelines do not even mention surveys as a possible source of data.[220]

If comprehensive data on rights violations against children in war-affected countries were being collected by other parts of the UN or other international agencies, the MRM failure to do so would be of little consequence. But no such data are being collected elsewhere.

What Do We Know?

The most comprehensive information on the extent of sexual violence in poor war-affected countries comes from well-run population surveys. But as we noted earlier, few of these surveys have been undertaken, and of these only a handful have sought to estimate the prevalence of sexual violence against children.

Some of the major surveys discussed previously—those that examined the incidence of wartime sexual violence in Liberia and the DRC published in the *Journal of the American Medical Association*, for example—provided no data on sexual violence perpetrated against children.[221]

The influential Demographic and Health Survey (DHS) organization has a domestic violence module that asks a series of questions about sexual violence, of which some answers can be disaggregated on the basis of age.[222] In principle, this module could be used to determine the prevalence of sexual violence against children—but it has not been included in many surveys in war-affected countries, and it collects no data on sexual violence against men or boys.

Moreover, in the very small number of war-affected countries where the violence module *has* been included in a DHS survey, the data in the public domain on sexual violence against children do not appear to have been disaggregated on the basis of age.

> Only a handful of well-run population surveys have sought to estimate the prevalence of sexual violence against children.

UNICEF also conducts major surveys focusing on women's and children's health. Unlike DHS, however, UNICEF's Multiple Indicator Cluster Surveys (MICS) do not collect any data on sexual violence perpetrated against children. This is somewhat remarkable since child protection, including protection from sexual violence, is central to UNICEF's mandate.[223]

Findings on the Prevalence of Sexual Violence against Children

The most comprehensive research effort to estimate the global prevalence of sexual abuse against children (here defined as individuals under 18 years old) published to date was based on a meta-analysis of the prevalence data from 217 studies published between 1980 and 2008.[224] Most of these studies were undertaken in developed countries that were not war-affected.

The meta-analysis, whose key findings were published in 2011 in the journal *Child Maltreatment*, found that the prevalence of sexual abuse of all children (girls and boys) worldwide was 11.8 percent. For girls, the rate was 18 percent; for boys, 7.6 percent.[225] If the definition of sexual violence included only acts that involved penile or other forms of penetration of the victim, the rate for girls under 18 drops to 15 percent. The rate for boys drops to approximately 7 percent.[226]

Reflecting the findings of other studies, the results of this study revealed significant differences between continents with respect to rates of sexual violence against children. North America (USA/Canada), Australia/New Zealand, and Africa had the highest prevalence rates; Asia, the lowest.[227]

> A recent study found that there are significant differences in the rates of sexual violence against children between genders, and across continents.

This relatively new analysis has, as yet, attracted relatively little attention. The best known study to date that has cross-national data on sexual violence and also looks at girls aged 15 years and under is the WHO (World Health Organization) *Multi-Country Study on Women's Health and Domestic Violence against Women* noted in Chapter 1.

The WHO research program was initiated in 1997 and drew on questionnaire data from 24,000 women respondents in 10 countries around the world.[228] The fact that the WHO surveys, unlike many others referred to earlier, used a common methodology and definitions meant that the results are commensurable and can be used for comparative analysis.

One limitation of the WHO surveys is that in most of the countries the areas that were surveyed were not nationwide—although they are usually treated as if they were nationally representative, both in media reporting and by many researchers. In half of the countries two sizable surveys were carried out, one taking place in a major city and the other taking place in a province with a mix of urban and rural populations. In four other countries, only a city or a province was surveyed, while there is only one country—Samoa—for which the survey was designed to be representative nationwide.

The countries surveyed were Bangladesh, Brazil, Ethiopia, Japan, Namibia, Peru, Samoa, Serbia and Montenegro, Thailand, and Tanzania—a group that is both culturally and geographically diverse. Approximately half of these countries had been involved in conflict at some time in the lifetimes of many of the respondents.

> The WHO surveys, unlike many others, used a common methodology and definitions. Hence, the results can be used for comparative analysis.

Unusually, the WHO surveys collected data on prevalence rates of sexual abuse against girls—here defined as females under 15 years of age. Women respondents—the age group was 15–49 years—were asked not only if they had been sexually abused in their lifetime but also if they had been sexually abused before the age of 15. Figure 3.1 below shows the results.[229]

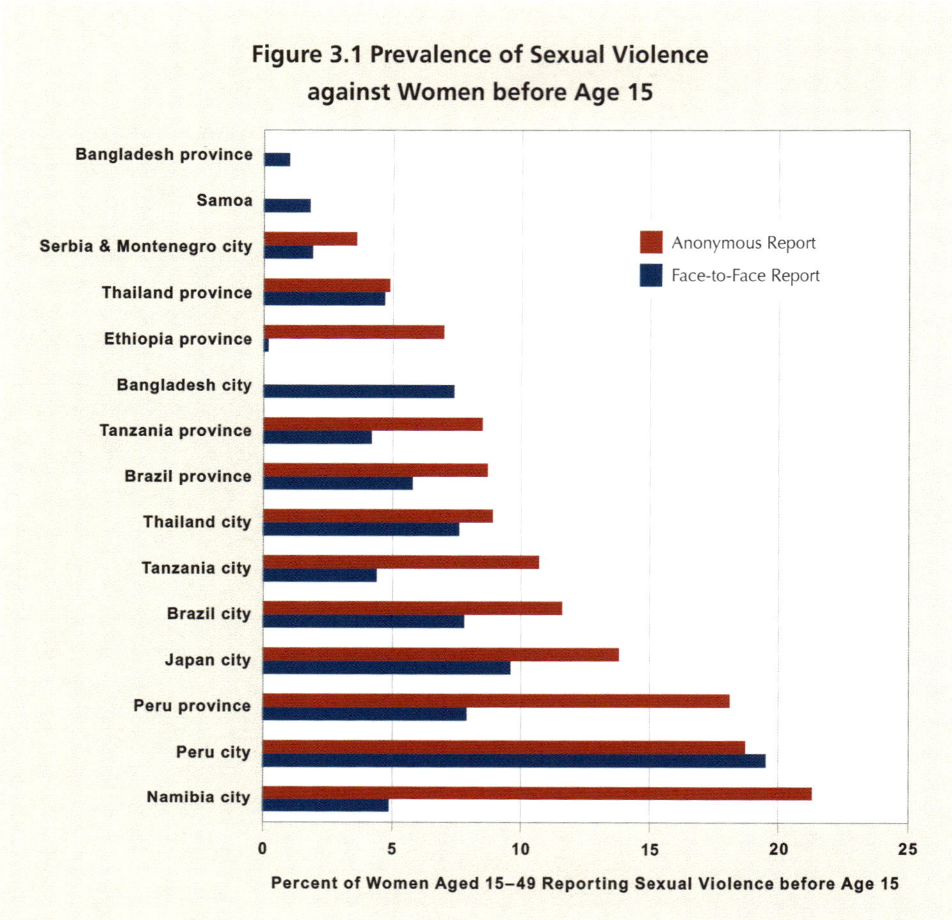

Figure 3.1 Prevalence of Sexual Violence against Women before Age 15

Data Source: WHO.[230]

Women are more likely to report that they were sexually abused as children if allowed to answer questions anonymously. The prevalence rates of sexual violence for children are still significantly lower than for adults.

Note: No data from anonymous reports were available for Bangladesh and Samoa.

There are three notable findings here. First, the data reveal the remarkable extent of cross-national—and sometimes also within-country—variation in the sexual violence prevalence rates of female children younger than 15. This is similar to the cross-national variation in the sexual violence prevalence rates for adult females noted in Chapter 2.

Second, the rates of sexual violence for girls under 15 are sharply lower than those for women aged 15–49 years. We discuss this further below.

Third, the WHO survey researchers gave women respondents the opportunity to respond anonymously to sensitive questions about their exposure to sexual violence as children.[231] Where both face-to-face and anonymous data are available, the differences between the responses to the questions that could be answered anonymously (the red bars in Figure 3.1) and those that were asked directly are striking. In all but two cases—one being Peru city and other being Thailand province—the anonymous responses recorded child sexual violence rates that were appreciably higher than the face-to-face responses.

The findings from the WHO survey provide compelling evidence that even well-run population surveys are likely to underestimate the true extent of sexual violence—unless they give respondents the opportunity of answering questions anonymously. Very few currently do so.

Sexual Violence against Girls Is Less Common Than against Adult Women

The above-cited 2009 report on children and armed conflict, co-published by the Office of the Special Representative of the Secretary-General for Children and Armed Conflict and UNICEF, claims that "almost half of all sexual assaults are against girls 15 years of age or younger."[232] In spite of the fact that no evidence was ever produced to support this extraordinary—but quite incorrect—assertion, it has been has been repeatedly cited by advocacy groups, governments, and major international organizations.

> Well-run surveys can still underestimate the extent of sexual violence if respondents are not given the chance to answer anonymously.

There are no reliable global data on the number of sexual assaults against children or adults. The prevalence data from the WHO multi-country study however, tell a story very different from the assertion that was made in the UNICEF report.

When we compare prevalence rates of sexual violence among adult women, on the one hand, and female children (under 15 years old), on the other, the WHO data show that far smaller percentages of girls under 15 than adult women were victims of sexual violence.

Figure 3.2 reveals that across the 15 sites surveyed by the WHO, between 8 and 44 percent of female respondents experienced sexual violence as adults, i.e., from ages 15 to 49.[233] The data on sexual violence against females before age 15 reveal much lower levels of sexual violence. Figure 3.1 above shows that prevalence rates recorded in the anonymous reports ranged from 4 to 21 percent.[234] The total prevalence rate of sexual violence against adult women across all surveyed areas was 33 percent: three times higher than the average prevalence rate of sexual violence against children at just 11 percent for the anonymous reports and 5 percent for the face-to-face reports.[235]

The WHO study did not specifically address sexual violence against children during wartime, but as we will see below, there is evidence to suggest that the rate of sexual violence against children is also lower in the context of armed conflict.

> There are no reliable global data on the number of sexual assaults against either children or adults.

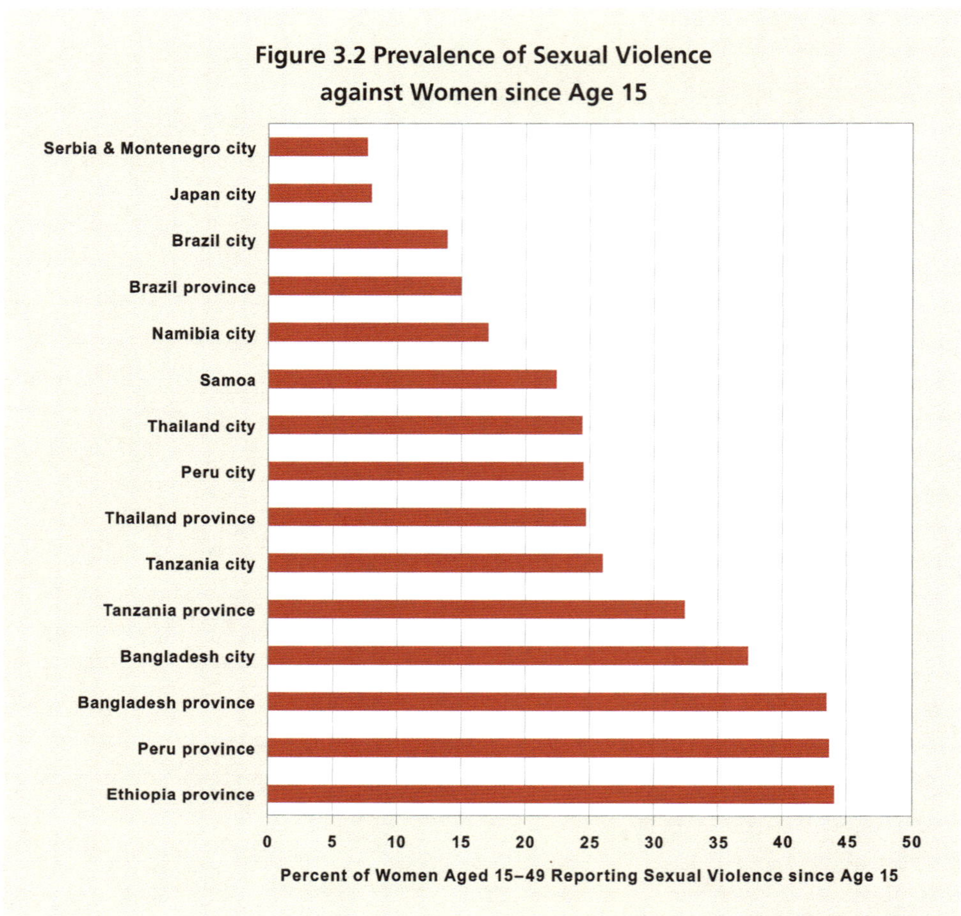

Figure 3.2 Prevalence of Sexual Violence against Women since Age 15

Data Source: WHO.[236]

In the countries surveyed, one-third of women reported having been sexually abused as adults, with rates ranging from less than 10 percent to more than 40 percent in the worst affected areas.

Sexual Violence against Children in War-Affected Countries

Most studies on the impact of war on sexual violence ignore children, while most studies of child sexual violence ignore the impact of war. In the remainder of this chapter, we discuss the findings of the few surveys that can help us gain some understanding of the extent of sexual violence against children during wartime.

To the best of our knowledge, no researchers have examined differences in the overall prevalence (or incidence) rate of sexual violence against children as a country moves from peace to war. The very small number of quantitative studies that have collected data on children and sexual violence in wartime tend to confirm the findings of research on child sexual violence in peacetime and the findings on sexual violence against adults in wartime discussed in Chapter 1.

The neighbourhood-method surveys[237] that collect data on sexual violence against children in war-affected countries are briefly reviewed below. Their results support the general finding revealed by the WHO data—namely that there are very large variations between rates of sexual abuse from country to country, but that in all cases the rates at which children are victimized in war-affected countries are substantially lower than the rates at which adults are victimized.

> Neighbourhood-method surveys indicate variations in rates of sexual abuse between countries, and lower rates of victimization for children than for adults.

Moreover, as is the case with the findings on sexual violence against adults in war, there is evidence to suggest that girls are more likely to be sexually abused by family members or someone known to the family than by combatants—rebels, militias, or government soldiers. Note, however, that there are only a few surveys that have collected and published data on perpetrators of sexual violence against children.

The much lower levels of reported sexual violence for children than for adults are also evident in studies of hospital and care centre patients in individual countries in conflict, such as the DRC, as a major study published in 2009 makes clear. Malteser International's relief program for rape victims in the DRC's South Kivu province registered some 20,500 female rape survivors between January 2005 and December 2007.[238]

Figure 3.3 below reveals that cases of child rape appear to constitute a very small percentage of female rape victims in one of the conflict areas in the DRC that is worst affected by war. Even if we assume that rape cases of children are less likely to be reported, there appears to be a clear difference between the victimization rates for adults and children—who constitute almost half of the population in the DRC and on average between 30 and 40 percent in developing nations generally.[239]

Girls aged 15 and under constituted 1.5 percent of the rape survivors for whom the survey collected age information.[240] For every girl under 16 who is raped, the study finds that 66 adult women are raped. Even if we add the 16- to 20-year-olds, the share of the 20-year-olds and under is still only 13 percent of the total number of survivors.

> Child rape constitutes a very small percentage of female rape cases in South Kivu, one of the worst affected conflict regions of the DRC.

It is important to note that because this sample of sexual violence victims is not randomly selected, the results of the study should be viewed with appropriate caution. But if the data are not completely misleading, it would appear that children—including teenagers—were at a much lower risk of being affected by sexual violence in South Kivu.

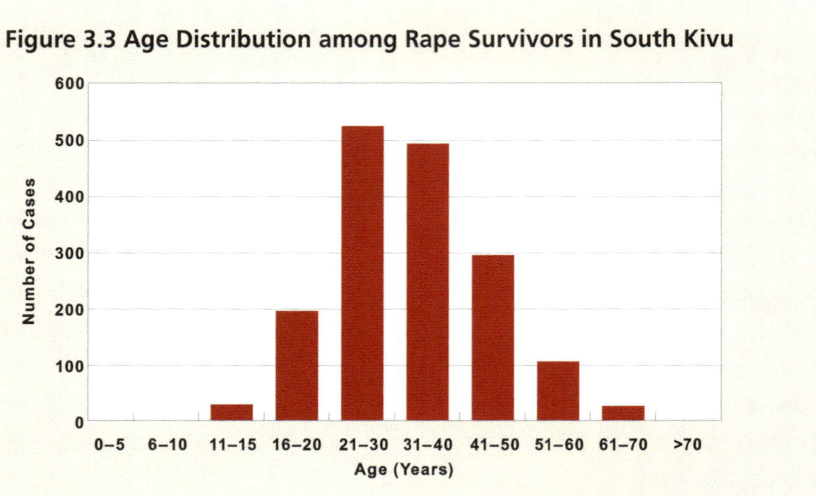

Figure 3.3 Age Distribution among Rape Survivors in South Kivu

Data Source: Birthe Steiner et al.[241]

Sexual violence against children is much less common than against adults. In one of the regions of the DRC worst affected by war, those under 16 made up only 1.5 percent of rape survivors.

This may suggest that even in severely war-affected areas children receive a considerable degree of protection from sexual violence simply by virtue of being children. If the data from the WHO multi-country study and the Malteser study in the DRC are indicative of overall patterns, there appears to be a norm against engaging in sex with children, even those who are sexually mature. Like all norms, this would be far from being universally respected, but it may serve to reduce the risk of young children being directly assaulted.

A second study based on hospital data on the sexual abuse of children in the war-affected eastern region of the DRC found that 81 percent of the perpetrators were civilians, while only 13 percent were described as wearing a military uniform. Records about the reported relationship between the victim and the assailant revealed that 74 percent of the perpetrators were known to the the family of the victim while 26 percent were strangers.[242] We know this pattern to be the case for adults, but this study, and some of the neighbourhood-method surveys discussed below, are among the very few that indicate that even in areas highly affected by warfare, most sexual violence against children is perpetrated by family members or acquaintances, not members of armed groups.[243]

The Neighbourhood Survey Method

One of the few sources of data on sexual violence against children in war-affected countries comes from a series of surveys of sexual violence in a number of countries using the novel low-cost neighbourhood methodology developed by Columbia University's Program on Forced Migration and Health.[244]

The findings of surveys using the neighbourhood method are subject to a considerably greater degree of uncertainty than surveys that use a more conventional data collection methodology and a larger number of respondents. The survey results are robust enough to detect major differences in rates of sexual violence, however.

The data from these surveys do in fact confirm other research that finds that while the incidence of sexual violence against female children varies greatly between countries, it is almost always much less than for adult females. In these studies, children are conventionally defined as being less than 18 years old.

The principal findings of the surveys include the following:

- In 2008 a neighbourhood survey of an internally displaced persons (IDP) camp in Trincomalee, Sri Lanka, found that less than 1 percent of girls (one out of 483) had become rape victims over an 18-month period—a remarkably low figure. In a village-based survey, the incidence of rape was even lower—a single rape victim under 18 in the sample of 1,022 girls.[245] The proportion of adult women in both samples who had been raped was also low—just over 3 percent—but still much higher than the rate for children.[246]

- A 2008 survey of Somali refugees in the Aw Barre camp in the Somali region of Ethiopia found that 2 percent of females under 18 were raped over an 18-month period. For females 18 years or over, the rate was 40 percent—20 times higher. In the Kebribeyah refugee camp, 3 percent of girls under 18 were victims of rape, while 35 percent of women who were 18 or over were raped.[247] In all sites, the most common perpetrators of rape against females under 18 were—unusually—strangers (32 out of 63 cases in total).[248]

- A neighbourhood survey undertaken in two war-affected counties in Liberia in 2007 examined, among other things, rates at which women and girls experienced rape outside marriage over an 18-month period. In Montserrado County, 13 percent of girls under 18, and 23 percent of women aged 18 or over, were identified as having experienced rape or sexual abuse outside of marriage. In Nimba County, the rate for girls under 18 was 11 percent; for women 18 or over, it was 32 percent.[249] The survey report includes information about the perpetrators of rape, but it does not distinguish between women and children in this regard. Overall, the vast majority of rape and sexual abuse was perpetrated by family members and acquaintances, while a maximum of 2 percent was attributed to strangers.[250]

- A 2009 neighbourhood survey taken in the Central African Republic found that the *annual* rape rate for girls between five and 17 in the severely war-affected north was 1.7 percent; for women 18 and over it was 3.4 percent.[251] In the south of the country, which was less affected by war, the annual rape rate for girls was approximately 0.75 percent; for women 1.8 percent. Almost half of all reported rapes in the war-torn north were committed by family members and neighbours, while only 26.5 percent were attributed to armed groups. In the south, there was only one case (1.6 percent) of rape by a member of an armed group. Note, however, that again the perpetrator data were not listed for women and girls separately.[252]

The fact that these surveys include information on large numbers of individuals from neighbouring households who are not questioned directly presents a particular challenge when dealing with sensitive topics like sexual violence. For this and other reasons, the findings of these surveys are subject to considerable uncertainty.[253]

Conclusion

As we have shown, the available data suggest that sexual violence is committed against children to a much lesser extent than against adults, but sexual violence against both adults and children is very similar in other respects. Most of the findings—and related policy implications—that derive from our analysis of the impact of war on sexual violence against adults are also relevant to wartime sexual violence against children.

First, the large cross-national variations in wartime sexual violence rates that are evident for adults are also evident with respect to children.

In the case of children, it is—in principle at least—possible that the variation in rates between countries could be due to differences in the efficacy of child protection policies.[254] But since effective protection policies are extremely rare in war-affected poor countries, this is not very likely.

Second, there is compelling evidence to suggest that for children as well as adults, the greatest threat of sexual violence in wartime comes from family members, friends, and acquaintances, not from armed combatants. Yet, as is the case for adult survivors, the child victims of domestic sexual violence receive a disproportionately small share of attention—and assistance—from the international community.

Third, as indicated in Chapter 1, the issue of sexual violence against men in wartime is rarely dealt with—not least by the UN. The same is true with respect to boys. The landmark Security Council Resolution on conflict-related sexual violence, Resolution 1325 on Women, Peace and Security, and subsequent documents that determine UN policy on sexual violence, ignore boys completely. Yet, if the worldwide peacetime ratio of sexual violence prevalence rates among girls to those among boys (found in the meta-analysis discussed earlier)[255] prevails during periods of conflict as well as peace, then the Security Council is ignoring the plight of a significant proportion of children victimized by wartime sexual violence.

> Most of the findings and policy implications on the impact of war on sexual violence against adults are also relevant to sexual violence against children.

Finally, we noted that every survey we have examined indicates that sexual violence prevalence rates among children are substantially lower than those among adults, despite the fact that children are more vulnerable than adults. This suggests that there may be normative constraints in place that provide children, particularly young children, with a greater degree of protection from sexual violence than is the case for adults.

Policy Implications

The policy implications of these findings are similar to those for adults:

- Understanding if, how, and why societal norms protect children from sexual violence in wartime to a much greater degree than adults could provide important insights for child protection policies.

- If policy-makers and researchers—wrongly—believe that sexual and other violations against children are increasing in war-affected countries, effective evidence-based policy becomes impossible.

- Not knowing whether the incidence of sexual violence against children is increasing or decreasing means that national governments in war-affected countries, international agencies, and donor governments have no way of determining the overall impact of their policies to prevent or reduce such violence.

- The absence of reliable information on the extent of sexual violence against children in war-affected countries greatly hampers the task of needs assessment and equitable resource allocation for assisting the survivors. As noted earlier in this chapter, the data collected by the UN's MRM on conflict-related sexual violence and other human rights violations against children severely underestimate the true extent of the problem.[256] Insofar as these data are used for needs evaluation, the amount of assistance needed will be severely underestimated. And if only a very small fraction of cases of sexual violence are reported—a necessary condition for bringing their perpetrators to justice—this will do little to break down the culture of impunity that protects sexual predators in so many war-affected countries.

Addressing the Knowledge Gaps

A key lesson from this review is that the absence of reliable cross-national data on the extent of sexual violence against children—and adults—means that the aspiration of donor governments and international agencies for policy in this area to be evidence-based cannot be realized.

Evidence-based policy needs evidence.

The UN's current approach to collecting data on wartime sexual violence—with respect to both children as well as adults—cannot, by its very nature, provide reliable nationwide data on the extent of sexual violence, domestic or conflict-related.

The population surveys reviewed in this *Report* can, in principle, provide far more realistic estimates of the extent of sexual violence in wartime than the reporting methods used by the UN and human rights organizations.

As we have pointed out, however, very few such surveys have been carried out—and almost all have been undertaken in the last decade, which means that conflicts of previous periods are rarely covered. And aside from the series of neighbourhood-method surveys cited above, both methodology and definitions (e.g., the definition of "children" and "sexual violence") vary to a considerable degree between surveys in different war-affected countries. As a result, the findings are rarely directly comparable.

Only sensitively implemented population surveys that are specifically designed for the purpose can determine the nationwide extent of sexual violence in war-affected countries with a degree of accuracy sufficient to usefully inform policy.

As the UN Statistics Division notes in a 2009 report on using surveys to estimate the extent of violence—including sexual violence—against women:

> Compared to the two other sources of statistics—censuses and administrative records—statistical sample surveys have the advantage of being less costly; more flexible in terms of the depth of investigation of certain topic[s]—survey instruments can accommodate larger number of more detailed questions; producing statistics of better quality as a consequence of the fact that interviewers can be better trained and prepared compared to census enumerators.[257]

Ideally, the incidence and prevalence of sexual violence in war-affected countries would be estimated by surveys dedicated wholly to this issue. In reality, despite the cost advantages of surveys compared to censuses and administrative records, they may be too expensive. The alternative is to incorporate a sexual violence module in general-purpose surveys. As noted earlier, the DHS organization has a violence module that can be incorporated into one of its standard surveys. The module includes questions about sexual violence—though not against males.

In the last *Human Security Report*, we addressed the more general information deficit that confronts international agencies and policy-makers embarked on peacebuilding and development programs in post-conflict societies. These actors rarely have access to timely and reliable nationwide data on livelihoods, health, education, security, and human rights violations—including sexual violence.

> ## The mandate of new UN peace operations should require nationwide retrospective population surveys to create an evidence base for policy.

We proposed that the mandate of new UN peace operations should therefore include a requirement to undertake a nationwide retrospective population survey addressing the knowledge gaps noted above. Such a survey would have a violence module—including questions on sexual violence against males as well as females. Data on sexual violence perpetrated against children could be gathered, as we saw with the multi-country WHO survey, by asking respondents whether or not they had been subject to sexual violence as a child. Children would not be questioned directly.

The data thus collected could be used for needs assessment and policy formation, and the baseline data collected would provide benchmarks measuring progress, given follow-up impact evaluation surveys at appropriate intervals.

Such surveys would, in other words, create an evidence base for policy where none currently exists.

Roger Lemoyne / UN Photo. AFGHANISTAN.

War Is Not "Development in Reverse": The Impact of Conflict on Children's Education

This chapter continues the investigation of the impact of war on human development that began with the last *Human Security Report*. Part II of that *Report*, "The Shrinking Costs of War," analyzed the apparent paradox of child mortality rates that decline in wartime.

In the first three chapters of this *Report*, we have argued, among other things, that the impact of war on the worldwide incidence of sexual violence has likely declined since the end of the Cold War.

In this final chapter of Part I we focus on how conflict affects children's education and find a similar counterintuitive pattern—a development indicator that again appears to *improve* during many periods of warfare.

It is certainly the case that wars can have hugely damaging impacts on entire educational systems. Indeed, major reports have described the overall impact of war on educational systems as highly damaging, even "devastating,"[258] "disastrous,"[259] and causing the destruction of educational opportunities on "an epic scale."[260]

But this is not the case for most countries, most of the time. Indeed, Paul Collier's memorable phrase, war is "development in reverse," is not an accurate description of the impact of war on educational outcomes.[261] Data from a major 2011 study of 25 countries by the UNESCO (United Nations Educational, Scientific and Cultural Organization) Institute for Statistics show that during the majority of conflict periods there is no clear decline in educational outcomes.[262]

In fact, the indicators used in the study show educational outcomes *improving* during a substantial number of conflict periods. An analysis by the Washington, DC-based Education Policy and Data Center (EPDC), released in 2010, found that many conflict-affected countries experienced improving educational outcomes, even in the regions *worst affected* by conflict.[263] Both studies are reviewed later in this chapter.

The fact that, on average, educational outcomes improve in wartime does not mean that conflict has *no* impact. The impact may be evident in a slowing of the rate of improvement in educational attainments that prevailed in the pre-war situation.

But there is an important difference between wartime situations in which nationwide educational attainments decline *absolutely,* and those in which they continue to improve, albeit at a slower rate than in peacetime.

In both cases, war has an impact, but in the latter case the societal effect of conflict on educational outcomes—i.e., a slower average rate of improvement—can hardly be described as "devastating" or "disastrous" in national terms.

The finding that conflict has a less dramatic impact on educational outcomes than is claimed in the literature is similar to the finding on child mortality in wartime that was analyzed in the last *Human Security Report*. In the latter case, we found that in approximately 90 percent of the years in which countries around the world experienced high-intensity conflicts between 1970 and 2008, under-five mortality rates declined.[264] The evidence suggests that educational outcomes in most wars follow a similar trend.

The claim that both child health and educational outcomes appear to improve during periods of conflict is profoundly counterintuitive—indeed, it may suggest that war is good for children's health and education. This is, of course, not the case.

The reality is that in most developing countries there is a strong, though far from universal, tendency for educational attainments and children's health outcomes to improve in peacetime, and the evidence suggests that these benign trends continue during many periods of conflict, in large part because very few of today's wars are deadly or destructive enough to reverse them.

Another possible explanation is that war *does* have the expected negative impact but that this is more than counterbalanced by other factors. In Afghanistan, for example, a dramatic improvement in school enrolments followed a massive infusion of international assistance to the educational sector after the overthrow of the Taliban in 2001, despite the ongoing insurgency.

This pattern—of development outcomes improving during periods of warfare—is true not only for child health and education. A recent cross-national statistical study undertaken for the World Bank's 2011 *World Development Report* examined the impact of war on progress towards achieving the Millennium Development Goals (MDGs).

It found that, on average, indicators for malnutrition, life expectancy, infant and maternal mortality—and access to sanitation and potable water—all improved in war-affected countries.[265]

These positive findings have received little publicity, however. Indeed, the fact that student educational attainment and attendance rates often improve in wartime is rarely even mentioned in the major reports on education in the developing world that are produced by international agencies like UNESCO and UNICEF (United Nations Children's Fund), by advocacy groups, and many researchers. In what we refer to as "mainstream narrative," the focus is on the worst affected countries where the damage to educational systems has been greatest.

Our Focus

In reviewing the impact of war on children's education, we examine three different approaches to describing and explaining it.

First, we examine the detailed and contextually rich case-study literature that provides much of the material that informs the mainstream narrative on the many ways in which conflict can affect educational systems.

Second, we examine two recent studies that use comparative descriptive statistics to examine the relationship between conflict and education. Both were undertaken for UNESCO's flagship 2011 Education for All report, *The Hidden Crisis: Armed Conflict and Education*.[266]

Third, we review the findings of the very small number of econometric analyses of the impact of war on education, notably the major background study undertaken by the Peace Research Institute Oslo (PRIO) for the World Bank's 2011 *World Development Report*.[267]

Each of these approaches provides different insights. The country case-study material that informs the mainstream narrative provides a deep, contextualized understanding of the very different impacts of conflict in particular countries at different times. Indeed, most of what we know about how war affects educational systems comes from the country case-study research that we discuss below.

However, the mainstream narrative that derives from this rich case-study literature suffers from selection bias in that it focuses—understandably enough—on the worst cases where the need for resources is greatest. It devotes little attention to countries where war appears to have little impact on educational attainments—or to asking why this might be the case. Yet, understanding how and why educational outcomes can continue to improve in periods of conflict is of obvious policy relevance.

The multi-country descriptive statistics studies we examine here derive their educational data primarily from nationwide population surveys, mostly UNICEF's Multiple Indicator Cluster Surveys (MICS) and those of the Demographic and Health Survey (DHS) organization. Because these surveys use similar methodologies, their findings can be compared cross-nationally.

The background research undertaken by the Montreal-based UNESCO Institute for Statistics (UIS) for UNESCO's *Hidden Crisis* report, and examined in detail below, uses descriptive statistics to reveal how educational attainments within countries may vary:[268]

- Between periods of war and peace.
- Between genders and between levels of income.
- Between areas of war-affected countries that are directly affected by conflict and those that are not.

The second comparative study examined here was undertaken for the same UNESCO report by EPDC. It focuses on the impact of armed conflict on school attendance and enrolment rates and other educational indicators at the subnational level in some 19 different countries.

In particular, it compares educational outcomes in regions of a country that were the worst affected by conflict with all other regions—where conflict had less impact.

Both studies analyze a limited number of the countries in conflict around the world during the periods that are covered. For this reason, and because the samples of countries examined are not randomly selected, we cannot be confident that their findings, while striking and suggestive, are necessarily representative of the impact of conflict on educational attainments and attendance in *all* war-affected countries.

Econometric studies on the impact of war on educational systems—like that undertaken by PRIO for the World Bank's 2011 *World Development Report*—avoid the possibility of unintended selection bias noted above by including virtually all countries in conflict over a given period.[269] Plus, regression analysis enables researchers to examine the association between possible causal factors—such as conflict—and educational outcomes while holding other factors (e.g., income) constant.[270]

Econometric studies that use all available cases of the phenomenon being studied— or a representative sample—can in theory be used to make generalizations about average impacts of conflict on education. Individual, or a series of, case studies and analyses that use descriptive statistics to compare limited numbers of countries that have not been selected randomly cannot be used to make such generalizations. But, as we pointed out in Chapter 2 of the previous *Human Security Report*, econometric analysis confronts its own theoretical and methodological challenges.

Case-study, comparative descriptive statistics, and econometric approaches to explaining the impact of war on children's education all have limitations, as this chapter makes clear. But drawing on the findings and insights of all three provides us with a deeper understanding of the war and education nexus than relying on any single approach on its own.

The Mainstream Narrative

As noted previously, we use the term, "mainstream narrative" as a shorthand way of referring to how issues are framed, perceived, and explained. It refers to the assumptions that international agencies, donor governments, and major NGOs (nongovernmental organizations) share with respect to the negative impacts of armed conflict on children's educational opportunities.

UNESCO's 2011 report, *The Hidden Crisis: Armed Conflict and Education*, provides the most compelling recent iteration of the mainstream narrative. Drawing on a wide range of research resources, it provides a comprehensive overview of the many different ways in which conflict adversely affects children's schooling. Its research leads it to conclude that "the 'scourge of warfare' … is destroying opportunities for education on an epic scale."[271]

The mainstream narrative is informed in considerable part by the detailed, and often evocative, descriptions of the ways in which war can affect children's education. These accounts are frequently buttressed with statistics from individual country case studies—for example, the percentage of schools destroyed during a period of warfare.[272]

The cumulative impression created by these detailed investigations does indeed suggest that war destroys educational opportunities on "an epic scale."

Nine Ways That War Affects Children's Education

First, and most obviously, war kills children, and injures others so seriously they cannot attend school. As we pointed out in Chapter 3, the frequently cited figures indicating that 6 million children were disabled and seriously injured and a further 2 million killed in recent wars are of dubious provenance.[273] But no one doubts that the costs that conflict imposes on children can be extremely high.

Second, teachers may be killed, injured, or subject to forced displacement in wartime environments. More than two-thirds of Rwanda's primary and secondary school teachers reportedly fled or were killed as a result of the genocide.[274] In Cambodia's genocide, teachers, along with other "intellectuals," were specifically targeted by the Khmer Rouge regime.[275] In less extreme circumstances, teachers are still at risk of conscription by government or rebel forces, or of losing their jobs because of war-driven cuts in educational spending.

Third, children in war are often displaced to refugee or internally displaced person (IDP) camps. IDP camps, which tend to have a high concentration of children, typically have far fewer educational resources than refugee camps. Moreover, many children, particularly those who have lost homes, parents, and siblings, may be deeply traumatized by their experiences. The scope of the problem is evident in the sheer numbers of displaced children—an estimated 13.5 million around the world are internally displaced[276] plus several million refugee children.[277]

Fourth, armed conflict affects education indirectly; for example, through conflict-related sexual violence. Sexual violence against children can have, "a devastating impact on education: it impairs victims' learning potential, creates a climate of fear that keeps girls at home and leads to family breakdown that deprives children of a nurturing environment."[278]

Fifth, war can destroy or seriously damage schools and other educational institutions:

- In Iraq the Ministry of Education reported that there were 31,598 attacks on educational institutions between March 2003 and October 2008.[279]
- In Afghanistan the number of attacks on schools increased from 242 to 670 between 2007 and 2008.[280]
- In Thailand attacks on schools almost quadrupled between 2006 and 2007, rising from 43 to 164.[281]
- In Timor Leste 95 percent of schools had to be repaired or rebuilt after the violence that followed the independence referendum in 2000. In Iraq the figure was 85 percent; in Kosovo, 65 percent; in Bosnia-Herzegovina, 50 percent; and in Mozambique, 45 percent.[282]

School buildings that are not destroyed or badly damaged may be commandeered by government or rebel forces and used as headquarters, as barracks, for storage, or to house IDPs who have lost their homes.[283]

Sixth, parents affected by war-exacerbated poverty, finding it difficult to pay school fees, may choose to take their children out of school and put them to work at home.

Seventh, child soldiers, who lose far more years of education than other children in war-affected countries, have special educational needs. These needs are rarely met.[284]

Eighth, in wartime, military budgets typically increase; educational budgets get cut. As a consequence, teachers go unpaid (causing many to quit), funding for teaching materials and routine maintenance of schools dries up, and system-wide management and development of educational systems degrades and sometimes grinds completely to a halt.[285]

Finally, warfare destroys human capital throughout the educational system. This is arguably an even greater challenge than damaged and destroyed buildings.

In what follows, we focus on three indicators used to measure the impact of warfare on education—school enrolment, attendance, and pupils' educational attainment (i.e., average years of education). If the mainstream narrative is correct, we would expect the impact of conflict would be reflected in declines in all three indicators.

A One-Sided Picture?

The above descriptions are very similar to those in many—not all—major reports from international agencies and NGOs that have examined the various impacts of armed conflict on children's education. Indeed, many of the above examples are drawn from these reports, which in turn draw on the findings of a range of detailed case studies that have investigated what happens to educational systems in times of war.

No one doubts that the negative impacts that war imposes on education are shockingly large in some cases. But the problem with the mainstream narrative, as we saw in the case of sexual violence, is that the worst cases are presented in such a way as to suggest that they are the norm.

Thus, the descriptions of how teachers may be vulnerable to attack in wartime are illustrated with reference to Cambodia, Iraq, Rwanda, and Afghanistan—four countries that have endured some of the deadliest wars in the past 40 years.

The references to the wartime destruction of school buildings are to Timor Leste, Iraq, Kosovo, Bosnia, and Mozambique—all countries in which the destruction of educational property was severe.

References to the impact of sexual violence on education are drawn from the Democratic Republic of the Congo (DRC), which, as we pointed out in Chapter 1, has been afflicted by extraordinarily high rates of wartime rape.

The strong tendency in most major reports to describe impacts of armed conflicts on educational systems in worst-case terms is no accident. What we are seeing here is essentially the same phenomenon we examined in looking at the impact of war on sexual violence. The international organizations and NGOs whose work is discussed above are not simply involved in reporting and analyzing the impact of war. They are also committed to trying to protect both children and their opportunities to be educated in war-affected countries.

These agencies and NGOs have every reason to seek greater international support for the underfunded educational needs of children in war-affected countries. The needs are great, and at the current rate of progress, the MDGs' education target—which calls for all children to have access to primary schooling by 2015—is unlikely to be met.[286]

So, it is also understandable that reporting concentrates on cases where the threats to education are greatest and the need for greater international assistance is most compelling. The consequence, however, is that the narrative of the impact of war on educational outcomes, like that on wartime sexual violence discussed in Chapters 1 and 2, becomes one-sided—biased by the strong focus on the worst cases. This, as we point out later, has important implications for policy.

One consequence of what might be called the "worst-case bias" in the mainstream narrative is that few nonspecialist readers of the major reports by UNESCO, other international agencies, or major NGOs will have any idea that there is compelling evidence to suggest that, on average, educational outcomes *improve* in conflict-affected countries.

There is another possible reason why the mainstream narrative overstates the impact of conflict on educational systems, namely a misunderstanding of current trends in armed conflict around the world.

As Oxford University's Julia Paulson and Jeremy Rappleye point out in a 2007 literature review of the relationships between education and conflict, many of the key studies—undertaken by education specialists rather than conflict researchers—are premised on the assumption that conflicts have been intensifying and increasing in frequency.[287] Clearly, if this were the case, it is likely that the threat to education would also be increasing. In fact, as this *Report* and others have made clear, the reverse is true: conflicts that are deadly and destructive enough to seriously affect educational outcomes have become much less frequent.

> It is understandable that reporting concentrates on cases where the threats to education are greatest and the need for assistance is most compelling.

Comparative Statistical Studies Reveal a Very Different Picture

To gain a rather different perspective on the impact of conflict on education, this section reviews the findings of a number of statistical studies on the effects of war on school enrolment, attendance, and attainment that use educational data drawn from population surveys.

The survey-based studies offer a more comprehensive picture of the extent of war's impact on education, because they draw on nationwide quantitative data rather than anecdotal accounts of particular impacts in particular countries—often in the worst affected areas. And the survey data reveal a very different picture from that depicted in the mainstream narrative.

The surveys on which the comparative statistics studies are based use similar definitions and methodologies that permit cross-national comparisons. (This practice stands in sharp contrast to the surveys on wartime sexual violence, which, as we pointed out in Chapter 1, often lack common definitions and methodologies, making cross-national comparisons difficult, if not impossible.)

All of the statistical studies reviewed here enrich our understanding of the variety of ways in which conflict affects education. Each offers a corrective to the bias inherent in the mainstream narrative.

The UNESCO Institute for Statistics

In 2011 the UIS produced a 25-nation comparative analysis of the impact of war on education. The study, which was commissioned for UNESCO's *Hidden Crisis* report, was entitled, *The Quantitative Impact of Conflict on Education.*

The UIS research team drew on the findings of nationwide population surveys undertaken in the new millennium in 25 war-affected countries. The aim was to provide a better understanding of the negative impact of conflict on educational attainments.[288]

The study drew attention to the many negative impacts of war on education in a careful review of the literature. But the most interesting fact to emerge from the cross-national data it reviews is that in a substantial proportion of cases in which the 25 countries it examined had experienced conflict since 1950, the indicators of educational attainment *were higher at the end of the conflict period than at the beginning.*[289]

Yet, this rather remarkable pattern is ignored in UNESCO's *Hidden Crisis* report, and, to the best of our knowledge, it is never mentioned in other reports on war and education that inform, and are in turn part of, the mainstream narrative.

> Data on the total number of years of education are rarely available in war-affected poor countries.

The methodology that the UIS researchers employed to detect the impact of war on education since the 1950s was ingenious. In the early post-World War II years, reliable government statistics on national educational attainments in developing countries were—at best—very rare. Absent official data, there were few other sources of information available—international population surveys, like those of the DHS, did not start collecting nationwide educational attainment data until the mid-1980s; MICS surveys did not start until the 1990s.

Although there are little or no survey data prior to the 1980s, each of the population surveys the UIS drew on had collected data on the total number of years of education that individual respondents attained. Such data are rarely available from other sources in war-affected poor countries.

Knowing the number of years of education that individuals have acquired in their lifetime, plus their age at the time of the survey, makes it possible to gain some idea of the years of education that successive cohorts of students may have lost due to warfare.

The UIS research team used educational attainment data from DHS and MICS surveys undertaken between 2000 and 2008.[290] The attainment measures used were the average number of years of formal education completed, or the percentage of the population that had received no formal education at all.

For some countries, data were collated to reveal differences in educational attainments depending on whether the respondants lived in war-affected or non-war-affected regions of the country, or by gender, ethnicity, or wealth.

However, the DHS and MICS data do not provide a direct measure of the impact of conflict on education.

The survey data that the UIS analyzed are for the average number of years of education attained by different age cohorts in their lifetime (i.e., up to the time when the survey was undertaken). Primary and secondary education is normally completed by the age of 15. And so the UIS data show the average number of years of education attained by all those individuals who were 15 years of age in a particular year. For example, the data for the year 1995 display the average number of years of education attained at the time of the survey by all respondents who were born in 1980.[291]

> The UIS data measure the total years of education attained during the lifetime of the respondent.

If the country in this example experienced conflict during, say, the first half of the 1990s, we would expect the data for the age cohort that turned 15 in 1995 to show lower educational attainments as a result of the disruptions caused by the fighting.

But since the data measure years of education attained during the *lifetime* of the respondents, rather than those attained *by the age of 15*, the figures may mask reductions in average attainments as a result of war.[292] This is because not all individuals achieve all of their lifetime years of education by the age of 15. Some may lose years of education because of conflict but are able to regain them by going back to school between the end of the conflict and the time when the survey was conducted. Where this is the case, the negative short-term impact of conflict will not be revealed by the UIS data.

These caveats mean that few *definitive* conclusions can be drawn from these data. Nevertheless, the broad trends that the data-derived graphics for individual countries describe offer valuable insights into the very different ways that conflict can affect educational systems and that are sometimes sharply at odds with the assumptions of the mainstream narrative.

The main conclusion of the UIS study was that there is:

> [a] significant negative impact of conflict on the proportion of the population with formal education, the average years of education attained, and the literacy rate. This legacy of conflict is visible at the national and sub-national level in household survey data from all countries analyzed, with the exception of six countries.[293]

Trend data displayed in the graphics in the report clearly show educational attainments worsening substantially in some countries, often during long periods of conflict. This is very evident in the cases of Afghanistan, Iraq, and Cambodia—countries that have experienced some of the deadliest conflicts in the past 40 years. In other countries, periods of declining attainment are much shorter, less steep, and take place within longer periods of improving attainments.

The belief that the impact of war reduces educational attainments is uncontroversial, supported by evidence as well as common sense, and is a central theme of the mainstream narrative on education and conflict. But while it is true, it is far from being the whole truth.

An Extraordinary Finding

In almost a quarter of the 25 countries reviewed, UIS's researchers found "no visible impact of conflict on education." They suggest that in these cases what is required is "a more fine-grained municipal-level analysis to pinpoint the conflict-exposed population."[294]

But, as noted earlier, what is perhaps most remarkable about the UIS data is that they demonstrate that in only 11 percent of conflict periods was there a clear deterioration in educational attainment indicators. In almost half the cases the trend was unclear or varied across different indicators. But in more than 40 percent of cases, educational attainment indicators were higher at the end of the conflict period than the beginning. In some of these latter cases there was a fairly steady improvement; in others, there were some periods in which educational attainments worsened, but there was nevertheless a net improvement from the beginning to the end.

> Only 11 percent of conflict periods saw a clear deterioration in educational attainment.

The finding that emerges from the UIS study that educational outcomes often improve during wartime is so counterintuitive, and so much at odds with the mainstream narrative, that it is open to question. One obvious counterargument is that increasing educational attainments in periods of warfare do *not* mean that conflict has no negative impact. The relevant issue is, one might argue, whether attainment rates improve or worsen *relative to the pre-war trend.*

It is evident from the UIS case studies that educational attainments may be negatively affected by the disruptive and destructive effects of conflict but not sufficiently to reverse any long-term improvement evident in the pre-war period. In these cases, educational attainments continue to increase but at a slower rate than in peacetime. Here conflict clearly has a negative effect, but, as we argued earlier, a slower improvement in attainments is still a much better outcome than an absolute decline.

In fact, as we show later, the major study undertaken by PRIO for the World Bank's 2011 *World Development Report* found that, on average, the rate of increase in educational outcomes in conflict-affected countries appears to be little different from that in countries at peace. This suggests that war has little impact on educational outcomes. This finding is important because the PRIO study included almost all countries in conflict in its review, while the UIS study was restricted to 25.

Some caution is necessary here. The pre-war peacetime educational attainment trend—the so-called counterfactual against which the in-conflict trend can be compared—can be very difficult to determine with confidence, since the pre-war trend is rarely linear. The same applies to in-conflict trends as well.

Educational Attainments in War-Affected Regions versus Unaffected Regions

There are two reasons why the impact of conflict on education in war-affected countries may be difficult to detect in nationwide trend data on educational attainments. First, as we noted earlier, today's predominantly low-intensity wars may be neither deadly nor destructive enough to have any discernible nationwide impact on educational attainments.

In other words, the impact may be there, but may be so small as to be indistinguishable from data uncertainties due to survey error at the national level. But if this is indeed the case, then the impact of war can hardly be described as "devastating" or "disastrous."

This argument is most compelling with respect to the past two decades—particularly since the beginning of the new millennium—compared to the Cold War years when war death tolls were much higher on average.

Second, there may be a negative impact of war on educational attainments in regions badly affected by conflict, while in the rest of the country educational attainments continue to improve. Where this happens, especially if the impact of the conflict on attainments is highly localized, the effect may not be discernible in the aggregated nationwide survey data. The impact is real in these cases, but not visible at the national level.

In what was in effect a test of this idea, the UIS research team examined the differences in educational attainments in war-affected versus non-war-affected regions in a number of the countries experiencing conflict.

> Today's predominantly low-intensity wars may not be deadly enough to have any visible impact on education at the national level.

The expectation here is that the war-affected areas will have lower educational attainments than those not directly affected by conflict. This is, in fact, the case in most war-affected countries, as the UIS graphics make clear, although there were a surprising number of cases where educational outcomes improved even in the worst affected regions.

If educational attainments are lower in the war-affected areas than in those that are at peace, we might reasonably expect that the death, disruption, and destruction associated with the war are responsible for the difference.

This would be a mistake—as UIS's graphics again clearly suggest.[295]

Take the case of Turkey. As Figure 4.1, replicated from the UIS study, clearly indicates, 13- to 17-year-old children in the war-affected Kurdish-inhabited provinces experienced worse educational outcomes during the conflict period than the rest of Turkey.[296]

This is what we would expect given the mainstream narrative's assumption that war affects education negatively. But the low level of access of children to education in the Kurdish region *preceded the conflict*; and thus, conflict cannot have been its primary cause. Children in the war-affected Kurdish provinces were certainly at an educational disadvantage, but this is largely because they were *already* disadvantaged before the conflict began.

This pattern is evident in the large majority of the cases where conflict-affected and non-conflict-affected regions were compared in the UIS's report.

The lower educational outcomes in the Kurdish areas in both peacetime and wartime were almost certainly caused by some combination of poverty, economic and gender inequality, and governmental neglect—all factors that preceded the conflict—and likely contributed to its onset.

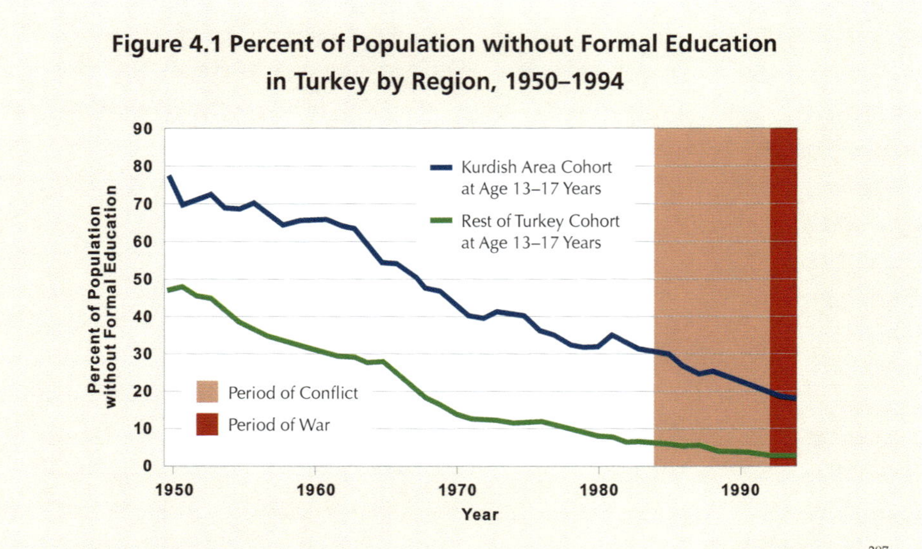

Figure 4.1 Percent of Population without Formal Education in Turkey by Region, 1950–1994

Data Source: UIS.[297]

Surprisingly, school attainment improves in many conflict zones. In Turkey's war-affected Kurdish area, the share of the population with no education fell by over a third among those who were at school-going age during conflict.

Moreover, if the conflict was affecting education more negatively in the conflict-affected Kurdish areas than in other parts of Turkey, we would expect the percentage of individuals with no formal education to shrink more slowly during the conflict than before the conflict. In fact, as Figure 4.1 makes clear, this is not the case.[298] Educational outcomes improved during conflict at a rate that is similar to that before the conflict.

In Turkey this positive trend may in part be a function of the substantial improvement in female educational attainments that had been underway since the 1970s, when female literacy levels started rising more rapidly in the war-affected Kurdish provinces than in the rest of the country.[299] However, while this trend is somewhat surprising, it is not uncommon in other conflict-affected countries.[300]

In Guatemala, which was continuously embroiled in armed conflict from the mid-1960s to the mid-1990s, educational attainments for male students improved, though somewhat unevenly throughout the war and in both the war-affected and non-war-affected regions of the country.

The male students in war-affected regions experienced lower educational attainments than those in non-war-affected regions. But, as was the case in Turkey, the gap in attainments *preceded* the war period, which means that conflict could not have been the primary cause of this gap. Moreover, the rate of improvement in educational outcomes during the 30-plus years of conflict was slightly greater for the war-affected than the non-war-affected regions over this period, again the opposite of what might be expected.[301]

In India the average number of years of education attained per person in the war-affected Jammu and Kashmir region improved through almost all periods of violence.[302] Attainments improved at a *faster* rate in this region than the rest of India from the mid-1980s onwards.[303]

In Ethiopia there was no clear difference in average educational attainments between the conflict-affected Tigray province and the rest of the country before the period of war that started in the mid-1960s. But both regions saw educational attainment rates improve throughout most of the conflict period. But while war-affected Tigray lagged behind the rest of the country during the first years of conflict, its attainment rates subsequently increased and actually exceeded those in non-war-affected parts of the country.[304]

Since these trends are both counterintuitive and very much at odds with the mainstream narrative, it is worth summarizing and briefly reflecting on them:

- In more than 40 percent of cases included in the survey, educational indicators for cohorts of school-age children were better at the end of a conflict period than at the beginning. In only 11 percent were they worse.

- In most countries affected by conflict, the war-affected regions showed lower educational outcomes than the non-war-affected regions. Yet, in almost all countries in which comparisons between war-affected and non-war-affected regions were made in the UIS study, the low outcomes in the war-affected regions preceded the conflict and must therefore have had different causes. Factors other than the impact of war—most obviously poverty and poor governance—appear to be the likely determinants of low outcomes both before and during conflicts.

- In a number of countries, the rate at which educational outcomes improved in conflict-affected areas *during* a conflict was similar to or greater than the rate of change during the same period in the nonconflict areas. If this finding based on a limited sample of countries is indicative of overall patterns, it again suggests that the impact of conflict is far less dramatic than what we would expect. In many cases, the impact may be too small to be measured with the data we have available.[305]

War Is Only One Factor among Many Affecting Educational Outcomes in Wartime

In focusing attention on the impact of war on education it is easy to forget that other factors also affect educational attainments—and may have a much greater impact. It is quite possible, for example, that low educational attainment scores in war-affected regions of a country are caused by factors that have little to do with the war—an economic crisis caused by persistent drought, for example.

In other cases, the impact of the destruction and displacement caused by warfare on aggregate educational outcomes may be more than offset by the positive effect of other factors—increased income per capita, for example, or a big infusion of international assistance to the educational sector. Where this happens, the trend line indicating that educational attainments in war were improving does *not* necessarily mean that war has no negative impact but simply that this impact was hidden by the positive countervailing effect on educational attainments of other factors.

In Colombia, for example, poverty appears to have been a far more important determinant of educational attainment than the continued presence of armed conflict. During the 40-plus years of conflict in Colombia, rising educational attainments have been associated with a steady and substantial increase in GDP (gross domestic product) per capita. So, it is quite possible that the positive effect of rising incomes on education has more than offset the negative effects of the war.

The most obvious demonstration of the negative impact of nonconflict factors on educational attainments is found in those cases where attainments decline for long periods in peacetime.

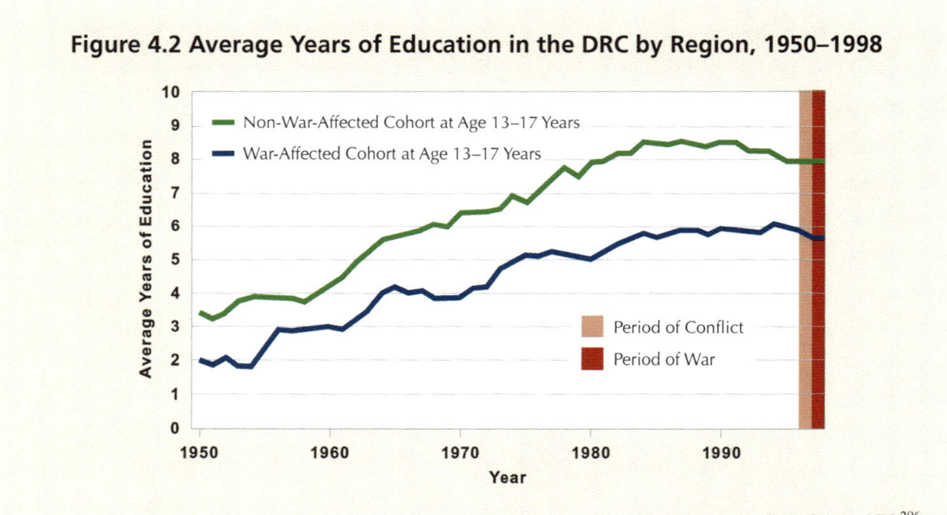

Figure 4.2 Average Years of Education in the DRC by Region, 1950–1998

Data Source: UIS.[306]

The conflict in the Eastern DRC inflicted a heavy toll on the civilian population. But educational attainments started to stagnate and decline prior to the war— likely as a result of bad governance and economic crisis.

Educational attainments have, on average, been increasing worldwide. Yet, in some countries—even those not afflicted by war—progress can stall, stagnate, and be reversed for long periods. The DRC is a case in point. Here, as Figure 4.2 makes clear, progress in education slowed in the 1980s and stagnated for more than a decade prior to the civil war that started in the late 1990s.

This decline in educational attainments was the result of a decades-long progressive collapse of governance—along with a drop in copper prices—that drove the DRC's GDP per capita down from approximately $300 per capita (in constant USD 2000) in the 1970s, to approximately $100 at the beginning of the periods of civil war that started in the late 1990s.[307]

Interestingly, as we show later, between 2000 and 2007—a period of continuous violence—primary and secondary school educational attendance rates *improved* in parts of the DRC that were most affected by violence.

Average years of education achieved also declined for long periods in peacetime in the DRC's neighbour, the Republic of Congo (sometimes referred to as Congo-Brazzaville).[308] In both countries we witness lengthy declines or periods of stagnation in educational attainments that have nothing to do with conflict itself. The likely causes of the non-war-related educational decline are failures of governance and, relatedly, declining national incomes.

> The EPDC found no strong evidence that education indicators declined dramatically in conflict areas as compared to nonconflict regions.

It is difficult to determine the impact of different and sometimes conflicting factors on educational attainments in periods of conflict with descriptive statistics. To discern the concurrent effects of a range of different causal factors, researchers can turn to regression analysis. We examine this approach in the review of recent econometric research on the impact of war on education at the end of this chapter. It includes the major study undertaken for the World Bank's 2011 *World Development Report* by PRIO.

The Education Policy and Data Center

EPDC's analysis, like the UIS study, was prepared for UNESCO's *Hidden Crisis* report.[309] But the EPDC looks at school attendance and enrolment rather than at attainment, which was the focus of the UIS study.

The EPDC study examined the differences between conflict-affected and peaceful provinces and regions in 19 countries that experienced warfare between 2000 and 2010. It found that:

- As expected, weighted net attendance rates for primary schools were on average 11 percent lower in conflict areas than peaceful areas,[310] but the EPDC also noted that "it is not possible to establish whether the differences are caused by conflict."[311]

- Comparing trends in school attendance rates in pre-conflict periods with conflict and post-conflict periods does not show that on average "conflict areas experience weaker attendance growth/greater declines."[312]

- There is "no strong evidence that primary attendance rates, enrolment rates, pupil numbers, and pupil teacher ratios decline dramatically in conflict areas as compared to nonconflict regions."[313]

As the authors point out, there are a number of factors that might explain why the negative effect of conflict on education might have remained unobserved in this study, especially regarding issues of data quality and availability.[314]

However, the most surprising finding to emerge from the data is that in many of the countries examined, the regions that were worst affected by wartime violence had experienced *rising* levels of school attendance during conflict periods.

In other words, like the UIS, the EPDC researchers found patterns of association between conflict and educational outcomes that were both counterintuitive and frequently sharply at odds with the assumptions that underpin the mainstream narrative.

Interestingly, both research teams appear somewhat skeptical about their own counterintuitive findings.

The EPDC study covers a much shorter period than does the UIS (which tracks trends back to the 1950s). The EPDC data are also more fine-grained. In many countries in the EPDC study, there are 20 or more regions—in the UIS study, just two. Since the EPDC examined smaller geographical units than the UNESCO study, it should, in principle, have been better placed to detect localized impacts of conflict on education.

Within each country, the EPDC research team compared the trends in school attendance between the "primary" and "secondary" conflict regions, with those that were not directly affected by conflict.

Of the 17 countries for which there were data on primary attendance rates, almost half lacked data for analyzing trends in conflict regions. Since in these cases there was no information on trends, they are not included in this review.[315]

In three of the nine cases that have data for at least two years, Côte d'Ivoire, Afghanistan, and Colombia—attendance rates declined or stagnated during periods of warfare in conflict-affected regions. This is what common sense and the mainstream narrative would lead us to expect.

But in four countries—Senegal, Central African Republic, the DRC, and Rwanda—educational attendance *increased* during periods of warfare in the regions affected by conflict.

In two cases, Uganda and Pakistan, the trend is not sufficiently clear to determine either an overall increase or decrease in attendance.[316]

The EPDC study notes that secondary educational attendance may be "more sensitive to system shocks"[317] than primary school attendance, so it also examines the differences in secondary school attendance between war-affected and non-war-affected regions over time. The pattern turns out to be very similar to that for primary education.

In two countries—Côte d'Ivoire and Rwanda—we find the decline in school attendance that might be expected during periods of warfare.

In four countries—Central African Republic, Colombia, the DRC, and Pakistan—we see attendance rates counterintuitively *rising* during conflict periods, although the increase in some of these cases is very small.[318]

In the remaining countries there are no trend data or the trend is not sufficiently clear.[319]

The EPDC data appear to confirm what the UIS data reveal—namely, that the effect of warfare on education is far more complicated and variable than the mainstream narrative, with its stress on worst affected countries, assumes. We stress, however, that the sample sizes in both the EPDC and the UIS studies are not large enough for any definitive conclusions to be drawn, especially since the countries examined were not randomly selected, creating the possibility of inadvertent selection bias.

Moreover, like is not being compared with like in these studies in two important respects. First, the UIS is examining educational *attainments*, while EPDC's focus is school *attendance*. Second, the time periods are very different—several decades in the case of the UIS, less than 10 years in the case of the EPDC. The more recent period covered by the EPDC studies saw far less deadly and destructive wars than the period examined by the UIS. So, we would expect conflicts to have a lesser impact on education during this period.

In the next sections we look at four of the EPDC's case studies, two that reveal the expected negative impact of war on school attendance and two that do not.

Côte d'Ivoire: Primary School Attendance and War

The association between conflict and school attendance in Côte d'Ivoire is exactly what the mainstream narrative would lead us to expect. Figure 4.3 shows the variation over time in gross primary school attendance rates.[320]

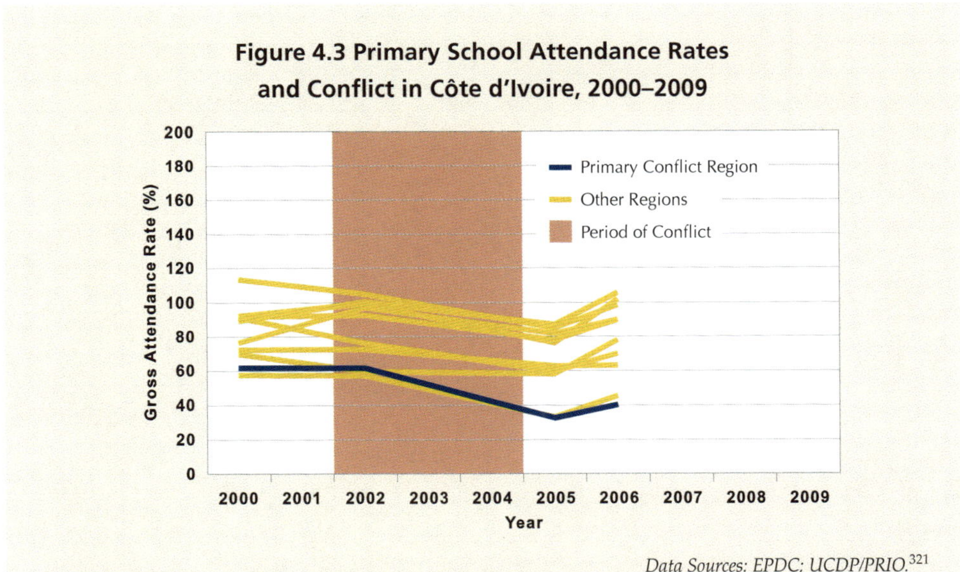

Data Sources: EPDC; UCDP/PRIO.[321]

Côte d'Ivoire's educational system was seriously affected by the armed conflict of the early 2000s. In the most heavily affected region, the primary school attendance rate dropped by almost half.

In the primary conflict region—the blue line on the graph—the gross attendance rate starts to decline shortly after the war begins and continues to decrease throughout the period of conflict. This most-war-affected region also had one of the lowest levels of primary school attendance. The nonconflict regions also witnessed a decline in attendance during the war, suggesting that the deaths, destruction, and disruption caused by the conflict had indirect, as well as direct, negative impacts. After the fighting is over, attendance increased again in all regions.

Afghanistan: Primary School Attendance and War

In Afghanistan the data also support the commonsense assumption that regions worst affected by wartime violence will see declines in educational attendance. As Figure 4.4 shows, in two of the three worst affected regions (namely Helmand and Kandahar), attendance rates dropped dramatically, while in the third region, Khost, the decline was less pronounced.

Afghanistan is unusual in that education suffers in considerable part because schools—and students—are deliberately targeted by insurgent groups.

Much of the insurgent violence against schools in Afghanistan has taken place in the provinces of Helmand, Kandahar, and other parts of the southern and eastern region of the country where there is a strong Taliban presence. In 2011, according to the country's Education Ministry, some 400 schools remained closed in this region because of security concerns.[322]

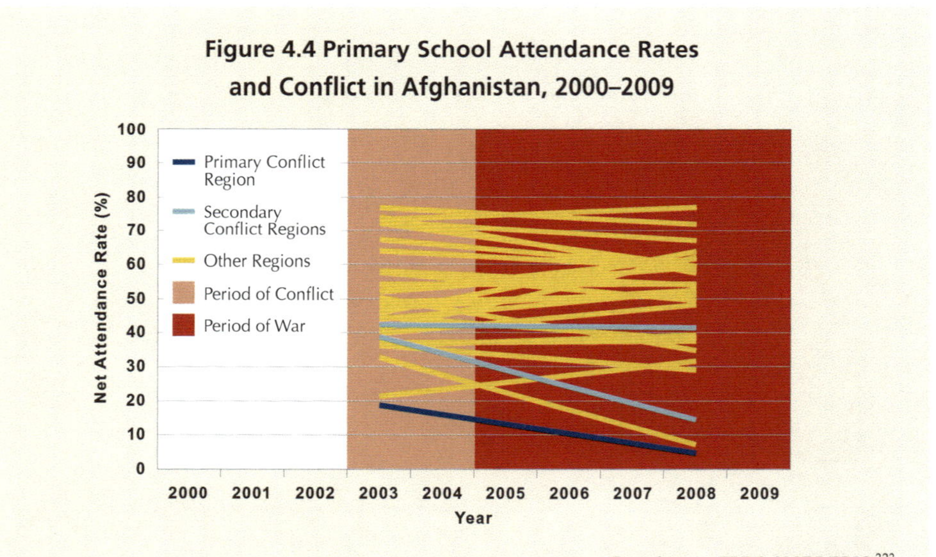

Data Sources: EPDC; UCDP/PRIO.[323]

Three war-affected Afghan provinces experienced declines in primary school attendance: Helmand, Kandahar, and Khost. They also witnessed many targeted attacks on children and their schools.

Note: This graph shows the net attendance rate while Figures 4.3, 4.5, and 4.6 show the gross attendance rate.

In the Taliban-influenced areas, educational attendance rates are among the lowest in Afghanistan, and militants have mounted campaigns of violence, including acid attacks, to deter girls from attending schools. In Helmand girls made up just 5 percent of school enrolment in 2004, compared with the national average of 35 percent.[324]

Senegal: Primary School Attendance and War

The association between war and educational attendance in Senegal, as Figure 4.5 below shows, is dramatically different from that which both common sense and the mainstream narrative would lead us to expect.

In most war-affected countries analyzed in the UIS report above, the regions most afflicted by armed conflict have, as we might expect, educational outcomes that are worse than non-conflict-afflicted regions.[325]

But surprisingly, in Senegal's worst affected conflict region (Ziguinchor in the Casamance area), the gross primary school attendance rate was the highest in the country throughout the conflict period and continued to rise over time.

It is not clear what accounts for this truly surprising outcome. But two points are worth noting. First, the level of political violence in Senegal was *very* low. The best estimate of reported battle deaths for the two periods of warfare in Senegal averaged just 40 per year. We would not expect a conflict with such low battle deaths to have a discernible impact on educational outcomes.[326]

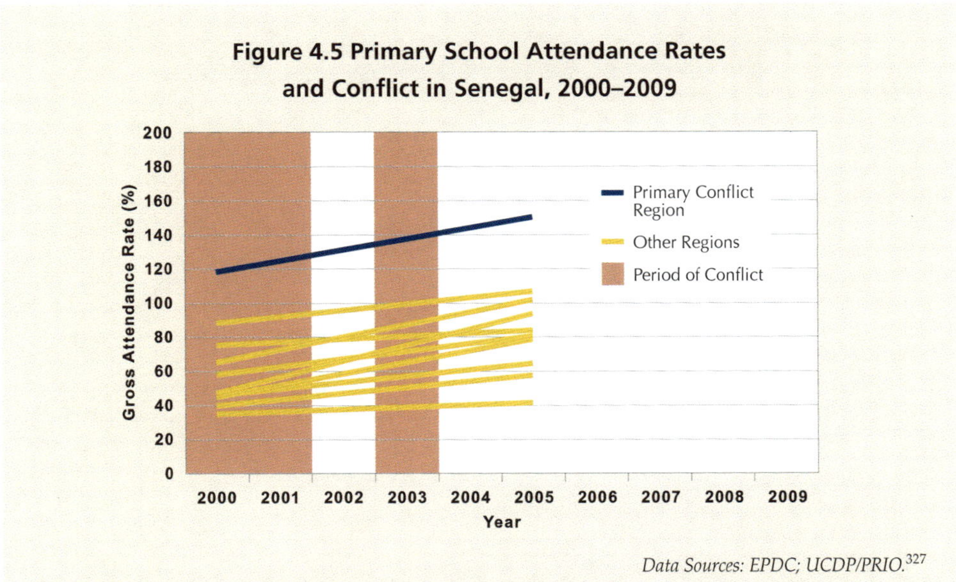

Data Sources: EPDC; UCDP/PRIO.[327]

In the conflict-affected Senegalese territory of Casamance, school attendance rates were higher than in nonconflict regions and actually appear to have increased between 2000 and 2005.

But secondly, while this may help explain why educational attendance levels in the primary conflict region did not *decline* during the war periods, it cannot explain why they were so much higher than the rest of the country.

We do not know the answer to this question, but the higher rates in Ziguinchor may have existed prior to the war (which started in the early 1990s). We note, however, that the gross attendance rate in the primary conflict region in 2005 was a remarkable 150 percent; i.e., it was 50 percent higher than would be the case if all primary school aged children—and only children of that age group—attended school. The additional 50 percent of students were those who missed years of schooling when they were younger—likely for reasons related to the conflict—and were now catching up. If this was the case, the high attendance rates during the conflict period were as much an indication of past educational failure as of current success.

The DRC: Primary School Attendance and War

In the DRC, as Figure 4.6 shows, we witness school attendance not only increasing in the regions worst affected by political violence but doing so at a rate greater than nearly all of the other regions in the country.

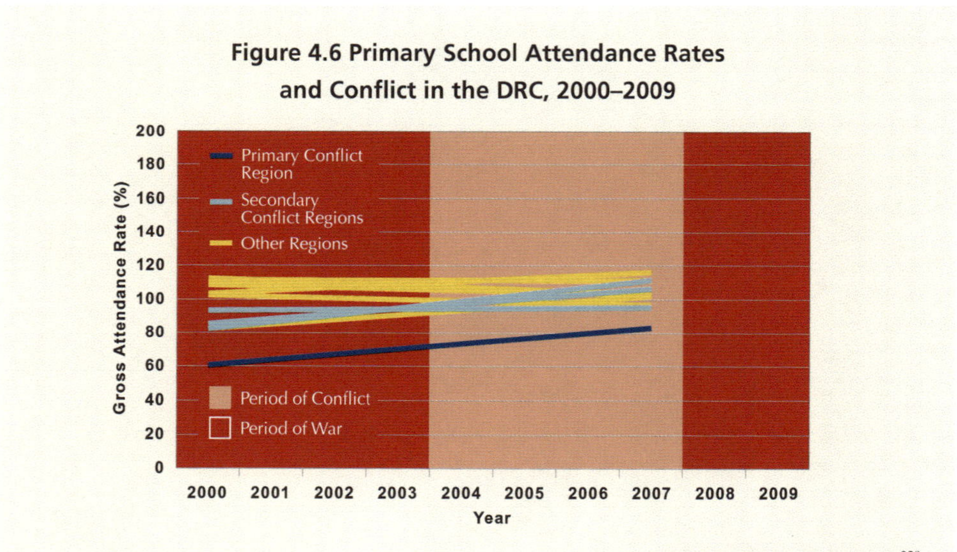

Data Sources: EPDC; UCDP/HSRP.[328]

Primary school attendance in the DRC's conflict-affected North Kivu region increased by over a third from 2000 to 2007—likely because of reduced violence and increased international aid following the 2002 peace deal.

Note: Conflict and war periods in this graph include deaths from all three types of organized violence because the DRC experienced a high level of non-state and one-sided violence between 2002 and 2005 while no state-based armed conflict was recorded. In Figures 4.3, 4.4, and 4.5, however, only state-based deaths are used.

As we noted previously, a catastrophic decline in the DRC's economy that started in the 1970s was responsible for the subsequent stagnation, then decline, in educational attainments.

Between 1980 and 2002, spending per pupil per year in primary and secondary schools fell by 96 percent as governance of the country progressively collapsed.[329] During the 1960s and 1970s, educational spending had amounted to more than 20 percent of total government expenditure; during the 1990s, it had shrunk to just 1 percent.[330] But by the beginning of the new millennium, spending on education had risen again to between 5 and 8 percent of government expenditure.[331]

The increased share of the state budget going to education was not, however, evident in increased gross school attendance rates for most of the country. As Figure 4.6 clearly indicates, in most nonconflict regions, school attendance rates remained stagnant in the new millennium, while some actually declined.

Paradoxically, however, two regions worst affected by conflict, North Kivu (the primary conflict region) and South Kivu (one of the secondary conflict regions), experienced the largest increases in attendance rates in the country.[332]

We do not have enough information to understand why this should be the case, but two possibilities suggest themselves. First, North and South Kivu have not only been the epicentre of conflict in the Eastern DRC but they have also received the lion's share of post-conflict reconstruction assistance, including assistance for education. It is quite possible that the regions most affected by the conflict have also benefitted most from the increase in government spending on education.

Second, according to one report, an extraordinary 81 percent of the population of the Eastern DRC has been displaced at some point since 1993.[333] Since children under 15 make up almost half the population in the DRC, the impact of displacement on education must have been very large, not least because most IDPs lack access to education.[334] So, the big increase in gross primary school attendance in the Kivus, evident in Figure 4.6, may have been due to children who had been displaced and subsequently returned to the classroom to catch up on years of education lost.

These examples illustrate two of the most persuasive explanations for educational outcomes that improve during periods of conflict (we discuss additional explanations below). First, as was the case in Senegal, the extent of death and destruction generated by today's wars may simply be too small to have any discernible nationwide, or even regional, impact on educational outcomes. Second, the positive effect of a recovery in government spending, coupled with a surge in international assistance in the wake of a peace agreement, can more than offset the negative impact of ongoing political violence on school attendance rates, even in the worst affected regions. This seems to have been the case in the DRC.

Descriptive Statistics and the Impact of War on Education

The descriptive statistics approach adopted by the UIS and EPDC focuses on trend data in a series of country case studies and provides a substantial amount of information on the variety of very different educational outcomes associated with periods of armed conflict. The data used by these studies challenge the mainstream narrative that depicts the impact of war on educational outcomes by using terms like "devastating" and "disastrous."

To summarize briefly: the discussion of the UIS data reveal that educational attainments *improved* during periods of conflict in a substantial percentage of the cases examined. Educational outcomes improved during the fighting, even in regions directly affected by the fighting.

As mentioned earlier, EPDC's analysis is more fine-grained. Instead of comparing educational outcomes in just two very broad categories (conflict-affected and non-conflict-affected), EPDC researchers compare "primary and secondary" conflict-affected regions with a large number of nonconflict regions—20 or more in many cases.

In principle, the impact of geographically localized conflict on educational outcomes should be easier to detect in the considerable smaller regions EPDC surveyed. Surprisingly, however, EPDC-collated data reveal that educational outcomes even improved in many of the regions *worst affected* by conflict.

Both the UIS and EPDC make the case that there *is* an impact of conflict on educational outcomes, but they note that in many of the countries analyzed, the methodology they use may be insufficiently sensitive to detect the impact.

The UIS report suggests that a "municipal-level analysis" may be necessary to discern the localized impact of conflict.[335]

EPDC's researchers note that "It may be that the effects of violence on the provision of education … can only be measured at *the most local levels of disaggregation*."[336]

> The UIS data reveal that educational attainments improved during periods of conflict in a substantial percentage of the cases that were examined.

It is clearly true that nationwide survey data can fail to detect the impact of war in some cases—a small town where schools may have been completely destroyed and teachers killed, for example. Such individual impacts may be undetectable in the aggregated nationwide, or even region-wide, data on educational outcomes. But if there is a sufficient number of such impacts, the nationwide impact *will* be detected in the data.

But if such events are rare, the consequences, while tragic for the local inhabitants and devastating for the local educational system, will have no discernible impact on nationwide educational outcomes. And it is *national* educational challenges and achievements that are the focus, not only of this study but of the mainstream narrative as well.

The EPDC researchers appear somewhat skeptical about their own findings, since they stress on several occasions that possible shortcomings in the survey data may be preventing the relationship between conflict and education from becoming apparent.[337]

In addition to concerns noted above, they point out that the surveys whose findings they draw on may not collect data in areas directly affected by violence. Data that are only drawn from peaceful areas will clearly be biased.

The EPDC research team reviewed data from 37 household surveys and found that in six of 16 cases for which there was documentation on sampling, "regions or portions of regions had been left out of the survey due to security concerns."[338] However, they also pointed out that there was not sufficient evidence to show that the missing data in these cases would have had a major impact on the study's findings.[339]

The most important limitation of both the UIS and the EPDC's studies is that they are relatively small nonrandom samples of the universe of possible cases of conflict affecting educational outcomes.

This, as the EPDC study notes, "is not sufficient to serve as the basis for global generalizations about the relationship between conflict and education."[340]

> PRIO researchers found that conflict had no statistically significant impact on education.

Only with regression analyses that draw upon the universe of possible cases can we make generalizations with any degree of confidence. In the next section we review the small number of econometric studies that have used regression analysis to seek to determine the average impact of conflict on education.

Econometric Studies of the Impact of War on Education

In this section we examine the remarkable, but little-publicized, findings of the few large-N econometric studies that have examined the impact of war on educational outcomes based on a large sample of countries and observations. (The term *Large-N* simply refers to large numbers. In conflict research it is often used to describe datasets that include most countries in the international system over a period of several decades or more. *Small-N* studies typically involve qualitative comparative case studies of a small number of countries.)

To the best of our knowledge, just three studies have used regression analysis and cross-national data to determine possible associations between conflict and educational enrolment and attainment. Two of these studies include all or nearly all countries that have experienced conflict over the time span of a decade or more.

The aim of these analyses is to identify whether, in general, conflict has a negative effect on education, and whether this effect is independent; i.e., whether it holds true when we control for other factors that might also cause a decline of educational outcomes.[341]

The most recent econometric study on the impact of war on the achievement of the MDGs—including education—was undertaken by researchers from PRIO for the World Bank's 2011 *World Development Report*. The PRIO team found that, on average, conflict had no statistically significant impact on educational attainments at the primary or secondary school levels.[342]

The contrast between this finding and the claims associated with the mainstream narrative, to the effect that the impact of war on educational systems is "devastating" and "disastrous," etc., could hardly be greater.

Figure 4.7, which we reproduce from the PRIO study, shows that countries in conflict had lower educational attainments than countries at peace, which is unsurprising. The attainment rates for countries at peace increase steadily, which is again not unexpected. The PRIO researchers found that, on average, educational attainments improved by about 2 percent in every five-year period.[343]

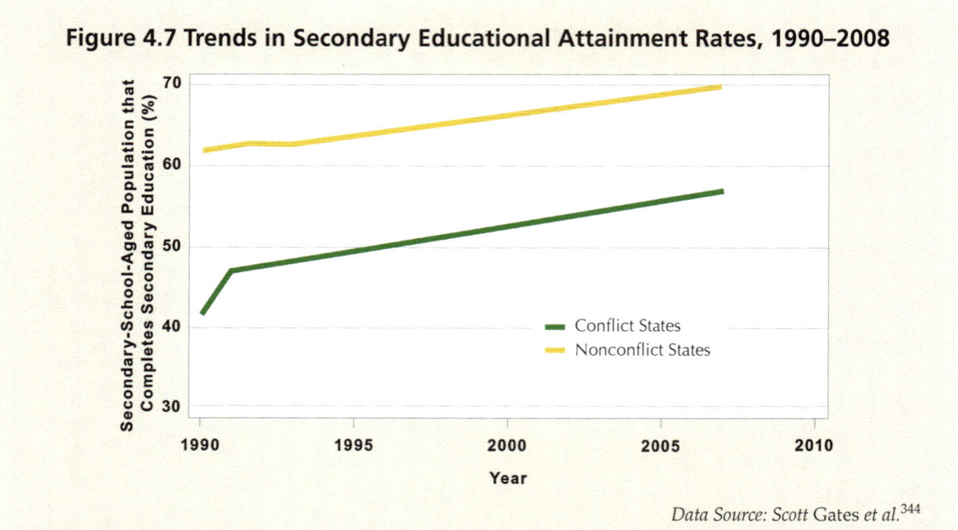

Figure 4.7 Trends in Secondary Educational Attainment Rates, 1990–2008

Data Source: Scott Gates *et al.*[344]

Educational outcomes in conflict countries are lower on average than in nonconflict countries. Remarkably, however, school attainment increased at a similar rate in both conflict countries and nonconflict countries.

What *is* surprising is that, as Figure 4.7 shows, secondary school educational attainments in the war-affected countries improved, again on average, at the same rate as they improved in the nonconflict countries.

This suggests that wartime violence was having little or no impact on the rate of improvement in educational attainment—or that any negative impact on the rate was so small that it is not visible in the graph.

If conflict were having a net negative impact on educational attainments, then the educational attainment trend line for the conflict countries would have declined relative to the trend line for the nonconflict countries.

The PRIO research team's regression analyses on the effect of conflict on primary school enrolment and secondary school attainment confirm what the graph above suggests. They demonstrate that conflict has no statistically significant impact on educational outcomes at either the primary or secondary level.[345]

The fact that the PRIO researchers found that warfare had no *statistically significant* impact on educational outcomes does not mean that they found no impact at all. In fact, the PRIO team's regression analyses revealed that conflict was associated with a very small reduction in educational outcomes, on average. But the association was not statistically significant—i.e., it was discernible, but it could have been determined purely by chance.

If this analysis is correct, it means that the average effect of conflict on educational outcomes is, at most, a minor decrease in the rate at which they improve.

An earlier cross-national statistical study that examined the impact of war on a range of development indicators was undertaken by the World Bank and published in the *World Bank Economic Review* in 2008. Among other things, it examined the trend in median educational enrolments at the primary and secondary school levels in seven-year periods of peace before and after periods of armed conflict.[346] It compared countries affected by war with control groups of other developing countries that were not war-affected.

It found that, on average, secondary school enrolments were appreciably higher for conflict countries in the post-conflict period compared to the pre-conflict period. This complements the findings of the PRIO study and the more tentative conclusions we drew from the UIS multi-country study.

The data in the *World Bank Economic Review* paper, like those of the PRIO study, indicate that countries in conflict have lower educational outcomes than nonconflict developing countries, which appears to support the mainstream assumption that conflict *causes* a decline in enrolments.

But the data also indicate that the low primary school enrolments of the *countries that were to become involved in conflict* were lower still *before* the conflict started. The *World Bank Economic Review* study is, however, limited by the fact that it includes only a relatively small number of countries in conflict in its analysis.

A reliable guide to the trend in educational outcomes for war-affected countries *before* they succumb to conflict comes from the data collected for the PRIO study referred to earlier. Although Figure 4.7 above shows only how educational attainments improve in the conflict-affected countries from 1990 to 2008, the PRIO researchers also analyzed data on average educational attainments of war-affected conflicts before they succumbed to war, which they shared with HSRP.

> The data indicate that the low primary school enrolments of the countries that were to become involved in conflict were lower still before the conflict started.

These trend data indicate very clearly that the major cause of the considerable gap between nonconflict and conflict countries is *not* the disruption and destruction of warfare between 1990 and 2008. The countries that were affected by war in this period had *even lower educational outcomes prior to the war*.

War in individual countries may indeed have had an impact, and wars in all countries may have slightly slowed the rate at which average educational outcomes improved, but warfare was *not* the reason that they were low in the first place.

The highly counterintuitive findings produced by these studies are uncontested but also largely unacknowledged. However, by themselves they tell us nothing about *why* the impact of armed conflict on education should appear to be so limited.

One explanation, already noted above, is that in recent decades wars have become far less deadly and destructive. Consequently, their impact is simply not great enough to reverse the long-term peacetime trend towards improving educational outcomes.

Second, conflict may have a negative effect if it slows the pre-war rate of improvement, but not sufficiently to reverse it. While this is likely true of a substantial number of countries in conflict, the PRIO study indicates that, on average, educational outcomes in conflict-affected countries improve at a very similar rate to nonconflict countries. This suggests that any negative effect is very small.

Third, a negative impact of conflict on education may be more common than the data that we review here suggest, but it may also be too short-lived to be easily detected. It is worth noting in this context that the surveys on which the studies reviewed here are based are typically not carried out every year. If a short-lived conflict erupted soon after one of these surveys were undertaken, the negative effects of the war might not be detectable in the subsequent survey.

Fourth, while war may well be destructive enough in some cases to have a negative impact on education, this effect may be offset by the impact of other factors that cause educational outcomes to improve. For example, in some countries national incomes continue to rise throughout periods of warfare. Where this is the case, the positive effect on education of rising incomes—which may enable more parents to send children to school, for example—may be stronger than the negative impacts of warfare.

A Challenge to the Finding That Educational Outcomes Do Not Decline during War

The two World Bank studies indicate that the overall impact of conflict on educational outcomes is much smaller than is assumed by the mainstream narrative.

However, an earlier econometric study published in the *Journal of Peace Research* in 2007 found that the impact of war on education is both statistically and substantively significant. Indeed, authors Brian Lai and Clayton Thyne argue that conflict is "devastating for a system of education, as both expenditures and enrolment decline during periods of civil war."[347]

Lai and Thyne note that across all the econometric models that they test, states in civil war experience a decline in educational enrolments of between 1.6 and 3.2 percent, dependent on the level of schooling.[348]

Both the PRIO study for the World Bank and the Lai and Thyne study rely on regression analysis in seeking to determine the impact of war on educational outcomes while holding constant other possible causal factors.

However, the two studies are different in many ways. They use different datasets, over different time periods and different econometric models. These differences, particularly with respect to the choice of econometric models, likely account for a substantial portion of the difference in findings.

Yet, upon closer examination, the differences between the two studies are not that great. Both find a negative effect of war on educational outcomes. PRIO finds a very small effect that is not statistically significant. Lai and Thyne find a small effect that *is* statistically significant.

A critical challenge for both studies is to determine to what extent the low educational outcomes that are evident in wartime are determined by the disruptive and destructive effects of conflict, as the mainstream narrative assumes, and to what extent they are determined by factors that are already pervasive in peacetime and continue to play a role in wartime.

Factors that might affect educational outcomes negatively in peacetime include generally weak governance structures; incompetent official management of the national educational system; deep poverty—which keeps children out of school because their parents cannot afford school fees or need them to work at home; and corruption within the school system—i.e., teachers being paid but not turning up for work. These factors are part of a broader system of state fragility, the effects of which we discuss in the conclusion.

It is important that the models and data sources that are used in the regression analyses take into account the impact on educational outcomes of *all* the major factors that may be driving educational outcomes downwards—these include the governance and poverty-related factors noted above. If important factors are left out of the study, the analyst will likely attribute the measured effect to the wrong "causal" factor. The attribution would be to a factor that—like conflict—is correlated with the omitted variables.

Consider a hypothetical case where the educational system in a particular country that had become embroiled in conflict suffered from increasingly incompetent management administration and pervasive corruption within the school system, and that these factors had driven educational outcomes downwards in peacetime and continued to do so in wartime.

Further suppose that the researchers had been unable to access reliable cross-national data on either managerial competence or corruption within the school system. This would mean that neither factor could be included as a control variable in the regression analyses that sought to determine the impact of war on educational outcomes.

It is not unusual for potentially important causal factors to be left out of regression analyses because data on indicators that can measure their variance is simply unobtainable.

In our hypothetical example, the impact of the important omitted variables on educational outcomes would therefore be hidden and would be attributed to other factors—likely the conflict itself.

> Conflict may slow the rate of improvement in educational outcomes, but not sufficiently to reverse it.

As we noted earlier, both the PRIO and the Lai and Thyne studies rely on different datasets, cover different time periods, and use different econometric models that have quite different approaches to meeting the challenge of omitted variable bias. These differences alone could be sufficient to account for their divergent findings. But to determine whether this is the case would require an in-depth methodological investigation that is beyond the scope of this *Report*.

Summing Up: Assessing the Evidence

There are, as we have shown, three quite different ways of examining the impact of warfare on education in the research literature.

First, there are the individual country case studies that explore the impact of war on national and local educational systems. These detailed case studies provide nuanced and contextualized analyses of the many ways in which conflict can disrupt and reduce children's educational opportunities.

The findings of these studies and the lessons that have been drawn from them inform what we have called the "mainstream narrative" on the impact of war on education. This narrative is associated with, and articulated by, major international organizations such as UNESCO and UNICEF, and by leading NGOs like Save the Children. These organizations play crucial roles in formulating policy, delivering service, and undertaking advocacy campaigns in this area.

> Generalizing from the particular is especially prone to error when the focus of research and policy is affected by selection bias.

Although critically important to our understanding of the wide variation in the impact of war on educational systems, the findings of small numbers of case studies should not be used—as they sometimes are—to make *general* claims about the effects of war on education. There is simply no way of determining whether the different impacts of conflict on education in a small number of war-affected countries are representative of the average impact of conflict on educational outcomes in *all* war-affected countries.

Generalizing from the particular, which is characteristic of the mainstream narrative, is particularly prone to error when the focus of research and policy is affected by selection bias.

The mainstream narrative is affected by selection bias in that it presents a picture of the impact of war on education that is—understandably—partial. Policy-makers, advocates, and researchers have focused most attention on countries and regions of countries where warfare has posed the gravest threats to children and their educational opportunities.

These extreme cases tend to be treated as the norm, with analysts, as well as advocates, using terms like "disastrous" and "devastating" as general descriptions of the impact of conflict on education. Such language is appropriate for the worst affected countries—Afghanistan, Iraq, Timor Leste, and Cambodia under the Khmer Rouge, for example. Yet, these countries, we have argued, are the exceptions, not the rule.

The second source of evidence on the impact of war on education examined in this chapter came from the multi-country studies undertaken by UIS and EPDC.

Unlike many of the individual case studies that inform the mainstream narrative, the surveys on which the UIS and EPDC studies rely use common methodologies and definitions. These data can therefore be used to reveal trends in educational outcomes across a substantial number of war-affected countries.

Both studies use statistical data on educational outcomes derived from population surveys in some 20 conflict-affected countries. In each case, the data are presented graphically to reveal the associations between conflict and educational outcomes.

The trend data published in the multi-country UIS and EPDC studies present a picture that is frequently at odds with core assumptions that underpin the mainstream narrative of the impact of war on education:

- In a large proportion of cases, indicators for educational outcomes *improve* during the periods of fighting.
- Even more counterintuitively, both the UIS and the EPDC studies reveal that educational outcomes in conflict-affected countries improve in many cases in regions that are *most affected* by the impact of warfare.
- Each study shows that, in general, educational outcomes are substantially lower in the regions that are worst affected by conflict than in regions that are not directly affected.
- The data in the UIS study also reveal, however, that in most cases the low outcomes in the worst affected regions were low—*or even lower*—in the pre-war periods. This indicates, contrary to the assumptions of the mainstream narrative, that the low educational outcomes in war are not driven primarily by warfare, but by factors that predate the war.

Although these are multi-country studies, and although there is no reason to assume they suffer from the sort of selection bias that is evident in the choice of the case studies that inform much of the mainstream narrative, their sample size is too small, and the descriptive trend analysis too coarse, to treat the results as more than highly intriguing and suggestive of general trends.

As the EPDC study's careful authors put it, because their study includes a relatively small number of countries its findings should not be used to make "global generalizations about the relationship between conflict and education."[349]

Generalizing about the impact of conflict on educational outcomes requires cross-national studies that have data on all, or nearly all, countries that experienced conflict over a period of at least several decades, plus data on a control group of nonconflict studies.[350]

We reviewed three such cross-national statistical studies that met these criteria and as we pointed out, some of their findings differ.

The descriptive statistics in the PRIO study reveal that educational outcomes generally improve in war-affected countries. The *World Bank Economic Review* study similarly finds that educational outcomes were higher in post-conflict periods compared to pre-conflict periods. The data from the UIS multi-country study show that in a substantial proportion of cases, educational outcomes were clearly higher at the end of a conflict period than at the beginning, while only a small percentage showed a clear deterioration.

The PRIO study's regression analyses finds that, on average, there was no *statistically significant* impact of conflict on educational outcomes. But there was a very small negative impact. The Lai and Thyne study finds there was a statistically significant negative association between conflict and educational outcomes, but that it was small.

Both studies show that, as might be expected, war-affected countries have lower educational outcomes than nonconflict countries. The mainstream narrative, on the other hand, assumes that war is the cause of the lower outcomes in the conflict-affected countries.

The *World Bank Economic Review* study finds that educational outcomes were higher in post-conflict periods compared to pre-conflict periods.

But the data from the PRIO study make it clear that the lower educational outcomes in wartime were also present in the pre-war period, indicating that they were largely determined by factors that preceded the war. In fact, educational outcomes are even lower in the periods of peace before the war than during the war itself. This finding fits with the data from the *World Bank Economic Review* study and the UIS study.

This critically important fact is ignored in the mainstream narrative, where the low educational outcomes in wartime are generally assumed to be caused by the disruption and destruction of warfare.

Finally, there is the Lai and Thyne finding that war does have a statistically significant impact on educational outcomes, albeit a small one. While this finding is in line with the mainstream narrative on the impact of war on education, it is somewhat at odds with the PRIO study, whose findings are supported by the *World Bank Economic Review* analysis, as well as the suggestive patterns that we find in the UIS and EPDC studies.[351]

Such differences in findings are common in the quantitative literature on the causes and consequences of civil war.[352] We suspect that the major source of the difference between the Lai and Thyne and PRIO studies lies in how their respective models correct for the challenging problem of omitted variable bias that we discussed earlier. But addressing this issue in more detail is beyond the scope of this chapter.

As far as we can determine, only three cross-national statistical studies have sought to determine the impact of war on education. This compares with a multitude of econometric studies on, for example, the causes of civil war onsets and duration.

The evidence suggests that conflict does not have the devastating impact on educational systems that is a central assumption of the mainstream narrative.

More research is needed to produce the robust conclusions about the impact of war on education that are currently lacking, and to resolve some of the differences between the current studies.

The evidence, we have argued, suggests that conflict does not have the devastating impact on educational systems that is a central assumption of the mainstream analysis. On average, educational outcomes actually improve during many periods of warfare. What explains this counterintuitive and rather remarkable finding remains far from clear, however.

Conclusion

A consistent theme in the mainstream narrative on conflict and education has been the hugely destructive impact of the former on the latter, with educational outcomes in conflict-affected countries being notably worse than those in nonconflict countries as a consequence.[353]

If, as it is claimed, the disruptive and destructive impacts of conflict are major drivers of low educational outcomes in war-affected countries, then protecting children and schools from these threats, and seeking to bring wars to an end, become obvious policy priorities. Indeed, UNESCO's *Hidden Crisis* report makes just such a case, calling for "a more robust defense of children, civilians and school systems on the front line of conflict."[354] The report further argues that:

> the most immediate challenge facing the international community is to strengthen protection and maintain access to education for those on the front line and for those displaced from their homes.[355]

While in the longer term:

> Peace and post-conflict reconstruction are the only viable foundations for achieving accelerated progress towards universal primary education and wider goals in conflict-affected countries.[356]

Protecting children and schools during wartime and seeking to end wars, and prevent those that have ended from starting again, are important and worthwhile goals in themselves. But neither address the very real possibility that the reason educational outcomes are, on average, lower in conflict-affected countries than nonconflict countries is because they were *already lower* before the war started. This suggests that the primary cause of low educational outcomes in wartime is not war itself, but factors that preceded it in peacetime.[357]

If policy-makers are concerned with low educational outcomes in wartime, then policy needs to address their root causes—i.e., those that predate the fighting.

Here an obvious candidate is state *fragility*, a term that describes the complex syndrome of interrelated governance challenges and pathologies that prevent, or slow down, the attainment of a broad range of development goals—including better educational outcomes.

> If policy-makers are concerned with low educational outcomes in wartime, they need to address their root causes—which predate the conflict.

Most states involved in civil wars would be designated as *fragile*, but definitions of fragility include countries that are not affected by conflict, but that also have weak institutions and governance. The PRIO study for the World Bank has its own category of fragile states that are *not* conflict-affected. Interestingly, as Figure 4.7 shows, these states turn out to have even lower educational attainments than the conflict-affected countries.[358]

There is no consensus definition of state fragility in the literature, but most analysts would agree that elements of fragility include:

- Weak and ineffectual national governance.
- The inability, or unwillingness, of national governments to provide basic security for citizens.
- Low governmental capacity—or will—to deliver other essential services, including education.
- Lack of legitimacy of the state in the eyes of citizens.
- Pervasive corruption.
- Armed conflict and other forms of organized violence.

These elements tend to be *mutually constitutive,* which means that each in part determines the other. From this it follows that addressing fragility and its consequences requires multidimensional and multi-stakeholder responses. This is precisely the direction in which the international development and security community has been moving since the end of the Cold War.

The increased commitment to multidimensional and multi-stakeholder policies in fragile states is most obviously evident in the dramatic post-Cold War shift from traditional peacekeeping operations—that often involved little more than UN "blue helmets" monitoring ceasefire agreements—to the present multidimensional and highly complex peacebuilding operations.

Addressing fragility as an interrelated syndrome, rather than as a series of discrete problems, is also central to the work of the Inter-Agency Network for Education in Emergencies (INEE) and the OECD's (Organisation for Economic Co-operation and Development's) International Network on Conflict and Fragility (INCAF).[359]

In all cases, the primary policy goal is to help to create effective, legitimate, resilient, and sustainable institutions of effective governance; i.e., the antitheses of fragile institutions. Such institutions help promote the realization of development goals—including better educational outcomes.

Conflict, from this perspective, is just one of many elements of state fragility and its associated low educational outcomes.

The mainstream narrative on conflict and education depicts the low educational outcomes in war-affected countries as being caused by the disruption and destruction of warfare. But viewing the association between war and low educational outcomes through the lens of state fragility suggests a very different picture.

Rather than seeking to determine if conflict is the cause of low educational outcomes, the fragility lens focuses our attention on the broad range of challenges to education posed by state fragility in peacetime—factors that are also major determinants of educational outcomes in wartime.[360]

But state fragility in peacetime does not explain why educational outcomes should, on average, continue to *improve* in periods of war. In some cases, the rates of improvement are comparable to, and sometimes even higher than, those in peacetime. Indeed, this is the most counterintuitive finding to emerge from our research.

How is the puzzle to be explained?

First, there is, as we have pointed out, a long-term average trend towards better educational outcomes in developing countries in peacetime—*even in those countries with fragile institutions*—and that few of today's wars are deadly or destructive enough to reverse this long-term trend.

Second, we noted the additional possibility that in particular cases the negative impact of conflict on educational outcomes could be offset by other factors, such as rising incomes or infusions of international assistance, that tend to improve enrolment and attainment rates during, and despite of, the armed conflict.

But there is another, more general, explanation for why educational outcomes improve in wartime. This explanation is somewhat conjectural. There is some evidence to support it, but not enough to be confident that it is correct.

Over the last 15 years, there appears to have been a substantial *decline* in state fragility, which is, as we point out, an important cause of low-performing educational systems.

The State Fragility Index produced by the Washington, DC-based Center for Systemic Peace (CSP) measures the fragility level of countries around the world. Between 1995 and 2010, its data indicate that overall state fragility decreased by over 20 percent worldwide.[361]

Over roughly the same period, there has moreover been significant progress towards achieving better educational outcomes and other key development goals in developing countries overall.

If high levels of state fragility are an important part of the explanation of low educational outcomes, we would expect that as fragility declines overall, educational outcomes will also tend to improve in fragile states. This is, in fact, what appears to be the case.

> Over the last 15 years, there appears to have been a substantial decline in state fragility.

While state fragility declined worldwide between 1995 and 2010, the PRIO study shows educational outcomes improving substantially in both conflict-affected and nonconflict fragile states, between 1990 and 2008.

Moreover, it is not just educational outcomes that often improve despite warfare. In the previous *Human Security Report*, we showed that child mortality rates declined in 90 percent of the years that countries were involved in war.

And, as we noted earlier in this chapter, the descriptive statistics from the PRIO report indicate that even though conflict may slow down—or even reverse—progress towards development goals in some countries, the general trend is towards improvement. Rates of malnutrition, life expectancy, infant and maternal mortality, plus access to sanitation and potable water all improve on average during periods of war.

These rather extraordinary findings have, to the best of our knowledge, not been replicated elsewhere, nor has their importance been assessed.[362] For students of both education and civil war, they are at once surprising, intriguing, and encouraging. They also suggest a clear need for more research to confirm—or challenge—the counterintuitive trends, and to examine their causes and policy implications more thoroughly.

PART I

ENDNOTES

OVERVIEW

1   References for all statistics and quotations in the Overview are found in the main body of the *Report* unless otherwise indicated.

2   Note that while conflict-related sexual violence declines when wars end, it may take significantly longer to stop completely.

3   For women aged 18 and above, the CDC found the rate for women was 18.3 percent—meaning that nearly one in five women had been victimized by sexual violence in their lifetimes. See Michele Black et al., *The National Intimate Partner and Sexual Violence Survey: 2010 Summary Report* (Atlanta: National Center for Injury Prevention and Control; Centers for Disease Control and Prevention, 2011), 18, http://www.cdc.gov/ViolencePrevention/pdf/NISVS_Report2010-a.pdf (accessed 3 September 2012).

4   Scott Gates et al., "Development Consequences of Armed Conflict," *World Development* 40, no. 9 (2012): 1713–1722, 1718, doi: 10.1016/j.worlddev.2012.04.031 (accessed 2 September 2012).

5   Japan International Cooperation Agency (JICA), "The Difficulty and Perils of Education in Afghanistan," http://www.jica.go.jp/english/news/focus_on/afghanistan/afghanistan_3.html (accessed 3 September 2012).

6   The particular measure of fragility that the PRIO researchers used did not, as do others, include conflict as one of its elements.

CHAPTER 1

7   Elisabeth Rehn and Ellen Johnson Sirleaf, *Women, War and Peace: The Independent Experts' Assessment on the Impact of Armed Conflict on Women and Women's Role in Peace Building* (New York: UNIFEM, 2002), 9, http://www.ucm.es/cont/descargas/documento7201.pdf (accessed 8 June 2012).

8   For a detailed description of the "narrative" concept, see Severine Autesserre, "Dangerous Tales: Dominant Narratives on the Congo and Their Unintended Consequences," *African Affairs* (2012): 6-9, doi: 10.1093/afraf/adr080 (accessed 8 June 2012).

9   Anne M. Goetz, "Introduction" (presented at the Wilton Park Conference, *Women Targeted or Affected by Armed Conflict: What Role for Military Peacekeepers?*, Sussex, UK, 27 May 2008), 1, http://www.unifem.org/attachments/events/WiltonParkConference_Presentations_200805.pdf (accessed 29 January 2012).

10   Wood's definition is based on that used by the International Criminal Court, see Elisabeth. J. Wood, "Armed Groups and Sexual Violence: When Is Wartime Rape Rare?" *Politics & Society* 37, no. 1 (2009): 5, doi: 10.1177/0032329208329755 (accessed 8 June 2012).

11   We do not include female genital cutting under this rubric since its motivation is very different.

12   Wynne Russell, who studies sexual violence against males, notes that although obtaining reliable data remains a major challenge, "the greatest difference between the male and female experiences appears to revolve around whether sexual violence is perpetrated with the body of the perpetrator, or with an object. The homosexuality taboo means that many captors of men will use objects to penetrate their victims, while captors of women are more likely to engage in penile penetration. Both are rape, by Wood's definition; both are also torture … Also, men appear to be more likely to be subjected to pain to the genitals or genital mutilation that does not involve a sexual assault, but that is designed to interfere with future sexual function or reproduction." Personal e-mail communication with Andrew Mack, 19 February 2012.

13   Because many studies do not clearly identify perpetrators as combatants, this will sometimes also include other cases of stranger rape perpetrated by civilians unknown to the victim. We note throughout the chapter where this is the case.

14   When presenting survey results, standard statistical practice is to provide not only the single best estimate but also some measure that indicates the degree of certainty about its accuracy. The conventional approach is to provide *95 percent confidence intervals* for the point estimate. Put simply, this means that if one were to sample the same population repeatedly, then the range within which 95 percent of the samples fall would constitute the confidence interval.

15   Dara Cohen, "Causes of Rape During Civil War: Cross-National Evidence (1980–2009)," University of Minnesota, 29 January 2012, unpublished manuscript, 50, table S1.

16   As we argue below, there is compelling evidence that reporting of human rights violations in general has increased over the last two decades, but no compelling independent evidence exists that actual violations have increased in this period.

17   United Nations Entity for Gender Equality and the Empowerment of Women, "Beijing and its Follow-up," http://www.un.org/womenwatch/daw/beijing/ (accessed 15 March 2012).

18   Domestic sexual violence that is perpetrated by intimate partners is sometimes treated as a separate category and referred to as intimate-partner sexual violence.

19   Domestic sexual violence is prevalent in wartime as well as in peacetime; indeed, it is often argued that its incidence increases in conflict and post-conflict environments. Such war-exacerbated rates of domestic sexual violence could, in principle, be included in a very broad definition of *conflict-related sexual violence*. However, since it would be very difficult to identify elevated levels of domestic sexual violence in war-affected countries or attribute them to armed conflict given the dearth of data, our discussion of conflict-related sexual violence is limited to that perpetrated by combatants.

20   Note that by using the term "war-affected," we do *not* limit the analysis to only those countries that experience *war* as defined by the Uppsala Conflict Data Program (UCDP), whose data we use in this report; i.e., a conflict with 1,000 or more battle deaths per year. We specify wherever we refer to a particular battle-death threshold.

21   As a recent study by the International Peace Research Institute Oslo, notes: "In the first five post-conflict years, there were reports of sexual violence by one-quarter of state armies and about one-third of all rebel groups and militias." See Ragnhild Nordås, "Sexual Violence in African Conflicts,"Peace Research Institute Oslo, January 2011, http://www.prio.no/sptrans/-1641546546/SVAC-CSCW-Policy-Brief-01-2011.pdf (accessed 13 August 2012).

22   In many surveys only women between 15 and 49 were questioned.

23   The lifetime prevalence rate of sexual violence is not a measure of the *wartime* prevalence, because it includes individuals who have experienced sexual violence in peacetime. The lifetime prevalence rate is, however, often the only available measure to estimate the extent of sexual violence in war-affected countries.

    In some surveys, respondents are asked if they have been victimized in the past 12 months—providing data to compute *annual* prevalence rates. This is not particularly useful with respect to understanding wartime sexual violence, however, since surveys are very rarely taken *during* a war. Post-war retrospective surveys could, in principle, ask respondents if they had been victimized by sexual violence during the conflict and if so in what year. But responses are likely to be affected by recall bias, and questions that require respondents to indicate in which year they were violated are rarely asked.

24   Claudia García-Moreno et al., *WHO Multi-Country Study on Women's Health and Domestic Violence against Women: Initial Results on Prevalence, Health Outcomes and Women's Responses* (Geneva: WHO, 2005), http://www.who.int/gender/violence/who_multicountry_study/en/ (accessed 18 July 2012).

25   United Nations Division for the Advancement of Women, United Nations Economic Commission for Europe, United Nations Statistical Division, *Indicators to Measure Violence against Women: Report of the Expert Group Meeting* (Geneva: United Nations, 2007), 21, http://www.un.org/womenwatch/daw/egm/IndicatorsVAW/IndicatorsVAW_EGM_report.pdf (accessed 14 August 2012). This report notes, "There are different understandings associated with prevalence and incidents of violence against women. There is no difference between them if each victim suffers just one incident in the given time period" (21). Many surveys include estimates of lifetime prevalence and prevalence over the past 12 months. Since the surveys are rarely taken during a conflict, the latter measure is of little value for measuring prevalence in wartime.

26   See, for example, the results of a survey in the Democratic Republic of the Congo (DRC) for data on the number of times that married, separated, or divorced women had been victims of physical or sexual violence in the 12 months preceding the survey. Ministère du Plan and Macro International, *Enquête Démographique et de Santé: République Démocratique du Congo 2007* (Calverton, MD: Ministère du Plan and Macro International, 2008), 308, http://www.minisanterdc.cd/fr/documents/eds.pdf (accessed 14 August 2012).

27 See WHO (World Health Organization), *WHO Ethical and Safety Recommendations for Researching, Documenting and Monitoring Sexual Violence in Emergencies* (Geneva, Switzerland: WHO, 2007), http://www.who.int/gender/documents/OMS_Ethics&Safety 10Aug07.pdf (accessed 15 March 2012), and Shana Swiss and Peggy J. Jennings, "Documenting the Impact of Conflict on Women Living in Internally Displaced Persons Camps in Sri Lanka: Some Ethical Considerations," Women's Rights International, 2007, http://www.womens-rights.org/Publications/Ethics_IDPSurvey.pdf/ (accessed 16 March 2012).

28 Indeed, as we point out in Chapter 3, unless surveys can provide respondents with the option of anonymously answering highly sensitive questions about being victimized by sexual violence, their responses can substantially underestimate the actual prevalence of sexual violence.

29 Dara Cohen, "The Incidence and Intensity of Wartime Sexual Violence," 6 March 2010, unpublished background paper prepared for the Human Security Report Project (HSRP), 3.

30 Jeanne Ward, Jackie Kirk, and Lisa Ernst, *Broken Bodies, Broken Dreams: Violence against Women Exposed* (Nairobi, Kenya: OCHA/IRIN, 2005), http://www.irinnews.org/ InDepthMain.aspx?InDepthId=59&ReportId=72831 (accessed 16 March 2012).

31 Cohen, "Causes of Rape During Civil War."

32 Ibid., 20.

33 The four levels were:
 - Level 0: no reported cases of rape related to the conflict.
 - Level 1: "some" reports, "isolated" reports of conflict-related rape.
 - Level 2: "widespread," "extensive," "common" reports of conflict-related rape.
 - Level 3: "systematic" and "massive" reports of sexual violence and references to rape being used as a "weapon," "tactic," or "tool" of war.

 See ibid., 50, table S1. As with all datasets, this one is subject to a number of limitations. These are discussed on pages 21–23 of the paper.

34 The data are provided by Dara Cohen. The dataset covers the years 1980–2009 and the respective figures for the entire period are 5 percent (Level 3), 19 percent (Level 2), 25 percent (Level 1), and 51 percent (Level 0). We, however, chose figures from the most recent decade because the Cohen data indicate that in the earlier years covered, especially the 1980s, there was little or no reported sexual violence in the large majority of years of active conflict, despite the fact that conflicts were far deadlier than in the 2000–2009 period. We believe that there is a strong possibility that the low levels of reported sexual violence in this period were almost certainly a function of low levels of reporting, *not* low levels of sexual violence. For this reason, we believe that the 2000–2009 period, where there is no doubt that reporting of wartime sexual violence had been far higher than in earlier periods, is likely to provide a more accurate picture of the cross-national variation in the intensity of sexual violence than the data from the 1980s and 1990s.

35   See Elisabeth Wood, "Variation in Sexual Violence during War," *Politics & Society* 34, no. 3 (2006): 307–341, doi: 10.1177/0032329206290426 (accessed 8 June 2012); Wood, "Armed Groups and Sexual Violence"; and Cohen, "Causes of Rape During Civil War."

36   Rehn and Johnson Sirleaf, *Women, War and Peace,* 10.

37   Ward, Kirk, and Ernst, *Broken Bodies, Broken Dreams.*

38   Office of the SRSG (Special Representative of the Secretary-General) for Children and Armed Conflict and UNICEF, "Ending Gender-Based Violence and Sexual Exploitation," in *Children and Conflict in a Changing World: Machel Study 10-Year Strategic Review* (New York: Office of the SRSG for Children and Armed Conflict and UNICEF, 2009), http://www.un.org/children/conflict/machel/english/811-ending-gender-based-violence-and-sexual-exploitation.html (accessed 26 February 2012).

39   Jan Egeland, "International Responsibilities," in "Sexual Violence: Weapon of War, Impediment to Peace," ed. Marion Couldrey and Tim Morris, special issue, *Forced Migration Review* 27 (January 2007): 8, http://www.fmreview.org/FMRpdfs/FMR27/full.pdf (accessed 26 February 2012).

40   Wilton Park Conference, ed., *Women Targeted or Affected by Armed Conflict: What Role for Military Peacekeepers? Conference Summary* (2008).

41   For a broad discussion of global trends in state-based armed conflict, see Chapter 5 of this *Report.*

42   Ward, Kirk, and Ernst, *Broken Bodies, Broken Dreams.*

43   Cohen, "Causes of Rape During Civil War," 31.

44   A third possibility is that both have increased.

45   Amber Peterman et al., "Rape Reporting During War: Why the Numbers Don't Mean What You Think They Do," *Foreign Affairs,* 1 August 2011, http://www.foreignaffairs.com/articles/68008/amber-peterman-dara-kay-cohen-tia-palermo-and-amelia-hoover-gree/rape-reporting-during-war?page=show (accessed 26 February 2012).

46   Howard Ramos, James Ron, and Oskar N.T. Thoms, "Shaping the Northern Media's Human Rights Coverage, 1986–2000," *Journal of Peace Research* 44, no. 4 (2007): fig. 1, 387, doi: 10.1177/0022343307078943 (accessed 6 March 2012). Reporting on human rights showed significant increases in other papers as well, ranging from 20 percent to 200 percent over the same period.

47   Ann Marie Clark and Kathryn Sikkink, "Information Effects and Human Rights Data: Is the Good News about Increased Human Rights Information Bad News for Human Rights Measures?" January 2011, unpublished manuscript.

48   Ibid., 24. The PTS relies in large part on the US State Department's human rights reporting, which Dara Cohen also uses in her study.

49   Clark and Sikkink, "Information Effects and Human Rights Data," 23–27.

50   Ibid., 27.

51   Severine Autesserre, "Dangerous Tales: Dominant Narratives on the Congo and their Unintended Consequences,"*African Affairs* (2012): 13, doi: 10.1093/afraf/adr080 (accessed 15 March 2012).

52   Ibid., 13.

53   Tara Gingerich and Jennifer Leaning have described some of the factors that may motivate strategic rape:

- It creates a sense of fear in the civilian population and restricts freedom of movement and economic activity.

- It can instill flight which facilitates the capture of land and killing of male civilians who are left more vulnerable to attack when fleeing.

- It demoralizes the population and reduces their will to resist and prolongs their forced exit from the land.

- It tears apart communities by breaking family and community bonds (thus diminishing the reproductive capacity of the community) and by "polluting"the blood line.

See Gingerich and Leaning,"The Use of Rape as a Weapon of War in the Conflict in Darfur, Sudan" (Boston, Program on Humanitarian Crises and Human Rights, Harvard School of Public Health, 2004), 17–18, http://reliefweb.int/sites/reliefweb.int/files/resources/B119C9EFB7DCAA2DC1256F5F004FBEA9-hu-sud-31oct.pdf (accessed 26 February 2012).

54   See Kofi A. Annan, *Women, Peace and Security: Study Submitted by the Secretary-General Pursuant to Security Council Resolution 1325 (2000)* (New York: United Nations, 2002), 2, http://www.un.org/womenwatch/daw/public/eWPS.pdf (accessed 26 February 2012). Emphasis added.

55   Tsjeard Bouta, Georg Frerks, and Ian Bannon, *Gender, Conflict, and Development* (Washington, DC: World Bank, 2005), 35, http://www.wds.worldbank.org/servlet/WDSContentServer/WDSP/IB/2004/11/15/000090341_20041115142901/Rendered/PDF/30494.pdf (accessed 26 February 2012).

56   Cited in Stephanie Nebehay, "Rape Used as Weapon in Libya and Elsewhere: U.N.," *Reuters Health News*, 10 June 2011, http://reuters_th.adam.com/content.aspx?productId =16&pid=16&gid=45497 (accessed 26 February 2012).

57   See Alexandra Stiglmayer, ed., *Mass Rape: The War against Women in Bosnia-Herzegovina* (Lincoln: University of Nebraska Press, 2011).

58   The 20 countries were not randomly selected, which means that the findings are not necessarily representative of all of sub-Saharan Africa, let alone the rest of the world. See Ragnhild Nordås,"SexualViolence in African Conflicts,"in *CSCW Policy Brief* 01 (Oslo, Centre for the Study of Civil War, PRIO, 2011), 3, http://www.prio.no/sptrans/-782981433/SVAC_policy_brief_Sexual%20Violence%20in%20African%20Conflicts.pdf (accessed 26 February 2012).

59   Ibid., 3.

60   Dara Cohen, for example, notes that in Sierra Leone many NGOs argued that wartime rape was an integral part of the military and political campaigns pursued by the rebels, particularly the notorious Revolutionary United Front (RUF). But in her own extensive interviews she found that while former rebels were quite frank about the fact that they had perpetrated sexual violence, there was little evidence of strategic rape. See Dara Cohen, "Explaining Sexual Violence During War" (Ph.D. diss., Stanford University, 2010), 95.

61   Maria Eriksson Baaz and Maria Stern, "The Complexity of Violence: A Critical Analysis of Sexual Violence in the Democratic Republic of Congo (DRC)" (working paper, Uppsala: Nordika Afrikainstitutet, 2010), 15–16, http://nai.diva-portal.org/smash/record.jsf?page=statistics&pid=diva2:319527 (accessed 27 February 2012). See also Maria E. Baaz and Maria Stern, "Why Do Soldiers Rape? Masculinity, Violence, and Sexuality in the Armed Forces in the Congo (DRC)," *International Studies Quarterly* 53, no. 2 (2009), doi: 10.1111/j.1468-2478.2009.00543.x (accessed 26 February 2012).

62   Baaz and Stern, "The Complexity of Violence," 14.

63   Ibid., 17–24.

64   Wynne Russell, "A Silence as Deep as Death: Sexual Violence against Men and Boys During Armed Conflicts" (background paper prepared for the Office for the Coordination of Humanitarian Affairs Expert Meeting, "Use of Sexual Violence in Conflict," New York, 26 June 2008), 1. This paper provides a concise overview of the key issues and a lengthy bibliography.

65   UN Security Council, S/RES/1820(2008), http://daccess-dds-ny.un.org/doc/UNDOC/GEN/N08/391/44/PDF/N0839144.pdf (accessed 18 May 2012). The resolution often referred to "civilians," which of course includes males, but in various instances limited the focus specifically to women and girls.

66   UN Security Council, S/RES/1325 (2000), http://www.un.org/events/res_1325e.pdf (accessed 16 May 2012).

67   Ibid., 619. See also Russell, "A Silence as Deep as Death."

68   See Lara Stemple, "Male Rape and Human Rights," *Hastings Law Journal* 60 (2009): 605–647.

69   UN Office for the Coordination of Humanitarian Affairs, "The Nature, Scope and Motivation for Sexual Violence against Men and Boys in Armed Conflict" (background paper prepared for the Office for the Coordination of Humanitarian Affairs Expert Meeting, "Use of Sexual Violence in Conflict," New York, 26 June 2008), http://ochaonline.un.org/OchaLinkClick.aspx?link=ocha&docId=1092305 (accessed 16 March 2012).

70   See, for example, UN Population Fund, *The State of World Population 2010: From Conflict and Crisis to Renewal: Generations of Change* (New York: UN Population Fund, 2010), Chapter 4, http://www.unfpa.org/swp/2010/web/en/pdf/EN_SOWP10.pdf (accessed 27 February 2012); and UN Office for the Coordination of Humanitarian Affairs, *The Nature, Scope and Motivation for Sexual Violence.*

71   Michele Leiby, "Principals, Agents, and Wartime Sexual Violence," (paper presented at the annual meeting of the American Political Science Association, Washington, DC, 2 September, 2010), 17. See also Pauline Oosterhoff, Prisca Zwanikken, and Evert Ketting, "Sexual Torture of Men in Croatia and Other Conflict Situations: An Open Secret," *Reproductive Health Matters* 12, no. 23 (2004), http://pramudithrupasinghe.weebly.com/uploads/4/2/1/8/4218922/sexual_torture_of_men_in_croatia_and_other_conflict.pdf (accessed 16 March 2012).

72   Lara Stemple points out that the abuse of males in wartime often takes place in prisoner of war camps and interrogation centres. The UN, for example, "reported that out of 5,000 male concentration camp detainees held near Sarajevo during the Bosnian conflict, 80 percent acknowledged having been abused sexually. In El Salvador 76 percent of male political prisoners told researchers they had experienced sexual torture." Lara Stemple, "The Hidden Victims of Wartime Rape," *New York Times*, 1 March 2011, http://www.nytimes.com/2011/03/02/opinion/02stemple.html?_r=1 (accessed 27 February 2012). For more details, see Stemple, "Male Rape and Human Rights."

73   Kirsten Johnson et al., "Association of Combatant Status and Sexual Violence with Health and Mental Health Outcomes in Postconflict Liberia," *JAMA: The Journal of the American Medical Association* 300, no. 6 (2008): 680, doi: 10.1001/jama.300.6.676, http://jama.ama-assn.org/content/300/6/676.full.pdf+html?sid=ae0751d1-ac0b-4f88-b7c7-2ced65a80382 (accessed 27 February 2012).

74   This extraordinarily high number may reflect the fact that many individuals served with government or rebel forces for a relatively short period of time—it does not mean that one-third of the population were serving as fighters or supporters all the time.

75   If only those who participated in combat are considered, the figure would be 14 percent. Note that in none of these figures, the combatants would be all serving at the same time, of course.

76   Johnson et al., "Association of Combatant Status and Sexual Violence," 681. The term *combatant* includes roles in the military that do not necessarily involve fighting—cooks, porters, messengers, etc.

77   These included "being forced to undress or being stripped of clothing." See ibid., 680.

78   Ibid., 683.

79   Ibid.

80   Kirsten Johnson et al., "Association of Sexual Violence and Human Rights Violations with Physical and Mental Health in Territories of the Eastern Democratic Republic of the Congo," *JAMA: The Journal of the American Medical Association* 304, no. 5 (2010): 557 doi: 10.1001/jama.2010.1086, http://jama.ama-assn.org/content/304/5/553.full.pdf+html?sid=3b1ab62a-616d-4232-816a-073af2b5a505, 557 (accessed 6 March 2012). The rape category excluded lesser forms of sexual violence, but the most commonly reported type of sexual violence was rape. Almost two-thirds of the male cases of sexual violence and three-fourths of the female cases of sexual violence were conflict-related, but the authors do not specifiy how this is measured.

81   This is beginning to change. A major new study on this issue is being undertaken by Laura Sjoberg of the University of Florida. Entitled *Rape Among Women: Genocidal Rape and Sex Subordination*, it will be published by New York University Press.

82   Cohen, "Explaining Sexual Violence During War," 165.

83   Johnson et al., "Association of Sexual Violence and Human Rights Violations," 557.

84   Dara Cohen, "Female Combatants and the Perpetration of Violence: The Case of Wartime Rape in the Sierra Leone Civil War," (unpublished manuscript), 2, 30.

85   The *neighbourhood method* uses household interviews to ask women not only about their own experiences of sexual violence but also those of others in their home and among their immediate neighbours. This method creates what is effectively a bigger sample size than is possible by questioning a single respondent about her own household. One obvious potential problem with the neighbourhood method is that the primary respondent may be misinformed about the prevalence of sexual violence among her neighbours. There is evidence from some of the surveys that this is in fact the case. See Ann Warner, "Incidence of Violence against Women and Girls in Liberia: A Quantitative Study Using the 'Neighborhood Method,'" International Rescue Committee and the Program on Forced Migration and Health, Mailman School of Public Health, Columbia University, 4, 19, http://www.forcedmigration.columbia.edu/research/documents/IRCReportonNeighbor hoodStudy_10-1-07.pdf (accessed 27 February 2012).

86   Care and Protection of Children in Crisis-Affected Countries (CPC) Learning Network, "Rethinking Gender-Based Violence," 7, http://www.forcedmigration.columbia.edu/ research/documents/GBV_Brief_winter_2010.pdf (accessed 27 February 2012).

87   Ibid.

88   Lindsay Stark et al., "Measuring Violence against Women amidst War and Displacement in Northern Uganda Using the 'Neighborhood Method,'" Program on Forced Migration and Health, Mailman School of Public Health, Columbia University; ChildFund International, 10–11, http://www.forcedmigration.columbia.edu/research/documents/ StarkRobertsAchamBoothbyAger2009MeasuringVioAgainstWomenJEpidemiol CommunityHealth.pdf (accessed 27 February 2012).

89   The rate at the national level was 12 percent. See Amber Peterman, Tia Palermo, and Caryn Bredenkamp, "Estimates and Determinants of Sexual Violence against Women in the Democratic Republic of Congo," *American Journal of Public Health* 101, no. 6 (2011): 1060–1067, doi: 10.2105/AJPH.2010.300070 (accessed 1 March 2012). The data for this study came from a 2007 study by the Demographic and Health Survey (DHS). See DRC Ministry of Planning (MoP) and Macro International Inc., *Democratic Republic of the Congo Demographic and Health Survey 2007: Key Finding* (Calverton, MD: DRC MoP and Macro International Inc., 2007), http://www.measuredhs.com/pubs/pdf/SR141/ SR141.pdf (accessed 1 March 2012); UN Women, *Violence against Women Prevalence Data: Surveys by Country* (New York: UN Entity for Gender Equality and the Empowerment of Women, 2011), http://www.endvawnow.org/uploads/browser/files/vaw_prevalence_ matrix_15april_2011.pdf (accessed 1 March 2012).

90   Inter Press Service News Agency, "Q&A: 'There Is Almost Total Impunity for Rape in Congo,'" 28 June 2010, http://www.ipsnews.net/2010/06/qa-there-is-almost-total-impunity-for-rape-in-congo/ (accessed 1 March 2012).

91   Uganda Bureau of Statistics (UBOS) and Macro International Inc., *Uganda Demographic and Health Survey 2006* (Calverton, MD: UBOS and Macro International Inc., 2007), 290, http://www.measuredhs.com/pubs/pdf/FR194/FR194.pdf (accessed 1 March 2012).

92   Unpublished data provided by the WHO based on Claudia García-Moreno et al., *WHO Multi-Country Study on Women's Health and Domestic Violence against Women: Initial Results on Prevalence, Health Outcomes and Women's Responses,* (Geneva: WHO, 2005), http://www.who.int/gender/violence/who_multicountry_study/en/ (accessed 15 August 2012). The survey undertaken in Ethiopia as part of the WHO's multi-country global survey of sexual violence was carried out in a largely rural district deemed "broadly representative of the country as a whole." See Yemane Berhane, "Ending Domestic Violence against Women in Ethiopia," *Ethiopian Journal of Health Development* 18, no. 4 (2004), 131–132.

93   UBOS and Macro International Inc., *Uganda Demographic and Health Survey 2006,* 290, 292.

     Even the notoriously violent Lord's Resistance Army (LRA) that abducted large numbers of girls and young women had a strictly enforced code governing sexual behaviour among its fighters. Sex was only permitted in forced "marriages" arranged between female abductees and LRA fighters. Sexual violence against other abductees and nonabducted civilians was strictly prohibited and rare, "and violations were severely punished, often with death." From Jeannie Annan et al., "Women and Girls at War: 'Wives,' Mothers, and Fighters in the Lord's Resistance Army," 10–11, http://www.prio.no/sptrans/185286780/blattman-women@war.1009.pdf (accessed 1 March 2012).

94   Unpublished data provided by the WHO based on Claudia García-Moreno et al., *WHO Multi-Country Study on Women's Health and Domestic Violence against Women: Summary Report of Initial Results on Prevalence, Health Outcomes and Women's Responses* (Geneva: WHO, 2005), 12, http://www.who.int/gender/violence/who_multicountry_study/summary_report/summary_report_English2.pdf (accessed 29 January 2012). A 2009 survey undertaken in seven regions of Ethiopia by the Population Council and the UN Population Fund (UNFPA) of some 8,000 women aged 15 and 49 asked who the perpetrators were when a woman's first experience of sexual intercourse was forcefully coerced. It found that "92 percent were husbands, 6 percent were boyfriends or fiancés, and 2 percent were acquaintances or classmates."

     See Population Council and UNFPA, *Ethiopia Gender Survey: A Study in Seven Regions* (New York: Population Council, 2010), 60, http://www.popcouncil.org/pdfs/2010PGY_EthiopiaGenderSurvey.pdf (accessed 6 May 2012).

95   Amber Peterman, Tia Palermo, and Caryn Bredenkamp, "Estimates and Determinants of Sexual Violence against Women in the Democratic Republic of Congo," *American Journal of Public Health* 101, no. 6 (2011), 1060-1067, doi: 10.2105/AJPH.2010.300070 (accessed 1 March 2012).

96   Pan African News Agency, "UN Chief Says Sexual Violence a Threat to Peace, Security," 23 September 2011, http://www.panapress.com/UN-chief-says-sexual-violence-a-threat-to-peace,-security--12-796358-25-lang2-index.html (accessed 1 March 2012).

97   Care and Protection of Children in Crisis-Affected Countries (CPC) Learning Network, "Rethinking Gender-Based Violence," 3.

98   Peterman, Palermo, and Bredenkamp, "Estimates and Determinants of Sexual Violence" 1065. This stands in contrast to the results of the *JAMA* study cited above, which found that in 72 (females) and 86 (males) percent of the cases, combatants were reported as perpetrators. The study was, however, based on a much smaller sample than the DHS data and undertaken in some of the regions worst affected by the civil war.

99   Dara Cohen, for example, stresses that gang rapes are used to build cohesion among combatants, something that obviously has little relevance for explaining domestic violence. Cohen, "Causes of Rape During Civil War," 4.

100 Peterman, Palermo, and Bredenkamp, "Estimates and Determinants of Sexual Violence," and Lori Handrahan, "Conflict, Gender, Ethnicity and Post-Conflict Reconstruction," Security Dialogue 35, no. 4 (2004): 429–445.

CHAPTER 2

101 LaShawn R. Jefferson, "In War as in Peace: Sexual Violence and Women's Status," in *Human Rights and Armed Conflict: Human Rights Watch World Report 2004* (New York, NY: Human Rights Watch, 2004), 324–350, http://www.hrw.org/legacy/wr2k4/download/wr2k4.pdf (accessed 14 April 2012).

102 For a more comprehensive analysis of how these incentive structures shape narratives and, as a result, policy-making, see Peter Andreas and Kelly M. Greenhill, eds., *Sex, Drugs, and Body Counts: The Politics of Numbers in Global Crime and Conflict* (Ithaca: Cornell University Press, 2010).

103 According to OECD (Organisation for Economic Co-operation and Development) and UN data, $6.7 billion was raised from governments around the world in 2000; by 2010 this had risen to an estimated $12.4 billion. Development Initiatives, *Global Humanitarian Assistance Report 2011* (Wells, UK: Development Initiatives, 2011), fig. 3, 12, http://www.globalhumanitarianassistance.org/wp-content/uploads/2011/07/gha-report-2011.pdf (accessed 14 April 2012).

104 Ibid., fig. 3, 55.

105 In 2010, for example, only 63 percent of the CAP request was actually allocated. Since the beginning of the new millennium, on average, 33 percent of annual requests have gone unfunded. Ibid., figs. 8–9, 60–61. The CAP is not the only source of humanitarian funding, of course, but the pattern it exhibits—of demand exceeding supply—is typical of almost all funding exercises.

106 Ian Smillie and Larry Minear, *The Charity of Nations: Humanitarian Action in A Calculating World* (Bloomfield, CT: Kumarian Press, 2004), 207.

107 Humanitarian Policy Group, "According to Need? Needs Assessment and Decision-Making in the Humanitarian Sector," *Overseas Development Institute Report* (London: Overseas Development Institute, 2003), 56, http://www.odi.org.uk/resources/docs/285.pdf (accessed 7 June 2012). Also cited in Smillie and Minear, *The Charity of Nations*, 204.

108 See Smillie and Minear, *The Charity of Nations*, 207. See also David Rieff, "Millions May Die ... Or Not: How Disaster Hype Became a Big Global Business," *Foreign Policy*, September/October 2011, http://www.foreignpolicy.com/articles/2011/08/15/millions_may_die_or_not?page=full (accessed 14 April 2012), and Human Security Report Project (HSRP), *Human Security Report 2009/2010: The Causes of Peace and the Shrinking Costs of War* (New York: Oxford University Press, 2011), 126.

109 Peter Andreas and Kelly M. Greenhill, "Conclusion: The Numbers in Politics," in *Sex, Drugs and Body Counts: The Politics of Numbers in Global Crime and Conflict,* ed. Peter Andreas and Kelly M. Greenhill (Ithaca: Cornell University Press, 2010), 265.

110   Nicholas D. Kristof, "After Wars, Mass Rapes Persist," *New York Times*, 20 May 2009, http://www.nytimes.com/2009/05/21/opinion/21kristof.html (accessed 16 August 2012). Kristof was not the first to cite a prevalence rate in the order of 75 percent for Liberia. A paper by Dara Cohen and Amelia Hoover Green investigates the questionable claim made by Kristof and others in more detail. See Dara Kay Cohen and Amelia Hoover Green, "Dueling Incentives: Sexual Violence in Liberia and the Politics of Human Rights Advocacy," *Journal of Peace Research* 49, no. 3 (2012): 445–458, doi: 10.1177/0022343312436769 (accessed 16 August 2012). See also the review posted on the blog *Feminist Critics*, "Have 75% of Women in Liberia Been Raped? (NoH)," 8 June 2012, http://www.feministcritics.org/blog/2009/06/08/have-75-of-women-in-liberia-been-raped-noh/ (accessed 31 July 2012).

111 Marie-Claire O. Omanyondo, "Sexual Gender-Based Violence and Health Facility Needs Assessment," WHO, September 2004, http://www.who.int/hac/crises/lbr/Liberia_GBV_2004_FINAL.pdf (accessed 15 August 2012). There are a number of other possible sources for Kristof's extraordinary claim, but none can be used to support it.

112 Ibid., 6, 16.

113 Liberia Institute of Statistics and Geo-Information Services (LISGIS), Ministry of Health and Social Welfare, National AIDS Control Program, Macro International, *Liberia Demographic and Health Survey 2007*, 230, http://www.measuredhs.com/pubs/pdf/fr201/fr201.pdf (accessed 16 August 2012).

114 Kelly M. Greenhill, "Counting the Cost: The Politics of Numbers in Armed Conflict," in *Sex, Drugs, and Body Counts: The Politics of Numbers in Global Crime Conflict*, ed. Peter Andreas and Kelly M. Greenhill (Ithaca, NY: Cornell University Press, 2010), 128. Greenhill argues that unreliable statistics can prove counterproductive from "political, humanitarian, juridical and scholarly perspectives" (127).

115 Ibid., 136.

116 See Rieff, "Millions May Die," (accessed 14 April 2012).

117 For a discussion of donor skepticism towards inflated humanitarian claims, see Smillie and Minear, *The Charity of Nations*.

118 Andreas and Greenhill, "Conclusion," *Sex, Drugs and Body Counts* 268.

119 See, for example, Elisabeth Wood, "Armed Groups and Sexual Violence: When Is Wartime Rape Rare?" *Politics & Society* 37, no. 1 (2009): 131–161, doi: 10.1177/0032329208329755 (accessed 13 July 2012); Dara Cohen, "Causes of Rape During Civil War: Cross-National Evidence (1980–2009)," University of Minnesota, January 2012: 1–45; and Ragnhild Nordås, "Sexual Violence in African Conflicts," in *CSCW Policy Brief* 01 (Oslo: Centre for the Study of Civil War, Peace Research Institute Oslo [PRIO], 2011): 1–4, http://www.prio.no/sptrans/-782981433/SVAC_policy_brief_Sexual%20Violence%20in%20African%20Conflicts.pdf (accessed 26 February 2012).

120 We pointed out that this assumption is at odds with the data on reported sexual violence compiled by Dara Cohen, based on US State Department reports and other reports. These data do indeed show that reported conflict-related sexual violence has increased over the past three decades. But, as we argued in Chapter 1, this increase is likely a function of better and more extensive reporting, rather than an increase in sexual violence.

121 In 2010 Jordan Ryan, assistant administrator of the United Nations Development Programme and director of the Bureau for Crisis Prevention and Recovery, stated, with what was an uncharacteristic candour for a senior UN official, that "we have not anywhere prevented sexual violence." See United Nations Population Fund (UNFPA), "Chapter Eight: And the Next 10 Years?" *State of the World Population 2010: From Conflict and Crisis to Renewal: Generations of Change* (New York: United Nations, 2010), 82, http://www.unfpa.org/swp/2010/web/en/ch8.shtml (accessed 18 June 2012).

122 In practice, however, the Security Council has shown little enthusiasm for imposing sanctions on known perpetrators of sexual violence in armed conflict. Security Council Report, "Cross-Cutting Report on Women, Peace and Security," 2010, 25, 28, http://www.securitycouncilreport.org/atf/cf/%7B65BFCF9B-6D27-4E9C-8CD3-CF6E4FF96FF9%7D/XCutting%20WPS%202010.pdf (accessed 27 February 2012).

123 Kathryn Sikkink argues that this may be an effective strategy for reducing rights abuses over the long term. Kathryn Sikkink, *The Justice Cascade: How Human Rights Prosecutions Are Changing World Politics*, 1st ed. (New York: W. W. Norton & Co., 2011).

124 For a comprehensive review of the UN's neglect of sexual violence against males, see Sandesh Sivakumaran, "Lost in Translation: UN Responses to Sexual Violence against Men and Boys in Situations of Armed Conflict," *International Review of the Red Cross* 92, no. 877 (2010): 259–277, doi: 10.1017/S1816383110000020 (accessed 13 July 2012).

125 United Nations, *Conflict-Related Sexual Violence: Report of the Secretary-General*, United Nations General Assembly and Security Council (New York: United Nations, 2012), 2, http://www.humansecuritygateway.com/documents/UNSC_ReportoftheSecretaryGeneral_ConflictRelatedSexualViolence_A66657.pdf (accessed 14 April 2012).

126 Ibid., 3. Emphasis added.

127 The omission of males from the Women, Peace and Security agenda 1325 is not surprising given that senior UN officials have argued strongly against including sexual violence against males as part of the 1325 policy agenda. See Anne M. Goetz, "Introduction" (paper presented at the Wilton Park Conference, *Women Targeted or Affected by Armed Conflict: What Role for Military Peacekeepers?* Steyning, UK, 27 May 2008), 3–4, http://www.unifem.org/attachments/events/WiltonParkConference_Presentations_200805.pdf (accessed 14 April 2012).

128 Study cited in Lara Stemple, "Male Rape and Human Rights," *Hastings Law Journal* 60, no. 3 (2009): 612, http://devhector.uchastings.edu/hlj/archive/vol60/Stemple_60-HLJ-605.pdf (accessed 27 February 2012). See also Wynne Russell et al., "Care and Support of Male Survivors of Conflict-Related Sexual Violence," Sexual Violence Research Initiative, http://www.humansecuritygateway.com/documents/SVRI_CareandSupportofMaleSurvivorsofConflictRelatedSV.pdf (accessed 27 February 2012).

129 R. Charli Carpenter, "Recognizing Gender-Based Violence against Civilian Men and Boys in Conflict Situations," *Security Dialogue* 37, no. 1 (2006): 95, doi: 10.1177/0967010606064139 (accessed 27 February 2012).

130 The subsequent Council resolutions were 1820 (2008); 1888 (2009); 1889 (2009); and 1960 (2010). See UN Women, "Resolutions & Instruments," http://www.unifem.org/gender_issues/women_war_peace/resolutions_instruments.php (accessed 19 June 2012).

131 United Nations Security Council, "Resolution 1325 (2000)," United Nations, 31 October 2000, 2, http://www.unfpa.org/women/docs/res_1325e.pdf (accessed 19 June 2012).

132 UN Security Council, *Women and Peace and Security: Report of the Secretary-General* (New York: United Nations, 2010), 1, http://www.un.org/ga/search/view_doc.asp?symbol=S/2010/173 (accessed 14 April 2012).

133 Ibid., 4.

134 Ibid., 14.

135 Ibid., 11.

136 UN Security Council, "Resolution 1960 (2010)," 4, http://daccess-dds-ny.un.org/doc/ UNDOC/GEN/N10/698/34/PDF/N1069834.pdf?OpenElement (accessed 14 April 2012).

137 UN, *Conflict-Related Sexual Violence*, 2. Emphasis added.

138 Ibid., 3.

139 Ibid. Aside from the information that UN field offices gather about incidents, the data collected may also include reports from rape survivors who present at clinics and hospitals.

140 Tia Palermo and Amber Peterman, "Undercounting, Overcounting and the Longevity of Flawed Estimates: Statistics on Sexual Violence in Conflict," *Bulletin of the World Health Organization* 89, no. 12 (2011), 925, doi: 10.2471/BLT.11.089888, http://www.who.int/ bulletin/volumes/89/12/11-089888/en/index.html (accessed 14 April 2012). Emphasis added. Note that the DHS data on the number of rapes over a 12-month period likely include some cases of intimate-partner sexual violence (which are also measured separately with specific questions). But even with this caveat, the rate of rape indicated by the DHS data was clearly many times higher than that which the UN reported.

141 UN Security Council, *Report of the Secretary-General to the Security Council on the Protection of Civilians in Armed Conflict: S/1999/957* (New York: United Nations, 1999), paragraph 68, http://www.un.org/Docs/sc/committees/sanctions/s99957.pdf (accessed 14 April 2012).

142 Victoria Holt, Glyn Taylor, and Max Kelly, "Protecting Civilians in the Context of UN Peacekeeping Operations: Successes, Setbacks and Remaining Challenges," (New York: United Nations, 2009), 4, http://www.peacekeepingbestpractices.unlb.org/pbps/Library/ Protecting%20Civilians%20in%20the%20Context%20of%20UN%20PKO.pdf (accessed 14 April 2012).

143 Ibid., 8–9.

144 See Victoria Holt and Tobias C. Berkman, *The Impossible Mandate? Military Preparedness, the Responsibility to Protect and Modern Peace Operations* (Washington, DC: The Henry L. Stimson Center, 2006), 12, http://www.stimson.org/images/uploads/research-pdfs/ Complete_Document-TheImpossible_Mandate-Holt_Berkman.pdf (accessed 14 April 2012). It took three years for this report to go through the UN's vetting process and be published as the Holt, Taylor, and Kelly paper cited above.

145 Goetz, "Introduction," 5. Emphasis added. UN peacekeepers have themselves been guilty of sexual abuse of civilians. But the UN states that reports of such cases have declined. UN News Centre, "Sexual Abuse Allegations Decline against UN Peacekeepers in DR Congo and Liberia," 27 July 2011, http://www.un.org/apps/news/story.asp?NewsID=391 64&Cr=peacekeeping&Cr1 (accessed 14 April 2012).

146 The Cohen data, for example, indicate that government forces are reported as perpetrators in more than three-quarters of the coded conflicts. In roughly 15 percent of conflicts government actors were reported to be solely responsible for very high levels of sexual violence. See Cohen, "Causes of Rape During Civil War," 51–52.

147 In her new book, *The Justice Cascade: How Human Rights Prosecutions Are Changing World Politics*, Kathyrn Sikkink discusses statistical data to support her claims that prosecutions of past human rights violations deter future violations.

148 For further details, see UN Development Fund for Women (UNIFEM), UN Action against Sexual Violence in Conflict, and UN Department of Peacekeeping Operations (DPKO), *Addressing Conflict-Related Sexual Violence: An Analytical Inventory of Peacekeeping Practice* (New York: United Nations, 2010), http://www.unifem.org/attachments/products/Analytical_Inventory_of_Peacekeeping_Practice_online.pdf (accessed 14 April 2012).

149 UN DPKO, "Protection of Civilians," http://www.un.org/en/peacekeeping/issues/civilians.html (accessed 14 April 2012).

150 See Chapter 4 in HSRP, *Human Security Report 2009/2010: The Causes of Peace and the Shrinking Costs of War* (New York: Oxford University Press, 2011), http://www.hsrgroup.org/human-security-reports/20092010/text.aspx (accessed 14 April 2012).

151 Ibid.

152 See, for example, Say NO—UNiTE to End Violence against Women, a social mobilization platform on ending violence against women and girls launched by UN Women. Say NO—UNiTE, "About Say NO," http://saynotoviolence.org/about-say-no (accessed 19 June 2012); WHO, *Addressing Violence against Women and Achieving the Millennium Development Goals* (Geneva, Switzerland: WHO, 2005), http://www.who.int/gender/documents/MDGs&VAWSept05.pdf (accessed 19 June 2012); and WHO, "Violence against Women: Intimate Partner and Sexual Violence against Women," factsheet, September 2011, http://www.who.int/mediacentre/factsheets/fs239/en/ (accessed 19 June 2012).

153 Goetz, "Introduction," 3. Emphasis in original.

154 Ibid., Emphasis added.

155 UN Entity for Gender Equality and the Empowerment of Women (UN Women), "Progress of the World's Women 2011–2012: In Pursuit of Justice: Executive Summary," (New York: United Nations), 33, http://progress.unwomen.org/pdfs/EN-Report-Progress.pdf (accessed 14 April 2012).

156 UN Development Programme, *Third Consolidated Annual Progress Report on Activities Implemented under the UN Action against Sexual Violence in Conflict Fund*, Report of the Administrative Agent of the UN Action against Sexual Violence in Conflict Fund for the period 1 January–31 December 2011 (New York: United Nations, 31 May 2012), 7, mdtf.undp.org/document/download/9099 (accessed 19 June 2012).

157 Physicians for Human Rights, *War-Related Sexual Violence in Sierra Leone: A Population-Based Assessment* (Boston: Physicians for Human Rights, 2002), 61, https://s3.amazonaws.com/PHR_Reports/sierra-leone-sexual-violence-2002.pdf (14 April 2012).

158 WHO (World Health Organization), Claudia García-Moreno et al., *WHO Multi-Country Study on Women's Health and Domestic Violence against Women*, (Geneva: WHO, 2005), 40, http://www.who.int/gender/violence/who_multicountry_study/en/ (accessed 23 August 2012).

159 Claudia García-Moreno et al., *WHO Multi-Country Study on Women's Health and Domestic Violence against Women: Initial Results on Prevalence, Health Outcomes and Women's Responses*, (WHO, 2005), 28, http://www.who.int/gender/violence/who_multicountry_study/en/ (accessed 18 July 2012).

160 WHO, "Preventing Intimate Partner and Sexual Violence against Women: Taking Action and Generating Evidence," (Geneva: WHO, 2010), 29, http://www.who.int/violence_injury_prevention/publications/violence/9789241564007_eng.pdf, (accessed 14 April 2012).

161 Ibid.

162 For more detail, see ibid., 30–31.

163 The idea that rape is hard-wired into male psychology was the central focus of a controversial study by Randy Thornhill and Craig T. Palmer. See Randy Thornhill and Craig Palmer, *A Natural History of Rape: Biological Bases of Sexual Coercion* (Cambridge, MA: MIT Press, 2000). For a critique, see Jerry A. Coyne and Andrew Berry, "Rape as an Adaptation: Is This Contentious Hypothesis Advocacy, Not Science?" *Nature* 404, no. 6774 (2000): 121–122, doi: 10.1038/35004636 (accessed 13 July 2012). Note that even though Thornhill and Palmer believe that males have an innate predisposition to rape, they believe that the incidence of rape can be reduced through strategies that stress education and deterrence.

164 See, for example, WHO, "Changing Cultural and Social Norms that Support Violence," (Geneva: WHO, 2009), 8, http://www.who.int/violence_injury_prevention/violence/norms.pdf (accessed 14 April 2012).

165 Ibid., 3.

166 Celia W. Dugger, "Senegal Curbs a Bloody Rite for Girls and Women," *New York Times*, 15 October 2011, http://www.nytimes.com/2011/10/16/world/africa/movement-to-end-genital-cutting-spreads-in-senegal.html?_r=1&ref=senegal (accessed 14 April 2012).

167 Ibid.

168 There is, in fact, some evidence to suggest that the ban in 1999 led to higher numbers of cuttings, at least in the short run, and may have damaged the community-driven efforts. See Monica Antonazzo, "Problems with Criminalizing Female Genital Cutting," *Peace Review: A Journal of Social Justice* 15, no. 4, (2003): 474, http://www.tandfonline.com/doi/pdf/10.1080/1040265032000156663 (accessed 13 June 2012).

169 Dugger, "Senegal Curbs a Bloody Rite for Girls and Women."

170 Lori L. Heise, "What Works to Prevent Partner Violence? An Evidence Overview," STRIVE Research Consortium, London School of Hygiene and Tropical Medicine (London: LSHTM, 2011), 27–28, http://www.dfid.gov.uk/R4D/PDF/Outputs/Gender/60887-PartnerViolenceEvidenceOverview.pdf (accessed 14 April 2012).

171 Ibid., 28.

172 Ibid., 29.

173 WHO, "Promoting Gender Equality to Prevent Violence against Women: Overview," (Geneva: WHO, 2009), 1, http://whqlibdoc.who.int/publications/2009/9789241597883_eng.pdf (accessed 14 April 2012).

174 Mary Caprioli, "Primed for Violence: The Role of Gender Inequality in Predicting Internal Conflict," *International Studies Quarterly* 49, no. 2 (2005): 161–178, doi: 10.1111/j.0020-8833.2005.00340.x (accessed 13 July 2012); and Erik Melander, "Gender Equality and Intrastate Armed Conflict," *International Studies Quarterly* 49, no. 4 (2005): 695–714, doi: 10.1111/j.1468-2478.2005.00384.x (accessed 13 July 2012).

175 Caprioli, "Primed for Violence," 171.

176 Melander, "Gender Equality and Intrastate Armed Conflict," 695.

177 James D. Fearon, "Governance and Civil War Onset: World Development Report 2011 Background Paper," (Washington, DC: World Bank, 2010), 35, http://wdr2011.worldbank.org/sites/default/files/pdfs/WDR%20Background%20Paper_Fearon_0.pdf?keepThis=true&TB_iframe=true&height=600&width=800 (accessed 14 April 2012).

178 Ibid., 36.

179 WHO, "Promoting Gender Equality," 1, 4.

180 World Bank, "Achieving Gender Equality at the Heart of MDGs," (Washington, D.C.: World Bank, 2010), http://data.worldbank.org/news/achieving-gender-equality-at-the-heart-of-mdgs (accessed 14 April 2012).

181 Heise, "What Works to Prevent Partner Violence?"

182 WHO, "Promoting Gender Equality," 4. See also R. B. Whaley and S. F. Messner, "Gender Equality and Gendered Homicides," *Homicide Studies* 6, no. 3 (2002): 188–210, doi: 10.1177/108876790200600302 (accessed 14 July 2012).

183 WHO, "Promoting Gender Equality," 9.

184 Heise, "What Works to Prevent Partner Violence?"

185 Heise, "What Works to Prevent Partner Violence?" 57–58; and Seema Vyas and Charlotte Watt, "How Does Economic Empowerment Affect Women's Risk of Intimate Partner Violence in Low and Middle Income Countries? A Systematic Review of Published Evidence," *Journal of International Development* 21, no. 5, 577–602, doi: 10.1002/jid.1500 (accessed 14 July 2012).

186 See Chapter 4 in HSRP, *Human Security Report 2009/2010: The Causes of Peace and the Shrinking Costs of War* (New York: Oxford University Press, 2011), http://www.hsrgroup.org/human-security-reports/20092010/text.aspx (accessed 14 April 2012).

187 For a wide-ranging and comprehensive analysis of other campaigns to reduce partner violence, including sexual violence, see Heise, "What Works to Prevent Partner Violence?"

CHAPTER 3

188 Dyan Mazurana and Khristopher Carlson, "The Girl Child and Armed Conflict: Recognizing and Addressing Grave Violations of Girls' Human Rights," United Nations Division for the Advancement of Women (DAW) in collaboration with UNICEF, 3, http://www.un.org/womenwatch/daw/egm/elim-disc-viol-girlchild/ExpertPapers/EP.12%20Mazurana.pdf (accessed 7 June 2012).

189 Note that Mazurana and Carlson claim that their figures were for the "last decade," when the source of their data—a UNICEF report—actually refers to the time period 1986–1996. Kelly Greenhill, in her revealing essay that we cited in the previous chapter, refers to similar figures as one example of the kinds of myths that surround the impact of armed conflict. See Kelly M. Greenhill, "Counting the Cost: The Politics of Numbers in Armed Conflict," in *Sex, Drugs and Body Counts: The Politics of Numbers in Global Crime and Conflict*, ed. Peter Andreas and Kelly M. Greenhill (Ithaca: Cornell University Press, 2010), 128–130.

190 Definitions of sexual violence against children are, in principle, the same as those against adults. We use the same definition for sexual violence used in Chapter 1 (see the box on page 23). But in some instances, particularly in advocacy reports, it is not always clear which definition is being used.

191 Jeanne Ward, Jackie Kirk, and Lisa Ernst, *Broken Bodies, Broken Dreams: Violence against Women Exposed* (Nairobi: OCHA/IRIN, 2005), 19, http://www.irinnews.org/InDepthMain.aspx?InDepthId=59&ReportId=72831 (accessed 16 March 2012).

192 Office of the United Nations High Commissioner for Human Rights (OHCHR), Convention on the Rights of the Child, Part I, Article 1, http://www2.ohchr.org/english/law/crc.htm (accessed 7 June 2012).

193 Office of the Special Representative of the Secretary-General for Children and Armed Conflict, "The Changing Nature of Conflict," http://www.un.org/children/conflict/english/the-changing-nature-of-conflict.html (accessed 7 June 2012).

194 United Nations Department for Policy Coordination and Sustainable Development (DPCSD), *Promotion and Protection of the Rights of Children: Impact of War on Children*, Note by the Secretary-General United Nations DPCSD, http://www.unicef.org/graca/a51-306_en.pdf (accessed 18 June 2012). The formal title of the Machel report was *Impact of Armed Conflict on Children: Report of the Expert of the Secretary-General, Ms. Graça Machel, Submitted Pursuant to General Assembly Resolution 48/157*, UN document A/51/306, New York, 26 August 1996.

195 The term "new war" derived from Mary Kaldor *New & Old Wars: Organized Violence in a Global Era*, 2nd ed. (Cambridge [England]; Malden, MA: Polity Press, 2006).

196 DPCSD, "Promotion and Protection of the Rights of Children," 5. The Machel report foreshadowed the claims of so-called new war scholars that there had been a fundamental change in the nature of armed conflict.

197 Office of the Special Representative of the Secretary-General for Children and Armed Conflict, "Introduction," http://www.un.org/children/conflict/english/issues.html (accessed 7 June 2012).

198 Office of the Special Representative of the Secretary-General for Children and Armed Conflict, "Engagement of Security Council on Children and Armed Conflict," http://www.un.org/children/conflict/english/security-council.html (accessed 7 June 2012).

199 Alastair Ager, Neil Boothby, and Megan Bremer, "Using the 'Protective Environment' Framework to Analyse Children's Protection Needs in Darfur," *Disasters* 33, no. 4 (2009): 567, doi: 10.1111/j.0361-3666.2008.01087.x (accessed 20 August 2012).

200 See Care and Protection of Children in Crisis Affected Countries Initiative Program on Forced Migration and Health, *Care and Protection of Children in Crisis Affected Countries: A Good Practice Policy Change Initiative* (New York: CPC, 2006), 17, http://www.forcedmigration.columbia.edu/research/documents/CPCSynthesisReport2008.pdf (accessed 22 August 2012).

201 Cited in ibid, 17.

202 See Greenhill, "Counting the Cost," 128–130.

203 See UNICEF, *Machel Study 10-Year Strategic Review: Children and Conflict in a Changing World* (New York: Office of the Special Representative of the Secretary-General for Children and Armed Conflict; UNICEF, 2009), http://www.un.org/children/conflict/_documents/machel/msr2_en.pdf (accessed 7 June 2012).

204 Ibid., 8.

205 The overall level of violence declined substantially, which—all else equal—should result in a lesser impact on children. From the 1990s to the 2000s, total death tolls from state-based conflict, non-state conflict, and one-sided violence decreased by 45, 24, and 49 percent, respectively (we exclude one-sided violence in Rwanda here to avoid skewing the result).

206 For example, the Office of the Special Representative of the Secretary-General for Children and Armed Conflict continues to refer to the "new wars" on its website. See "The Changing Nature of Conflict" (accessed 13 July 2012).

207 Kaldor, *New & Old Wars*.

208 Ibid., 107.

209 UN Population Division, Department of Economic and Social Affairs, *World Population Prospects: The 2010 Revision*, http://esa.un.org//wpp/Excel-Date/population.htm (accessed 11 June 2012).

210 Human Security Centre, *Human Security Report 2005: War and Peace in the 21st Century* (New York; Oxford: Oxford University Press, 2005), 75, http://www.hsrgroup.org/human-security-reports/2005/text.aspx (accessed 7 June 2012).

211 Erik Melander, Magnus Oberg, and Jonathan Hall, "Are 'New Wars' More Atrocious? Battle Severity, Civilians Killed and Forced Migration before and after the End of the Cold War," *European Journal of International Relations* 15, no. 3 (2009), 529, doi: 10.1177/1354066109338243 (accessed 22 August 2012).

212 Notable critiques of the new wars thesis include Mats Berdal, "How 'New' are 'New Wars'? Global Economic Change and the Study of Civil War," *Global Governance* 9 (2003); Stathis N. Kalyvas, "'New' and 'Old' Civil Wars: A Valid Distinction?" *World Politics* 54, no. 01 (2001), doi: 10.1353/wp.2001.0022 (accessed 7 June 2012); and Edward Newman, "The 'New Wars' Debate: A Historical Perspective Is Needed," *Security Dialogue* 35, no. 2 (2004), doi: 10.1177/0967010604044975 (accessed 7 June 2012).

213 For data on the decline in genocides, see Human Security Centre, *Human Security Report 2005*, 41.

214 See endnote 18.

215 Office of the Special Representative of the Secretary-General for Children and Armed Conflict, "Rape and Other Grave Sexual Violence against Children," http://www.un.org/children/conflict/english/sexualviolence.html (accessed 7 June 2012). Emphasis added.

216 There will clearly be individual conflicts in which levels of sexual violence have increased; our concern, however, is with overall trends.

217 UN Security Council, "Security Council Establishes Monitoring, Reporting Mechanism on Use of Child Soldiers, Unanimously Adopting Security Council Resolution 1612 (2005)," news release, 26 July 2005, http://www.un.org/News/Press/docs/2005/sc8458.doc.htm (accessed 31 July 2012).

218 Watchlist on Children and Armed Conflict, *Getting It Done and Doing It Right: A Global Study on the United Nations-led Monitoring & Reporting Mechanism on Children and Armed Conflict* (New York: Watchlist on Children and Armed Conflict, 2008), 18, http://www.watchlist.org/reports/pdf/global-v8-web.pdf (accessed 31 July 2012).

219 Even well-run surveys will underestimate the extent of sexual violence, especially if respondents are not given the opportunity of answering questions anonymously. But the degree of underestimation is still far less than with the type of reporting undertaken by the MRM task forces.

220 Office of the Special Representative of the Secretary-General for Children and Armed Conflict, UNICEF, and Department of Peacekeeping Operations (DPKO), *Monitoring and Reporting Mechanism (MRM) on Grave Violations against Children in Situations of Armed Conflict: MRM Field Manual,* http://s3.amazonaws.com/tdh_e-platform/assets/147/original/MRM_Field_Manual_16-04-10.pdf?1309159505 (accessed 7 June 2012).

221 Because these studies have recall periods of 10 years or more, some of the adult respondents may have been children when they were violated, but the data are not disaggregated to reveal the prevalence of sexual violence against children.

222 Two questions in the module are critical here for information on sexual violence against children in wartime. First, women respondents are asked, "How old were you the first time you were forced to have sexual intercourse or perform any other sexual acts?" Answers to this question will determine what percentage of females experienced sexual violence while still children—and at what age. A follow-up question asks about the identity of the perpetrator. These data could be used to derive a conservative estimate of the percentage of the under-age population that had experienced sexual violence, and who the perpetrators were—family members or acquaintances (most likely), or soldiers and other members of the security forces. This would, however, still underestimate the extent of sexual violence, especially if respondents were not given the opportunity to answer questions anonymously. See DHS, "Domestic Violence Module: Questionnaire and Interviewer's Manual," 3 January 2011, 5, http://www.measuredhs.com/pubs/pdf/DHSQM/DHS6_Module_Domestic_Violence_3Jan2011.pdf (accessed 23 August 2012).

223 The UNICEF surveys can include optional modules that collect data on *child discipline*—i.e., physical violence against young children—and on adult *attitudes* towards the use of disciplinary force against children, but nothing on sexual violence. See UNICEF, "Multiple Indicator Cluster Surveys: Questionnaires and Indicator List," April 2012, http://www.childinfo.org/mics4_questionnaire.html (accessed 23 August 12).

224 See Marije Stoltenborgh et al., "A Global Perspective on Child Sexual Abuse: Meta-Analysis of Prevalence around the World," *Child Maltreatment* 16, no. 2 (2011): 79–101, doi: 10.1177/1077559511403920 (accessed 7 June 2012).

225 See ibid., 84.

226 Ibid., 83, 88.

227 See Stoltenborgh et al., "A Global Perspective on Child Sexual Abuse," 87, 89.

228 Claudia García-Moreno et al., *WHO Multi-Country Study on Women's Health and Domestic Violence against Women: Initial Results on Prevalence, Health Outcomes and Women's Responses* (Geneva: WHO, 2005), 3, xiv, http://www.who.int/gender/violence/who_multicountry_study/en/ (accessed 18 July 2012)

229 Ibid., 50.

230 WHO (World Health Organization), Claudia García-Moreno et al., *WHO Multi-Country Study on Women's Health and Domestic Violence against Women,* (Geneva: WHO, 2005), 50, http://www.who.int/gender/violence/who_multicountry_study/en/ (accessed 23 August 2012).

231 In addition to being asked directly if they had experienced sexual violence before they were 15, the women could respond anonymously by placing the answer in a sealed envelope.

232 UNICEF, *Machel Study 10-Year Strategic Review,* 161.

233 Unpublished data provided by the WHO based on García-Moreno et al., *WHO Multi-Country Study on Women's Health and Domestic Violence against Women.*

234 There are only two sites where the rate of sexual violence against children was shown to be higher than that against adults.

235 Ibid., 50. The 33 percent figure for adults is high. We should, however, expect that the data broadly reflect the difference in prevalence rates between adults and children.

236 Unpublished data provided by the WHO (World Health Organization) based on García-Moreno et al., *WHO Multi-Country Study on Women's Health and Domestic Violence against Women*.

237 *Neighbourhood surveys* are so called because interviewers solicit information from female heads of households, not only about their own experience of sexual violence and that of other females in the household but also of the experience of women in three neighbouring households. This has the effect of increasing the sample size of the population being surveyed, but there is no guarantee that the single respondent's estimate of sexual violence in other households will be correct. For more information on neighbourhood surveys, see Child Protection in Crisis Network for Research, Learning and Action, "Neighbourhood Method," http://www.cpcnetwork.org/neighborhood-method.php (accessed 7 June 2012).

238 Birthe Steiner et al., "Sexual Violence in the Protracted Conflict of DRC Programming for Rape Survivors in South Kivu," *Conflict and Health* 3, no. 1 (2009) doi: 10.1186/1752-1505-3-3 (accessed 7 June 2012).

239 UN Population Division, *World Population Prospects: The 2010 Revision, Population Database*, http://esa.un.org/unpd/wpp/unpp/panel_population.htm (accessed 18 July 2012) and http://esa.un.org/wpp/Excel-Data/population.htm (accessed 11 June 2012).

240 This was done only for a short period from October to December 2005.

241 Steiner et al., "Sexual Violence in the Protracted Conflict of DRC Programming for Rape Survivors in South Kivu," 7.

242 Luc Malemo Kalisya et al., "Sexual Violence toward Children and Youth in War-Torn Eastern Democratic Republic of Congo," *PLoS ONE* 6, no. 1 (2011), Table 1, doi: 10.1371/journal.pone.0015911 (accessed 19 July 2012).

243 For the very small number of adult victims included in the Kalisya et al. study, the data show a high share of rape by strangers and perpetrators in military uniform (70 percent and 48 percent, respectively). Note that these figures are based on a total of only 54 adult cases, as opposed to the 440 "pediatric victims." See ibid., 3.

244 Child Protection in Crisis Network, "Neighbourhood Method."

245 Braeden Rogers et al., "Estimating the Incidence of Physical and Sexual Violence against Children and Women in Trincomalee District, Sri Lanka: The Neighbourhood Method," 14 January 2009, Heilbrunn Department of Population and Family Heath, Program on Forced Migration and Health, Mailman School of Public Health, Columbia University/ Save The Children, 18, http://www.cpcnetwork.org/learning-details.php?ID=1 (accessed 21 June 2012).

246 Ibid., 27. The two cases of rape of girls recorded in the survey were both perpetrated by family members, but the total number is too low to be meaningful. See ibid., 23.

247 Angela Parcesepe, Lindsay Stark, and Les Roberts, "Using the Neighbourhood Method to Measure Violence and Rape in Ethiopia," Heilbrunn Department of Population and Family Heath, Program on Forced Migration and Health, Mailman School of Public Health, Columbia University, 11, http://www.cpcnetwork.org/neighborhood-method.php (accessed 18 July 2012).

248 Ibid., 17.

249 Ann Warner, "Incidence of Violence against Women and Girls in Liberia: A Quantitative Study Using the 'Neighborhood Method,'" International Rescue Committee; Program on Forced Migration and Health, Mailman School of Public Health, Columbia University, 7, http://www.forcedmigration.columbia.edu/research/documents/IRCReportonNeighborhoodStudy_10-1-07.pdf (accessed 18 June 2012).

250 Ibid., 11–12.

251 Kathleen Myer, Alina Potts, and Les Roberts, "Grave Violations of Children's Rights and Mortality in the Central African Republic: Results of a Nationwide Survey," Heilbrunn Department of Population and Family Heath, Program on Forced Migration and Health, Mailman School of Public Health, Columbia University, 13, http://www.forcedmigration.columbia.edu/research/documents/CAR_1612_Survey_Report_17Sep09_FOR DISTRIBUTION.pdf (accessed 18 June 2012).

252 Ibid.

253 See Lindsay Stark et al., "Measuring Violence against Women amidst War and Displacement in Northern Uganda Using the 'Neighborhood Method,'" *Journal of Epidemiology & Community Health* 64 (2010): 1056–1061, doi: 10.1136/jech.2009.093799 (accessed 20 July 2012).

254 As Elisabeth Wood has argued, differences in the rate of rape committed by armed groups may also be determined by antisexual violence policies pursued by military authorities. However, there is insufficient cross-national data to determine the extent to which such policies have been implemented outside the relatively small number of case studies that have been carried out thus far. See Elisabeth J. Wood, "Armed Groups and Sexual Violence: When Is Wartime Rape Rare?" *Politics & Society* 37, no. 1 (2009): 131–161, doi: 10.1177/0032329208329755 (accessed 22 August 2012).

255 See Stoltenborgh et al., "A Global Perspective on Child Sexual Abuse," 89.

256 This is not to say that the MRM has no utility—simply that it is not useful for measuring trends in conflict-related sexual violence against children. For a description of the MRM and some of its roles, see Watchlist on Children and Armed Conflict, *Getting It Done and Doing It Right* (accessed 18 June 2012).

257 UN Statistical Commission, "Proposed Draft Outline for the Guidelines for Producing Statistics on Violence against Women, Part I: Statistical Survey," 3, http://unstats.un.org/unsd/demographic/meetings/vaw/docs/Item13.pdf (accessed 18 June 2012).

CHAPTER 4

258 Brian Lai and Clayton Thyne, "The Effect of Civil War on Education, 1980–97," *Journal of Peace Research* 44, no. 3 (2007): 289, doi: 10.1177/0022343307076631 (accessed 18 July 2012).

259 Marc Sommers, *Children, Education, and War: Reaching Education for All* (EFA) *Objectives in Countries Affected by Conflict*, Conflict Prevention and Reconstruction Unit (CPR) Working Papers 1 (Washington, DC: World Bank, 2002), Introduction, http://siteresources.world bank.org/EDUCATION/Resources/278200-1099079877269/547664-1099079993288/children_edu_war_efa02.pdf (accessed 18 July 2012).

260 UNESCO (United Nations Educational, Scientific and Cultural Organization) Education for All (EFA) Global Monitoring Report Team, *The Hidden Crisis: Armed Conflict and Education* (Paris: UNESCO, 2011), 13, http://unesdoc.unesco.org/images/0019/001907/190743e.pdf (accessed 4 September 2012).

261 See Paul Collier, *Breaking the Conflict Trap: Civil War and Development Policy* (Washington, DC; New York: World Bank; Oxford University Press, 2003).

262 UNESCO Institute for Statistics (UIS), "The Quantitative Impact of Conflict on Education," UIS technical paper no. 7 (Montreal: UIS, 2011), http://www.uis.unesco.org/Library/Documents/tp7-quantitative-armed-conflict-impact-education-2011-en.pdf (accessed 18 July 2012).

263 Education Policy and Data Center (EPDC), "How Do Violent Conflicts Affect School Enrolment? Analysis of Sub-National Evidence from 19 Countries" (Geneva: UNESCO, 2010), background paper prepared for the *Education for All Global Monitoring Report 2011—The Hidden Crisis: Armed Conflict and Education*, http://unesdoc.unesco.org/images/0019/001912/191248e.pdf (accessed 21 July 2012).

264 See Chapter 6 of Human Security Report Project (HSRP), *Human Security Report 2009/2010: The Causes of Peace and the Shrinking Costs of War* (New York: Oxford University Press, 2011), http://www.hsrgroup.org/human-security-reports/20092010/overview.aspx (accessed 13 September 2012). Note that the period studied was 1970 to 2008.

265 Scott Gates et al., "Consequences of Civil Conflict," *World Development Report 2011* Input Paper, World Bank, http://wdr2011.worldbank.org/PRIO (accessed 19 July 2012). A shortened and revised version of this study was published in September 2012. See Scott Gates et al., "Development Consequences of Armed Conflict, "*World Development* 40, no. 9: 1713–1722, doi: 10.1016/j.worlddev.2012.04.031 (accessed 14 September 2012).

266 UNESCO Institute for Statistics, "The Quantitative Impact of Conflict on Education; EPDC, "How Do Violent Conflicts Affect School Enrolment?"

267 Gates et al., "Consequences of Civil Conflict."

268 "Descriptive statistics" include the tables, charts, and graphics used to describe, summarize, and graphically present raw statistical data. They help summarize and support factual claims and are much easier to understand than the raw data.

269 Econometric studies may choose to exclude select countries where including them in the analysis would distort the results. The PRIO study, for example, excluded a number of developed countries, such as the UK, which experienced a small conflict in Northern Ireland. Development indicators in such highly industrialized countries are unlikely to improve significantly. See Scott Gates et al., "Consequences of Civil Conflict," 5.

270 *Regression analysis* seeks to determine associations between different phenonoma, with the assumption usually being that the association indicates an "average" causal effect.

271 Gates et al., "Consequences of Civil Conflict," 13.

272 Most of these statistics are from the Households in Conflict Network (HiCN), which has published studies on education and conflict in Burundi, Tajikistan, Nepal, Timor Leste, and Bosnia. See HiCN, "About," http://www.hicn.org/papers.html/ (accessed 21 July 2012). See also Francis Akena Adyanga, *The Catastrophe of Education in Civil War Areas, Uganda: The Impact of Civil War on Education: A Case Study of Acholiland, Northern Uganda* (Saarbrucken, Germany: Lambert Academic Pub., 2010); Avis Sri-Jayantha, "Impact of War on Children in Sri Lanka," Association of Tamils of Sri Lanka in the USA, http://www.sangam.org/ANALYSIS/Children_1_28_03.htm (accessed 21 July 2012); and Kate Wharton and Ruth U. Oyelere, "Conflict and Its Impact on Educational Accumulation and Enrollment in Colombia: What We Can Learn from Recent IDPs," Institute for the Study of Labor (IZA), http://www.iza.org/en/webcontent/publications/papers/viewAbstract?dp_id=5939 (accessed 21 July 2012).

273 World Bank, *Reshaping the Future: Education and Postconflict Reconstruction* (Washington, DC: World Bank, 2005), xi, http://siteresources.worldbank.org/INTCPR/Resources/Reshaping_the_Future.pdf (accessed 21 July 2012). Note that no sources were provided for these claims.

274 World Bank, *Reshaping the Future*, 13.

275 Ibid., 13, 22.

276 Internal Displacement Monitoring Centre (IDMC), "Internally Displaced Children," http://www.internal-displacement.org/8025708F004D404D/(httpPages)/6E780F0E0FE6BA1AC1257214003D980E?OpenDocument (accessed 21 July 2012).

277 United Nations High Commissioner for Refugees (UNHCR), *Global Trends 2010: 60 Years and Still Counting* (Geneva: United Nations, 2011), http://www.unhcr.org/4dfa11499.html (accessed 21 July 2012).

278 UNESCO, "Conflict Is Robbing 28 Million Children of a Future, UNESCO Report Warns," News Release, 1 March 2011, http://www.unesco.org/new/fileadmin/MULTIMEDIA/HQ/ED/pdf/gmr2011-press-release-main.pdf (accessed 21 July 2012).

279 UNESCO, "Education Under Attack 2010—Iraq," http://www.unhcr.org/refworld/docid/4b7aa9df5.html (accessed 21 July 2012).

280 Brendan O'Malley, *Education Under Attack 2010* (Paris: UNESCO, 2010), 43, http://unesdoc.unesco.org/images/0018/001868/186809e.pdf (accessed 21 July 2012).

281   Ibid.

282   World Bank, *Reshaping the Future*, 17.

283   Bede Sheppard and Kyle Knight, "Disarming Schools: Strategies for Ending the Military Use of Schools during Armed Conflict," *Disarmament Forum* 2011, no. 3 (2011): 23, http://unidir. org/bdd/fiche-periodique.php?ref_periodique=1020-7287-2011-3-en#biblio (accessed 21 July 2012).

284   Christopher Blattman and Jeannie Annan, "The Consequences of Child Soldiering," *Review of Economics and Statistics* 92, no. 4 (2010): 882–898, doi: 10.1162/REST_a_00036 (accessed 21 July 2012).

285   World Bank, *Reshaping the Future*, 18–19.

286   UN, "Millennium Development Goals: Goal 2: Achieve Universal Primary Education— Fact Sheet," http://www.un.org/millenniumgoals/pdf/MDG_FS_2_EN.pdf (accessed 21 July 2012).

287   Julia Paulson and Jeremy Rappleye, "Education and Conflict: Essay Review," *International Journal of Educational Development* 27, no. 3 (2007): 341, doi: 10.1016/j.ijedudev.2006.10.010 (accessed 21 July 2012).

288   UNESCO Institute for Statistics, "The Quantitative Impact of Conflict on Education."

289   Note that the study does not measure directly a country's overall national attainment rate but rather the educational attainments of cohorts of 15-year-olds at given points in time. We describe this indicator elsewhere in the chapter.

290   See UNESCO Institute for Statistics, "The Quantitative Impact of Conflict on Education," 13, for a detailed description of the methodology used by the UIS researchers—and some cautions about the conclusions that can be drawn from the data analysis. The conflict data come from PRIO and the Uppsala University Conflict Data Program (UCDP). The graphics in the study show periods of both minor conflict (in yellow) and major conflict (referred to as "war" here). *Major conflicts* or *wars* are those that incur 1,000 or more battle deaths in a calendar year.

291   In addition, the researchers also grouped the respondents in cohorts of 13- to 17-year-olds to smooth year-to-year fluctuations.

292   The data used in the UIS report can serve as an indicator of the effect of conflict on education, but as the authors note, they do not directly "reveal the educational attainment of 15 year-olds…at any time in the past." See UNESCO Institute for Statistics, "The Quantitative Impact of Conflict on Education," 13 (accessed 4 September 2012).

293   Ibid., 7.

294   Ibid.

295 The figures derived from the UIS study that are presented here do not extend as far in time as the UIS graphics. This is because, as the UIS report's authors explain, data immediately prior to the time of the survey are distorted. This is very evident in the UIS graphics, which all reveal a sharp decline in educational outcomes prior to, and following, the survey date. To avoid misinterpretation, the graphics used here only extend the year that is nine years *prior* to the year in which the survey was undertaken. This is the maximum period over which the UIS researchers believe the distortion will be evident.

296 To be more precise, the Kurdish areas had a greater percentage of individuals with no formal education than the rest of Turkey.

297 UNESCO Institute for Statistics (UIS), "The Quantitative Impact of Conflict on Education," UIS technical paper no. 7 (Montreal: UIS, 2011), http://www.uis.unesco.org/Library/Documents/tp7-quantitative-armed-conflict-impact-education-2011-en.pdf (accessed 18 July 2012).

298 By the time the conflict started, only a very small percentage of those living in the areas of Turkey not directly affected by war had received no education at all, which means that there was little room for improvement on this measure. But the counterintuitive process of educational attainments improving more rapidly in war-affected areas than in those that are not directly affected is evident in other graphs in the UIS study.

299 UNESCO Institute for Statistics, "The Quantitative Impact of Conflict on Education," 27 (Figure 4.6) (accessed 4 September 2012).

300 The UIS study did not examine the differences between war-affected and non-war-affected areas in all the countries it reviewed.

301 Attainment rates for women were broadly similar but from a lower base than males, and the attainment rate for women in the conflict zones, unlike for males, lagged somewhat behind the attainment rate for women in the nonconflict zones. UNESCO Institute for Statistics, "The Quantitative Impact of Conflict on Education," 38–40 (accessed 4 September 2012).

302 Exceptions were periods of violence in the 1960s and 1980s, during which the average years of education followed an unsteady, but largely stagnant, pre-war trend.

303 See UNESCO Institute for Statistics, "The Quantitative Impact of Conflict on Education," 45 (Figure 8.5) (accessed 4 September 2012).

304 The data for the male population without formal education represented an exception here, as it deteriorated during the 1970s but then caught up again with the trend in the rest of the country.

305 It could also mean that the negative impact of conflict on the rate of educational attainment is being offset by the positive impact of some other factor—e.g., rising incomes or improved educational attainment among girls.

306 UNESCO Institute for Statistics (UIS), "The Quantitative Impact of Conflict on Education," UIS technical paper no. 7 (Montreal: UIS, 2011), http://www.uis.unesco.org/Library/Documents/tp7-quantitative-armed-conflict-impact-education-2011-en.pdf (accessed 18 July 2012).

307 Andrew Mack, "Armed Conflicts," Perspective Paper, Copenhagen Consensus 2012, http://www.copenhagenconsensus.com/Files/Filer/CC12%20perspective%20papers/Armed%20Conflicts__Mack.pdf (accessed 21 July 2012).

308 See UNESCO Institute for Statistics, "The Quantitative Impact of Conflict on Education," 66 (Figure 9.20) (accessed 4 September 2012).

309 EPDC, "How Do Violent Conflicts Affect School Enrolment?"

310 This refers to 10 countries that experienced conflict in 2010 and for which conflict-affected as well as peaceful regions could be identified. See ibid., 2 (accessed 4 September 2012).

311 Ibid., 1 (accessed 4 September 2012).

312 Ibid. (accessed 4 September 2012).

313 Ibid., 2 (accessed 4 September 2012).

314 See the methodology section of ibid., 6–8 (accessed 4 September 2012).

315 The countries in question are Burma, Burundi, Chad, Indonesia, Liberia, the Philippines, Sierra Leone, and Sudan. In the case of Sierra Leone, there was trend data but no period of conflict; in the case of Chad, trend data existed only for the nonconflict region.

316 Note that for most of these countries, only two data points are available, or there are only data for the conflict period, which means that we cannot compare values for all periods; i.e., before, after, and during the conflict.

317 EPDC, "How Do Violent Conflicts Affect School Enrolment?" 27 (accessed 4 September 2012).

318 In addition, Ethiopia also shows increases in attendance rates. The EPDC does not show conflict periods in its Ethiopia graph covering the years 2000–2009. According to UCDP/PRIO data, however, the country continuously experienced conflict during that time period.

319 The countries in question are Burma, Burundi, Chad, Indonesia, Liberia, the Philippines, Senegal, Sierra Leone, and Uganda.

320 Gross attendance rates can be more than 100 percent, because in addition to the regular cohort of children, they include children older than the cohort who previously missed a year or more of education.

321 EPDC, "How Do Violent Conflicts Affect School Enrolment?" 12; Uppsala Conflict Data Program (UCDP), Uppsala University, Uppsala, Sweden/Center for the Study of Civil War, International Peace Research Institute Oslo, (PRIO).

322 See Ray Rivera and Taimoor Shah, "Taliban Attacks on Afghan Schools Lessen," *SFGate*, 9 June 2011, http://www.sfgate.com/world/article/Taliban-attacks-on-Afghan-schools-lessen-2368869.php (accessed 21 July 2012).

323 EPDC, "How Do Violent Conflicts Affect School Enrolment?" 12; UCDP.

324 World Bank, "In Afghanistan, Out of Conflict and Into School," http://web.worldbank. org/WBSITE/EXTERNAL/TOPICS/EXTEDUCATION/0,,contentMDK:20279607~menuP K:617572~pagePK:148956~piPK:216618~theSitePK:282386,00.html (accessed 30 August 2012).

325 However, as we pointed out previously, the limited evidence we have suggests that these outcomes usually precede the conflict.

326 Adding deaths caused by the intentional killing of civilians for the period covered by the survey does not significantly alter the average. If death tolls in minor conflicts are so low that the impact that they make on educational outcomes is not discernible, it might be useful to focus on high-intensity conflicts only. This is what we did in our analysis of under-five mortality in the last *Human Security Report,* where only *wars*—conflicts in which there were a reported 1,000 or more battle deaths in a calendar year—were included. The findings were very similar for both intensity levels. This time we include minor conflicts, primarily because the UIS and EPDC studies that we review include minor conflicts as well as wars in their analyses.

327 EPDC, "How Do Violent Conflicts Affect School Enrolment? 15; UCDP.

328 Ibid., and Human Security Report Project, School for International Studies, Simon Fraser University, Vancouver, Canada.

329 Gratien Mokonzi Bambanota and Mwinda Kadongo, *Democratic Republic of Congo: Effective Delivery of Public Services in the Education Sector: A Study* (Johannesburg, South Africa: Open Society Initiative for Southern Africa, 2010), 4, doi: 10.1177/00223433030405006 (accessed 21 July 2012).

330 Bambanota and Kadongo, *Democratic Republic of Congo: Effective Delivery of Public Services in the Education Sector,* 19 (accessed 30 August 2012).

331 Ibid. (accessed 30 August 2012).

332 The light blue South Kivu trend line is that which has the highest attendance rate in 2007 of the three secondary conflict region trend lines.

333 Lisa Bender, *Innovations in Emergency Education: The IRC in the Democratic Republic of Congo* (Geneva: UNESCO, 2009), commissioned background report prepared for the *Global Monitoring Report,* 3, http://ddp-ext.worldbank.org/EdStats/ZARgmrpap10.pdf (accessed 21 July 2012).

334 IDMC, "Democratic Republic of Congo: IDPs Need Further Assistance in Context of Continued Attacks and Insecurity," http://www.internal-displacement.org/countries/ drcongo (accessed 22 July 2012).

335 UNESCO Institute for Statistics, "The Quantitative Impact of Conflict on Education," 7 (accessed 4 September 2012).

336 EPDC, "How Do Violent Conflicts Affect School Enrolment?" 31 (accessed 4 September 2012). Emphasis added.

337 See ibid., 6–8 (accessed 4 September 2012) for a discussion of all EPDC's methodological concerns.

338 Ibid., 7 (accessed 4 September 2012).

339 In the Central African Republic there are only data for the two secondary conflict regions. In 2006 the primary conflict region was not surveyed. It is possible that the primary conflict region saw a decline, but both of the secondary conflict areas witnessed an appreciable *improvement* in educational outcomes in this period, as seems to be the case for all the other regions. In Uganda parts of the northern and western regions were omitted from the survey in 2001. However, this is unlikely to change the main finding much, since the data already show a decline in educational attainments for most of the period. Several areas of Indonesia were missed from the survey, but there were only data for one year on Indonesia so they are not discussed here. The same is the case with Sudan. In the cases of Pakistan and Colombia, there were missing data, but the EPDC states that the omission is unlikely to have affected the overall results in either case.

340 EPDC, "How Do Violent Conflicts Affect School Enrolment?", 6 (accessed 4 September 2012).

341 The terms *effect* and *impact*—which imply causality—are used both in this *Report* and in most other studies. Strictly speaking, we should be referring to an *association* between conflict and educational outcomes.

342 The PRIO study uses both cross-section and fixed-effects models, but the authors believe the latter are more appropriate (HSRP correspondence with Håvard Mokleiv Nygård, 29 May 2012). See Gates et al., "Consequences of Civil Conflict," 1. Cited earlier in the chapter, the updated Gates et al., "Development Consequences of Armed Conflict" corrects a minor error in the version that is cited here.

343 Gates et al., "Consequences of Civil Conflict," 40.

344 Gates et al., "Consequences of Civil Conflict."

345 Ibid., 43.

346 Siyan Chen, Norman V. Loayza, and Marta Reynal-Querol, "The Aftermath of Civil War," *The World Bank Economic Review* 22, no. 1 (2008): 63–85, doi: 10.1093/wber/lhn001 (accessed 14 September 2012). In this study, conflict periods sometimes included shorter interwar peace periods (less than 10 years).

347 Lai and Thyne, "The Effect of Civil War on Education," 277 (accessed 4 September 2012).

348 Ibid., 284 (accessed 4 September 2012).

349 EPDC, "How Do Violent Conflicts Affect School Enrolment?" 6 (accessed 4 September 2012).

350 The *World Bank Economic Review* study has a considerable smaller number of countries than the PRIO and Lai and Thyne studies, meaning that its findings are likely a less reliable guide of the overall effect of war on education.

351 There is also the possibility, canvassed by Lai and Thyne themselves, that the positive relationship that they find between conflict and low educational outcomes is affected by the omitted variable bias discussed above—i.e., that the association between war and educational outcomes that they report could be caused by factors that were not included in their statistical models. See Lai and Thyne, "The Effect of Civil War on Education," 289 (accessed 4 September 2012).

352 For a discussion of the differences in results in the literature on civil war onset, see Håvard Hegre and Nicholas Sambanis, "Sensitivity Analysis of Empirical Results on Civil War Onset," *Journal of Conflict Resolution* 50, no. 4 (2006): 508–535, doi: 10.1177/0022002706289303 (accessed 4 September 2012).

353 We reiterate a cautionary note here. The trends that we have been describing are averages—what is *generally* the case and certainly not what is *always* the case. The averages will, of course, include many cases where war does indeed have disastrous impacts on educational outcomes. These cases are the ones that receive the most attention from policy-makers, that generate the headlines, and that inform the mainstream narrative. Those cases where educational outcomes improve in conflicts at a more rapid rate than the average get no attention.

354 UNESCO EFA Global Monitoring Report Team, *The Hidden Crisis*, 126.

355 Ibid., 159.

356 Ibid.

357 However, even if conflict is *not* the primary cause of low educational outcomes in war-affected countries, it may well exacerbate them.

358 The nonconflict fragile states in the PRIO study have consistently lower educational attainments than those in conflict. See Gates et al., "Consequences of Civil Conflict," 41.

359 See INEE, http://www.ineesite.org/ (accessed 4 September 2012) and INCAF, http://www.oecd.org/dac/conflictandfragility/44282247.pdf (accessed 4 September 2012).

360 Some of the research of the INEE focuses on fragility in explaining educational and other development outcomes. See INEE, http://www.ineesite.org/ (accessed 4 September 2012). For an overview of the concept of state fragility as it applies to education, see Jacqueline Mosselson, Wendy Wheaton, and Paul St. John Frisoli, "Education and Fragility: A Synthesis of the Literature," *Journal of Education for International Development* 4, no. 1 (2009).

361 Monty G. Marshall and Benjamin R. Cole, *Global Report 2011: Conflict, Governance, and State Fragility* (Vienna, VA: CSP, 2011), 21, http://www.systemicpeace.org/GlobalReport2011.pdf (accessed 4 September 2012). The total global fragility score hides considerable variation between individual countries, of course. The CSP's 2011 *Global Report* points out that from 1995 to 2010, state fragility ratings improved for 115—or 72 percent—of the 161 countries on its list. For 27 countries (17 percent), the ratings stayed the same, while 19 (12 percent) showed a deterioration (23). Different fragility measures provide somewhat different results. The CSP index includes OECD countries, as well as developing states. On the other hand, Carleton University's Country Indicators for Foreign Policy (CIFP) shows data for developing countries only and finds that fragility increased from 1980 to 1997 and then stopped rising and stayed at about the same level until 2006. See David Carment and Yiagadeesen (Teddy) Samy, "Extent and Sources of State Fragility and Failure: Core Factors in Fragility and Failure," PowerPoint presentation, http://www4.carleton.ca/cifp/app/serve.php/1243.pdf (accessed 4 September 2012). Over an overlapping period (1995–2010), the CSP dataset shows a global decline in fragility of some 20 percent.

362 Note that the implications of the descriptive statistics in the PRIO study are not exactly the same as the findings of the econometric analysis. In the former case, the PRIO graphics simply show the net trend for a range of development indicators. These graphs—like Figure 4.7, for example—show how development outcomes differ between countries affected by conflict and nonconflict countries. But they do *not* tell us whether conflict has an impact on these development indicators that may be overridden by other factors.

Sven Torfinn / Panos Pictures. SOMALIA.

TRENDS IN HUMAN INSECURITY

Part II analyzes global and regional trends in organized violence. It sheds light on new research into the deadliness of external military interventions and scrutinizes recent claims that civil wars are becoming more difficult to resolve.

TRENDS IN HUMAN INSECURITY

Introduction

Civil wars in which external military forces fight in support of one of the warring parties are on average twice as deadly as other civil conflicts. Moreover, military interventions by minor powers can be just as deadly as those by major powers.

There is little support for recent claims that civil conflicts are generally becoming more difficult to end and thus more of a concern. Long-lasting conflicts are the exception rather than the rule, and conflicts that recur tend to be small in scale.

New data on non-state conflicts show no evidence to support claims that these generally low-intensity struggles are becoming either more frequent or deadly. They do show, however, that organized violence between groups tends to be very short.

The number of attacks on civilians in 2009 was the lowest level recorded since 1989, the first year for which data are available. Although death tolls increased slightly from 2008 to 2009, they have declined substantially since the mid-1990s.

INTRODUCTION

Part II of this _Report_ studies global and regional trends in the incidence and severity of armed conflict and other forms of organized violence. The analysis highlights, among other things, the deadly effect of military support for warring parties in civil wars and critically reviews claims that armed conflicts are becoming more difficult to resolve.

This part presents updated data on three important types of organized violence, which the _Human Security Report_ first analyzed in 2005:

- _State-based armed conflicts_—international conflicts and civil wars—in which at least one of the warring parties is the government of a state.
- _Non-state armed conflicts,_ which consist of fighting between two armed groups, neither of which is the government of a state.
- _One-sided violence,_ or targeted attacks on unarmed civilians.

The updated datasets confirm findings of our earlier editions of the _Report._ The deadliness of warfare has seen a marked decline over the last 50–60 years, and there are now significantly fewer armed conflicts around the world than during the peak of the early 1990s. Plus, contrary to popular notions, we find no evidence that non-state conflicts and one-sided violence have increased over the past two decades, the period covered by the datasets. The number of campaigns of one-sided violence, for example, reached a low point in 2009—the last year covered by the dataset used here.

Chapter 5 gives a global and regional overview of trends in the number and deadliness of state-based armed conflicts. It finds that the location of the world's deadliest conflicts has shifted over time. From the 1950s through to the end of the 1970s, most of the world's battle deaths occurred in East and Southeast Asia and Oceania. More recently, the conflicts in

Sri Lanka, Afghanistan, Pakistan, and Iraq make Central and South Asia and the Middle East and North Africa the deadliest regions in the world.

The analysis furthermore takes a closer look at external military interventions in *intrastate conflicts*: civil wars that involve the military forces of external powers fighting in support of one of the warring parties are shown to be twice as deadly as other intrastate conflicts. We argue that calls for intervention in support of a warring party in an ongoing intrastate conflict should therefore be viewed with caution.

Chapter 6 investigates the claim that civil wars are becoming increasingly difficult to end, which has caused concern among researchers and policy-makers in recent years. The chapter represents the first systematic analysis of trends in conflict duration and recurrence and finds that the data suggest a much less alarming picture. In contrast to what has been argued in the past, there is little support for an overall trend towards longer conflicts; civil wars that started since the end of the Cold War have tended to be less persistent than previous ones.

It is true that many contemporary conflicts stop only to start again after a short interruption. But we show that this is not so much, as some have suggested, because efforts to permanently resolve armed violence through negotiations are failing. Instead, the high rate of conflict relapse is in large part due to the fact that most of today's civil wars are very small in scale, involve weak rebel groups, and often take place in remote areas. Such struggles are less likely to end in victories or peace agreements, which are more stable outcomes.

Peace agreements reduce armed violence and save lives even when they fail to ensure lasting peace.

Chapter 6 also presents another important finding that has so far rarely been noticed: peace agreements are much more successful in reducing armed violence than is usually assumed, and they save lives even when they fail to ensure lasting peace. The intensity of a conflict drops by more than 80 percent if it restarts after a peace deal—a more dramatic change than for any other type of conflict termination.

Our data on non-state conflicts now cover the entire post-Cold War period between 1989 and 2009. Chapter 7 discusses the often volatile trends in the incidence of these conflicts and the number of victims. It looks more closely at the characteristics of this type of violence and the actors involved. The analysis highlights, among other things, that non-state conflicts are much shorter and less deadly than their state-based counterparts.

Finally, Chapter 8 reviews the data on targeted attacks against civilians. Although deaths from one-sided violence increased slightly from 2008 to 2009, these figures are substantially lower compared to the mid-1990s. Most campaigns of and deaths from one-sided violence were concentrated in sub-Saharan Africa between 1989 and 2009; however both campaigns and deaths in the region have decreased significantly in recent years.

Teun Voeten / Panos Pictures. AFGHANISTAN.

State-Based Armed Conflict

In this chapter, we analyze trends in the number and deadliness of *state-based armed conflicts*—those in which at least one of the warring parties is a government. We show how the geographic locale of the deadliest wars has shifted over time. In the first three decades that followed the end of World War II, most of the world's battle deaths were in East and Southeast Asia and Oceania. In the 1980s, the Middle East and North Africa was the most violent region; in the 1990s, it was sub-Saharan Africa. By the middle of the new millennium, Central and South Asia and the Middle East and North Africa had become the world's deadliest regions. Most recently, the deadliest conflicts in the world are concentrated in these two regions, notably the wars in Sri Lanka, Afghanistan, Pakistan, and Iraq.

Internationalized intrastate conflicts are civil wars in which external military forces fight in support of one warring side.

Finally, we examine the complicated phenomenon of *internationalized intrastate conflicts*—civil wars in which external military forces intervene and fight in support of at least one of the warring sides. These conflicts include many of the wars involving major powers that have dominated the media headlines for decades—the Vietnam War, the Soviet intervention in Afghanistan, the civil war in Iraq following the invasion in 2003, and the current conflict in Afghanistan.[1]

We find that these wars are consistently deadlier than civil wars in which there is no external military intervention. Given the large numbers of troops and heavy conventional weapons that major powers can bring to civil-war battlefields, this is perhaps not surprising. What *is* surprising is that civil wars in which there are military interventions by *minor* powers can be as deadly as those in which major powers are involved.

Global Trends in State-Based Armed Conflict

The last *Human Security Report* noted that the number of state-based armed conflicts rose by 25 percent between 2004 and 2008. While this was a significant increase, and clearly a source of concern, we cautioned against interpreting this five-year increase as a long-term trend towards an increased incidence of warfare around the world.

As Figure 5.1 below demonstrates, the number of conflicts in 2009 was a third lower, at 36, than in the peak year of 1992. The latest data, which we are currently analyzing for the next *Human Security Report,* show that the number of conflicts appears to be stabilizing roughly at this level—i.e., between 30 and 40 active conflicts per year—despite significant year-to-year fluctuations.

Data Source: UCDP/PRIO.[2]

The number of conflicts declined steadily after the Cold War, then rose from 2004 to 2008. There was a slight decrease in 2009; however this does not appear to mark the start of a downward trend.

Battle deaths also increased by around a third from 2005 to 2008.[3] But this increase should be seen in the context of the dramatic decline in battle deaths over the past 60-plus years, shown in Figure 5.2. The average number of battle deaths per conflict in the post-Cold War period[4] is some 76 percent lower than the average during the Cold War period.

A large part of this long-term, but uneven, decline in battle deaths has been a result of the reduction in the number of high-intensity conflicts, counted as wars in years when they cause at least 1,000 battle deaths. As shown in Figure 5.3, in the new millennium the average number of wars being fought each year was just over half that in the 1990s.

Wars also make up a decreasing share of all conflicts.[5] During the Cold War period—from 1950 to the end of the 1980s—31 percent of conflict years resulted in at least 1,000 battle deaths. That figure dropped to 25 percent in the 1990s, and even further to 19 percent in the new millennium.

Figure 5.2 Global Trends in Battle Deaths from State-Based Conflicts, 1946–2008[6]

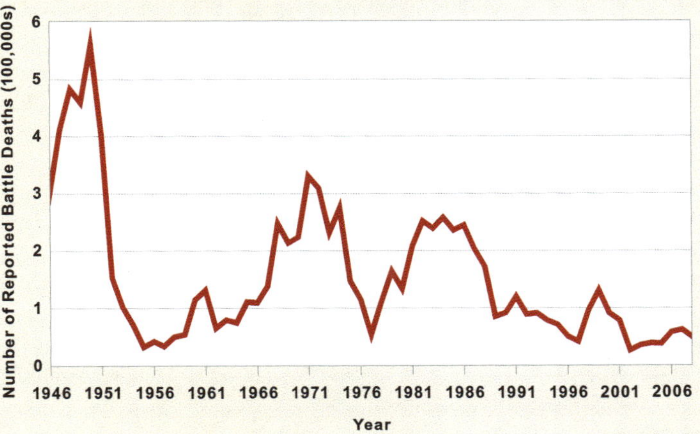

Data Source: PRIO.[7]

Battle deaths peaked in 1950 due to the Korean War, in the 1970s due to the Vietnam War, and in the 1980s due to the Iran-Iraq and Afghanistan wars. Despite these deadly wars, battle deaths have declined since 1946.

Figure 5.3 Trends in Wars, 1950–2009

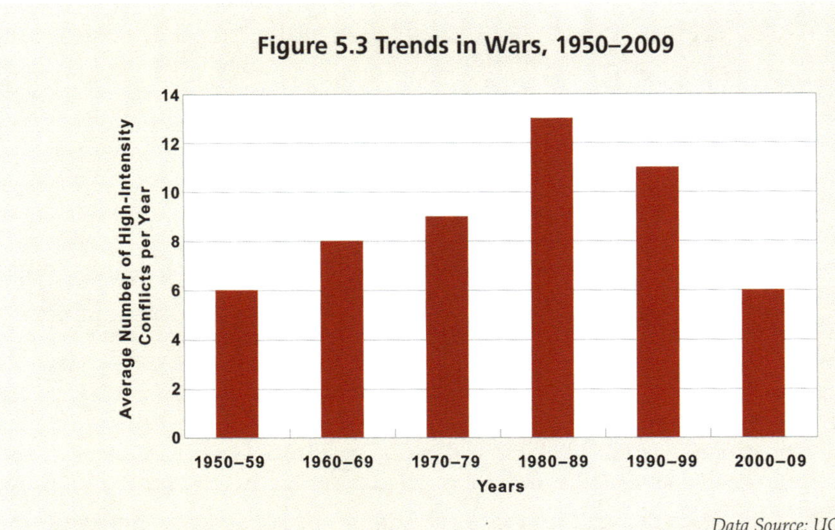

Data Source: UCDP/PRIO.

The average number of high-intensity conflicts per year—defined as conflicts that reach 1,000 or more battle deaths in a calendar year—halved from the 1980s to the new millennium.

The Deadliest Conflicts

In 2009 the three deadliest conflicts in the world were all in Central and South Asia—in Sri Lanka, Pakistan, and Afghanistan.

There were just three high-intensity conflicts outside of Central and South Asia in 2009: in Iraq, Somalia, and the Democratic Republic of the Congo (DRC), where Rwandan and Congolese forces battled the Democratic Forces for the Liberation of Rwanda (FDLR).[8]

Of these six high-intensity conflicts, those in Afghanistan, Iraq, Somalia, and the DRC are internationalized intrastate conflicts. This type of conflict, as we explain later, tends to be considerably deadlier than civil wars in which there is no military intervention by external powers.

Four of 2009's six most deadly conflicts, those in Afghanistan, Iraq, Pakistan, and Somalia, are associated with international and local campaigns against Islamist groups. The security implications of this association are discussed in the last *Human Security Report*.[9]

Regional Trends in State-Based Armed Conflict

Since the end of World War II, the location of the world's deadliest conflicts has shifted repeatedly.

From 1946 to the end of the 1970s, East and Southeast Asia and Oceania was by far the deadliest region in the world, with most of the deaths being caused by the Chinese Civil War, the Korean War, and the wars in Indochina. But, as we demonstrated in the last *Human Security Report*, with the effective ending of foreign military intervention (mostly by the US and China), the region's major wars were over by the early 1980s and battle-death tolls declined steeply. Since the end of the Cold War, East and Southeast Asia and Oceania has suffered fewer battle deaths than any other region.

In the early 1980s, the Middle East and North Africa became the deadliest region in the world, with the war between Iran and Iraq alone causing hundreds of thousands of battle deaths. But in the late 1980s, death tolls in the region declined sharply, driving the global death toll down in the process.

Half of the World's Battle Deaths in the Post-Cold War Period Have Occurred in Sub-Saharan Africa

The battle-death toll in sub-Saharan Africa declined in the late 1980s, but in the second half of the 1990s it increased again—this time dramatically. This increase meant that sub-Saharan Africa was by far the deadliest region in the world in the 1990s. And as Figure 5.4 indicates, nearly half of the world's state-based battle deaths between 1989 and 2009 were caused by wars in sub-Saharan Africa, most of them in the 1990s.

But in the new millennium there was another radical change as the number of people being killed in state-based conflicts across the region dropped dramatically. While the number of conflicts in sub-Saharan Africa has remained high, as Figure 5.5 demonstrates, the average number of battle deaths per conflict in the region has declined by 90 percent since 2000.

**Figure 5.4 Regional Trends in Battle Deaths
from State-Based Conflicts, 1989–2009**[10]

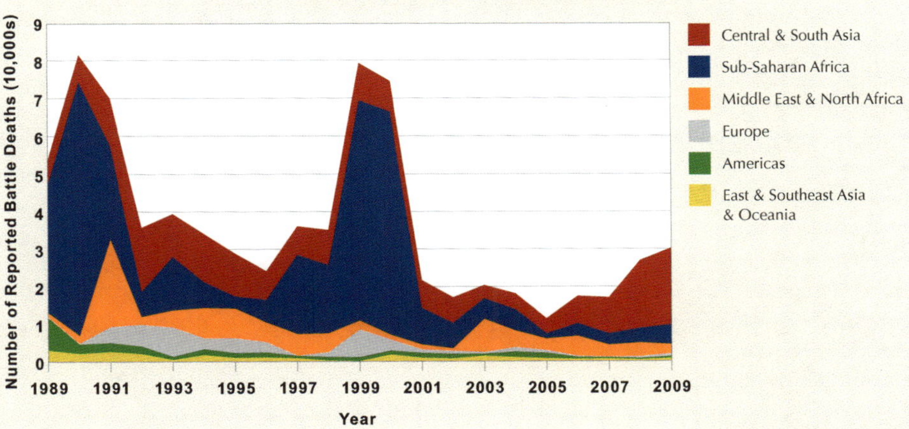

Data Source: UCDP/HSRP Dataset.[11]

Nearly half of the world's battle deaths between 1989 and 2009 took place in sub-Saharan Africa, but deaths there have declined since 2000. From the mid-2000s onwards, Central and South Asia has been the deadliest region.

Note: Figure 5.4 is a "stacked graph," meaning that the number of battle deaths in each region is indicated by the depth of the band of colour. The top line shows the global total number of battle deaths in each year.

**Figure 5.5 State-Based Conflicts and Battle Deaths
in Sub-Saharan Africa, 1989–2009**

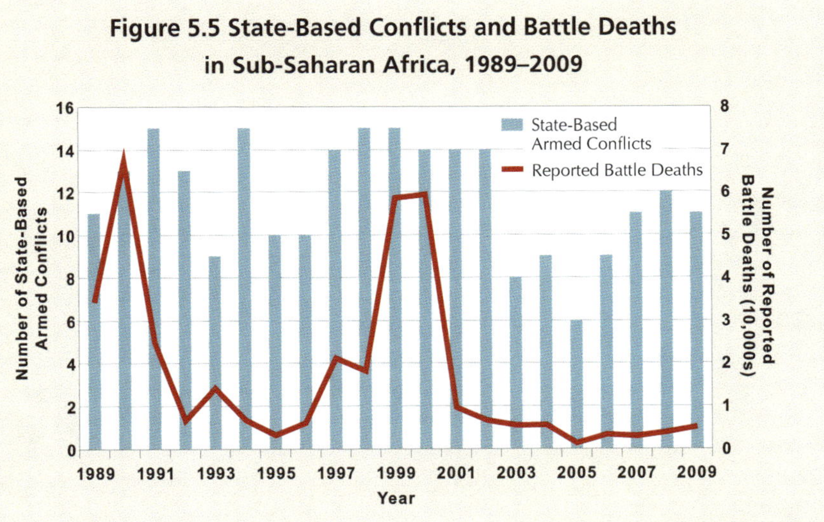

Data Source: UCDP/HSRP Dataset.

The number of conflicts in sub-Saharan Africa was high throughout the post-Cold War period. However, just five of those conflicts accounted for the majority of battle deaths in the region.

Sub-Saharan Africa has been by far the most conflict-prone region in the post-Cold War years, with nearly a third of the world's total conflicts.

However, over half of the region's battle-death toll has been due to just five conflicts, each of which caused at least 10,000 battle deaths in a calendar year at some stage in the conflict. Two of these wars were civil conflicts in Ethiopia. There was a single international conflict between Ethiopia and Eritrea, and civil wars in Angola and the Republic of Congo (sometimes referred to as "Congo-Brazzaville") that also exceeded 10,000 reported battle deaths in a year. Since the end of the Cold War, only one conflict outside sub-Saharan Africa has reached this level of intensity in at least one year: the war following the Iraqi invasion of Kuwait in 1991.

> Sub-Saharan Africa has been by far the most conflict-prone region in the post-Cold War years, with nearly a third of the world's total conflicts.

None of these conflicts have been active since 2002, however, and their ending has made a major contribution to the decline in global death tolls in the new millennium.

The list of the deadliest cases of organized violence also includes the 1994 Rwandan genocide and the violence in the DRC (sometimes referred to as "Congo-Kinshasa") during the late 1990s and early 2000s, the latter of which has been described as "the world's deadliest conflict since World War II."[12] In these cases, however, the majority of deaths resulted from one-sided attacks against civilians. Data on one-sided violence are discussed in more detail in Chapter 8 of this *Report*.

Central and South Asia Is Currently the World's Deadliest Region

In the mid-2000s, death tolls due to conflicts in Central and South Asia and in the Middle East and North Africa increased relative to all other regions. As the battle-death toll in Iraq decreased in 2007, however, Central and South Asia has clearly become the world's deadliest region.

Recently, death tolls in Central and South Asia have escalated significantly, more than quintupling between 2005 and 2009, as shown in Figure 5.6.

In 2009 Central and South Asia alone accounted for two-thirds of the world's total battle deaths from state-based armed conflict. The region had four times as many battle deaths as the next deadliest region, sub-Saharan Africa.

The fact that the number of armed conflicts in the region has remained fairly stable while the number of battle deaths has increased dra-

> Death tolls in Central and South Asia have escalated, more than quintupling between 2005 and 2009.

matically means that, on average, these conflicts are becoming deadlier. But this higher average is driven by just three conflicts. The wars in Sri Lanka, Pakistan, and Afghanistan were the three deadliest conflicts in the world both in 2008 and, as noted earlier, in 2009.

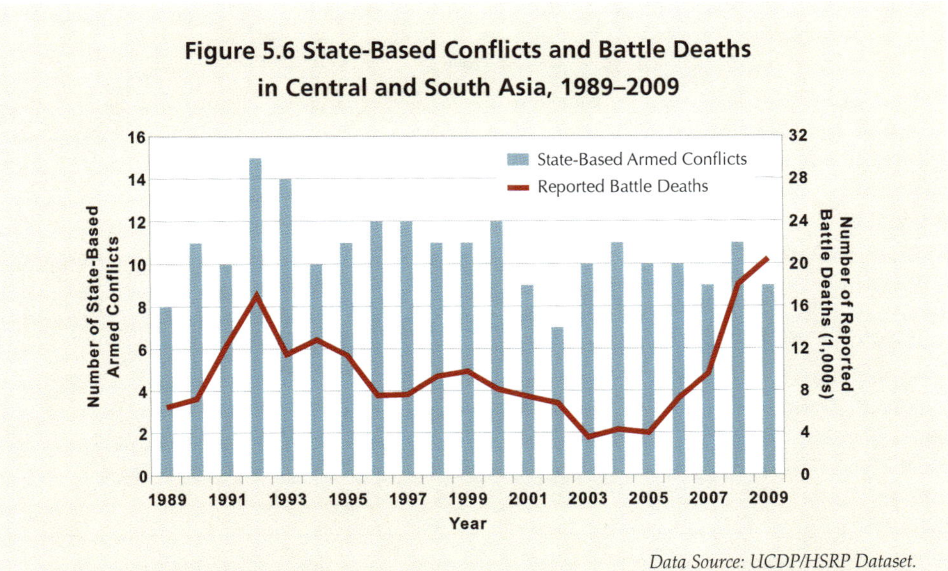

Data Source: UCDP/HSRP Dataset.

Although conflict numbers in this region have not changed much, death tolls quintupled from 2005 to 2009 due to conflicts in Sri Lanka, Pakistan, and Afghanistan, the world's deadliest conflicts in 2008 and 2009.

In 2009 the government of Sri Lanka decisively defeated the Liberation Tigers of Tamil Eelam (LTTE), and there have been no battle deaths associated with this conflict since mid-2009. However, the other two conflicts, both associated with international and local campaigns against Islamist groups, show no signs of abating.

While these conflicts are currently the world's deadliest, they cost far fewer lives than the deadliest conflicts in previous decades. For example, UCDP researchers estimate that the war between Ethiopia and Eritrea had a battle-death toll of nearly 50,000 in 1999 alone. In Sri Lanka it took some 18 years to reach a comparable cumulative death toll.

The Deadly Impact of Military Interventions

Many of the deadliest conflicts of the past two decades have involved external military forces fighting in civil wars. These internationalized intrastate conflicts are, on average, twice as deadly as intrastate conflicts where there is no military intervention.[13]

Interstate wars tend to have far higher battle-death tolls than civil wars with or without external military support, but as shown in Figure 5.7, conflicts between states have become extraordinarily rare. Since the end of the Cold War there have been three times as many internationalized intrastate conflicts as interstate conflicts.

Internationalized intrastate conflicts are a type of civil conflict in which the military forces of one or more external governments fight in support of one of the warring parties.[14] This includes so-called humanitarian interventions if external military forces officially take sides and support a party to the conflict with troops. However, the definition does not include most peacekeeping missions, which are usually deployed to support negotiated settlements—and sometimes to help protect the peace against spoilers—but not to further the goals of a combatant.[15]

States intervene militarily in civil conflicts in other countries for a variety of reasons. They may send forces to protect political or ideological interests, as was the case in the so-called proxy wars of the Cold War era, or in response to humanitarian crises. Intervening states often have a complex combination of motivating factors, many of which may remain unstated. Our data do not provide information on these motivations but rather enable us to focus on the common characteristic of these conflicts: the presence of external military forces supporting at least one of the warring sides.

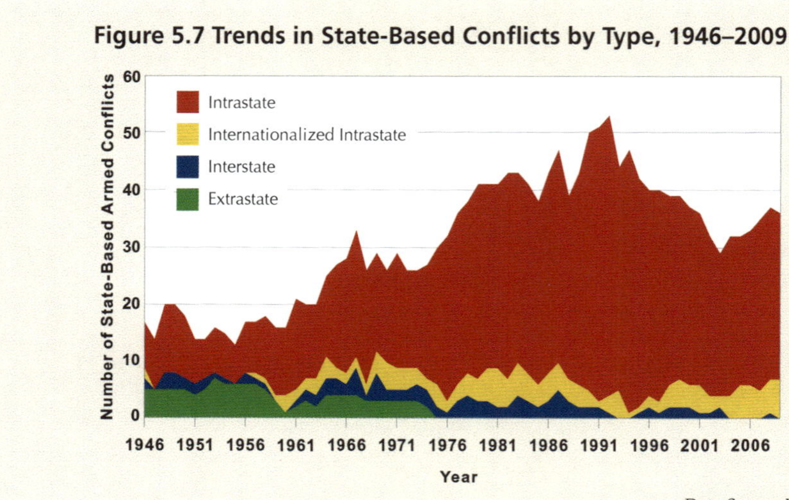

Figure 5.7 Trends in State-Based Conflicts by Type, 1946–2009

Data Source: UCDP/PRIO.

Extrastate—or anticolonial—conflicts ended by 1975, while interstate conflicts became rare in the 2000s. As a result of this shift, all conflicts in 2009 were intrastate, though nearly a quarter were internationalized.

Note: Figure 5.7 is a "stacked graph," meaning that the number of conflicts in each category is indicated by the depth of the band of colour. The top line shows the total number of conflicts of all types in each year.

The highest-profile internationalized intrastate conflict currently is in Afghanistan, where the United States and its allies intervened on behalf of the Northern Alliance and now support the current government against the Taliban. The US-led involvement in Iraq started as an interstate war with the foreign forces fighting to end Saddam Hussein's regime, but in 2004 the conflict shifted to a civil conflict in which the United States and its allies are militarily supporting the current government in its fight against rebel forces. Earlier examples of internationalized intrastate conflicts include the American intervention in South Vietnam in the 1960s and early 1970s and the Cuban presence in Angola in the 1970s and 1980s. France's reinstatement of Léon M'ba as president of Gabon in 1964 was a smaller-scale internationalized intrastate conflict.

As the Cuban example shows, intervening countries can be non-major powers. North and South Vietnam (and later the Socialist Republic of Vietnam) played a major role in the Cambodian civil war throughout the 1970s and 1980s, while the armed forces of a major power, the US, were also involved. In the DRC the armies of several neighbouring countries fought in the civil war in the late 1990s and early 2000s without the presence of a major power.

As we will show in the following section, civil wars with foreign military support differ from other intrastate conflicts in a number of ways. Most notably, they are on average twice as deadly as conflicts in which no external powers are involved.

Intervention is Associated with Intensified and Prolonged Conflict

The trend data on internationalized intrastate conflicts show a strong positive correlation between external involvement in a conflict and that conflict's battle-death toll, but this does not necessarily mean that the former caused the latter. The involvement of foreign combat troops and their weaponry in a civil war clearly has the *potential* to increase fatalities, but it may also be the case that foreign military support is more likely in conflicts that are already deadly.

The internationalized intrastate conflict in Iraq from 2004 to 2009 resulted in much higher battle-death tolls than any previous civil conflict in Iraq. In this conflict there is no doubt that the intervention was one of the major drivers of the huge death toll in the country. In other cases the pre-existing level of organized violence prompted the intervention that eventually stopped the fighting. Cases in point are the intervention of the US-led coalition in Kosovo in 1999 and the UK deployment of combat troops in Sierra Leone in 2000.

> The limited research findings provide little more than confirmation that external support is usually associated with high battle-death tolls.

Surprisingly little systematic research has been done on the impact of external military support on conflict intensity. The limited findings so far provide little more than confirmation that external support is usually associated with high battle-death tolls, but quantitative analyses tend not to draw strong conclusions about causality.

Bethany Lacina, of the University of Rochester, finds that "[a] strong predictor that a civil war will be severe is the availability of foreign assistance to the combatants"—but her findings do not include an analysis of external military support in civil conflicts since the end of the Cold War.[16] More recently, Kristine Eck, of Uppsala University, has found that the risk of conflict escalation—i.e., of higher death tolls—"increases by 192 percent if an external state intervenes militarily on the side of the rebels," suggesting that this is because "obtaining troops and military resources from an external state" increases the "strength of the rebel organization."[17]

A number of researchers have examined the impact of external military support on the duration of conflict. Patrick Regan, of Binghamton University, who has done extensive research on different types of intervention, finds for example that "longer running conflicts tend to have more outside interventions." But again, he notes that the research design of his study "cannot discriminate between the cause and effect."[18]

Some researchers argue that a one-sided intervention may increase the probability of victory for the warring party that receives the support and that this will shorten the conflict,[19] but this claim is contested.[20] Most agree that intervention leading to a balance of power between the warring parties is likely to prolong conflicts since neither side will have the forces necessary to defeat the other.[21]

David Cunningham, of the University of Maryland, offers a somewhat different perspective, finding that the effect of external military interventions on conflict duration results from cases "in which the intervener has an independent agenda." He argues that if there are separate agendas to be satisfied, the conflict will consequently be more difficult to settle.[22]

Cunningham uses the example of South African and Cuban involvement in Angola's civil war to illustrate how the presence of an external party can be an important obstacle to peace: with the winding down of the Cold War in the late 1980s, the political imperatives that had led South Africa[23] to support the National Union for the Total Independence of Angola (UNITA) rebels and the Cuban government to support the left-oriented Angolan government lost their salience. Following an agreement in 1988, Cuban and South African forces withdrew. As Cunningham notes, this "paved the way for an internal peace agreement in Angola in 1991, albeit one that broke down a few years later."[24]

In December 2011 UCDP released a new dataset that provides more information on the involvement of foreign powers in wars. This includes the provision of both military and economic assistance by external actors. UCDP's Therese Pettersson reviewed the new data, and preliminary findings "suggest that there is a positive relationship between external support and conflict intensity."[25]

Are Internationalized Intrastate Conflicts a Growing Threat?

Many scholars see military intervention in civil wars as a phenomenon associated primarily with the security politics of the Cold War. Bethany Lacina, for example, examines the impact of military assistance on conflict severity by comparing the death tolls of conflicts that started during the Cold War with those that started subsequently.[26] She finds that conflicts that started during the Cold War had 1.8 times as many battle deaths as compared to the post-Cold War era.[27] This makes intuitive sense: the high-stakes geopolitics of the Cold War drove many *proxy wars*—conflicts in which the US and the Soviet Union (or their allies) supported warring parties in the developing world. Support related to the ideology of the Cold War, which was often associated with extremely high death tolls, ended with the Cold War.

But while this might suggest that internationalized intrastate conflict numbers should have declined in the aftermath of the Cold War, the reverse has been true. The number of foreign military interventions in civil wars over the past two decades has actually increased, while the number of intrastate conflicts with no such intervention has decreased substantially. In the new millennium the number of conflicts in which external forces have intervened militarily is 70 percent higher than in the 1980s, the last decade of the Cold War.[28] Therese Pettersson, using UCDP's new data on external support, finds that the proportion of "active conflicts with external troop involvement" has gone from an average of 12 percent during the Cold War, to 7 percent in the 1990s, and up to 16 percent in the new millennium. If sustained, the rise in both the number and percentage of conflicts with external military intervention in recent years is a cause for concern.[29]

As the number of internationalized intrastate conflicts increased over the past two decades, their average deadliness showed no discernible upward or downward trend. As Figure 5.8 demonstrates, internationalized intrastate conflicts have remained, on average, deadlier than other intrastate conflicts throughout most of the post-Cold War period. The difference peaks in 1997, a year in which external military support was recorded in only two intrastate conflicts.[30] The civil wars in the DRC ("Congo-Kinshasa") and in the neighbouring Republic of Congo ("Congo-Brazzaville") each resulted in several thousands of battle deaths that year.

Figure 5.8 Death Tolls in Intrastate and Internationalized Intrastate Conflicts, 1989–2009

Data Source: UCDP/HSRP Dataset.

Intrastate conflicts with external military support on one side have been deadlier, on average, than those without. The dramatic spike in 1997 was due to deadly conflicts in the DRC and in the Republic of Congo.

While there are civil conflicts with no foreign military support that are quite deadly, this analysis shows that, on average, conflicts that do involve external armed forces tend to be deadlier. The number of these conflicts, and the proportion of all armed conflicts that involve foreign military support, appears to be increasing. Even though the limited evidence available does not prove that military intervention causes deadlier conflicts—foreign militaries may be more likely to intervene in already deadly wars—it does suggest that a significant risk of escalation may be associated with intervention on behalf of a party to a conflict.

The Surprising Deadliness of Minor Power Intervention

Since the end of World War II, France, the UK, the US, and Russia (USSR) have each shown the ability to independently project power over significant distances.[31] These four countries, which here we consider the major powers, have repeatedly dispatched military forces overseas to assist governments or rebels in fighting civil wars around the world.[32] Some of these interventions—such as those by the US in Vietnam and the Soviets in Afghanistan—have been associated with hundreds of thousands of battle deaths.

It is not surprising that major power interventions, which add highly trained troops and sophisticated weapons systems into ongoing civil wars, are sometimes associated with high battle-death tolls. What *is* surprising is that military interventions by *minor* powers are, in many cases, associated with battle-death tolls that are just as high.[33]

For example, the internationalized intrastate conflict in Angola involved the armed forces of Cuba, South Africa, and the DRC—none of which are here considered major powers. The conflict caused over 1,000 battle deaths every year from 1975 to 1989. This minor power intervention is far more deadly than some examples of major power intervention. The Russian intervention in Georgia's South Ossetia region in 2008 was associated with hundreds, not thousands, of battle deaths, while even fewer fatalities were recorded in the context of the UK's intervention in Sierra Leone in 2000.

> Major power interventions, which add troops and weapons to civil wars, are often associated with high death tolls.

High-profile major power interventions that cause extremely high death tolls—from Vietnam to Afghanistan—capture most of the media's attention. But, in fact, minor power interventions in civil wars are more often associated with high death tolls than major power interventions.

Some 61 percent of minor power interventions—by which we mean external military support that does not involve any of the major powers—in civil wars since 1946 were associated with battle-death tolls that crossed the high-intensity, thousand-battle-death threshold for a year or more. Over the same period, just half of the intrastate conflicts in which major powers intervened crossed this threshold.

Conclusion

Some scholars have suggested that international military interventions are an effective means of ending civil wars. Ann Hironaka, for example, argues that "decisive external intervention" represents a "promising possibility" to end civil wars, citing the NATO missions in Bosnia-Herzegovina and Kosovo as examples.[34] The doctrine of the Responsibility to Protect (R2P), which was endorsed in principle by the UN General Assembly in 2005, also envisages the possibility of Security Council-mandated military interventions by the international community to protect civilians from war crimes, genocides, or other gross violations of human rights, which tend to occur during civil wars.

However, we have shown in this chapter that the support of foreign military forces for a warring party in a civil conflict is very generally associated with higher death tolls than is the case where there is no intervention. While in some cases military intervention can save lives, the reality is that we know very little about the necessary conditions for successful military interventions.

By contrast, there is much evidence to suggest that international efforts to resolve conflicts through diplomacy, negotiations, and peace operations have overall been successful in reducing the number of wars worldwide—as we have discussed in detail in the last *Human Security Report*.[35] The following chapter analyzes trends in the duration and termination of civil wars and argues, among other things, that the large increase in the number of peacemaking and peace-building efforts since the end of the Cold War has helped make recent conflicts less persistent.

Dean Chapman / Panos Pictures. BURMA.

CHAPTER 6

Persistent Armed Conflict: An Increasing Threat?[36]

It is now widely accepted that the number of armed conflicts has declined substantially over the last two decades. But there are warnings of serious and even growing causes for concern: that wars are lasting longer than before and that, even when wars stop, violent conflict is increasingly likely to recur. In short, it is argued conflicts are becoming more difficult to resolve.[37]

This bleak assessment has certainly received support from some influential conflict researchers. For example, James Fearon noted in 2004 that "the average duration of civil wars in progress has been steadily increasing throughout the postwar period, reaching almost 16 years in 1999."[38] Paul Collier and colleagues, as well as Ann Hironaka, have made similar claims.[39] If it is indeed the case that conflicts are lasting longer on average, then this is bad news for efforts to end them.

It is true that numerous conflicts have remained unresolved for decades. The conflict between Israel and the Palestinians was recorded as active for 58 of the 64 years from 1946 to 2009, the period covered by the Uppsala Conflict Data Program (UCDP) and Peace Research Institute Oslo (PRIO) datasets on which we primarily rely for our analyses. Other conflicts that have lasted decades include those in Burma, the Philippines, and Colombia. And even civil wars in Algeria, India, and elsewhere that started more recently—in the 1980s or 1990s—have already continued for more than a decade.

An additional cause for concern is that in an increasing share of instances where conflicts have stopped, the violence starts up again within a short time. The World Bank *World Development Report (WDR)* noted in 2011 that repeated cycles of violence and recurring civil wars have become "a dominant form of armed conflict in the world today," pointing out that "90 percent of conflicts initiated in the 21st century were in countries that had already had a civil war."[40]

If these analyses are correct—if conflicts are becoming much more protracted, more likely to restart once stopped and therefore more difficult to resolve—this raises an important question. Were the vast number of international initiatives that were launched after the end of the Cold War to stop conflicts and prevent them from starting again as effective as the Human Security Report Project (HSRP) and others have argued?

However, while recognizing that conflict persistence is an important policy issue, we argue in this chapter that a closer examination of the data reveals a considerably more encouraging picture than other authors suggest. Most of today's conflict episodes are relatively short; long-lasting conflicts are increasingly the exception rather than the rule. Persistent conflicts are often very small in scale, and the higher rates of recurrence of conflict result in large part because conflicts have become more difficult to win—but not necessarily more difficult to resolve. An increasing proportion of conflicts is terminated by negotiated settlements, the majority of which prevent the recurrence of violence. We further find that even when peace deals collapse, the death toll due to subsequent fighting is dramatically reduced.

Defining and Measuring Conflict Persistence

What do we mean by *conflict persistence*? Generally, concern about armed conflicts arises not because governments and their non-state rivals have serious disputes, but primarily because they attempt to resolve such disputes through armed violence, which is highly destructive and disruptive. Simply speaking, a *persistent conflict* is therefore one that involves many years of fighting.

Conflicts that have resulted in armed combat for long periods without interruption are persistent according to this definition, but so too are those that repeatedly stop and then start again, accumulating many years of fighting in the process. We therefore approach persistence from different angles, looking at the duration of armed conflicts, as well as rates of conflict recurrence. Findings on how long conflicts last and how frequently they recur, however, depend to some extent on how onsets and terminations of conflicts are defined.

> Studies on duration and recurrence focus on civil wars because they are the most common conflict type and the most persistent.

Most studies on conflict duration and recurrence focus on civil wars—or *intrastate conflicts* as they are defined in the datasets used here—because they are not only the most common type of conflict but also the most persistent. Following this practice, the chapter will also be limited to conflicts that occur within rather than between states.[41] An armed intrastate conflict in UCDP/PRIO terms consists of state forces fighting one or more rebel groups over either government power or the control of a certain territory, leading to at least 25 battle deaths per year.

But how do we distinguish between a new conflict and a recurrence? And what exactly does "uninterrupted" fighting mean? Does a cessation of hostilities lasting for a few years mark the end of a conflict or simply the end of an episode within the same armed struggle?

Some researchers consider a conflict terminated when it causes fewer than 1,000 battle deaths within a calendar year; others apply lower casualty thresholds and require a two-year break in the fighting to qualify as a termination.[42] One dataset may record certain events as a single long-lasting conflict, another might count the same events as a series of violent episodes within one conflict, while a third may count these events as two separate conflicts. Trends and analytical findings based on these definitions differ as a result.

> When the conflict's battle-death toll falls below 25 deaths for one calendar year, this marks the end of a conflict *episode*.

The UCDP/PRIO armed conflict dataset and the related UCDP conflict terminations dataset that we primarily use here avoid this problem by allowing the study of both distinct episodes of fighting as well as conflicts consisting of several such episodes of fighting between the same actors or over the same issues.[43]

The datasets code a conflict as *active* for each year in which it results in at least 25 battle deaths. When the conflict's death toll falls below this threshold for one calendar year—and thus the fighting is interrupted—this marks the end of a conflict *episode*.[44]

Even when the fighting dies down below this death-toll threshold, the conflict is not necessarily over. The dispute between Israel and the Lebanese group Hezbollah, for example, was last active (using the UCDP/PRIO definition) in 2006, but few would argue that the conflict—the core antagonism between the rival parties—is really over. The cessation of hostilities in 2006 is counted in the UCDP/PRIO dataset as the end of an episode. If violence breaks out again between these two parties, the dataset will list a new episode within the same conflict. A new conflict, on the other hand, is recorded when fighting erupts between any two parties over an issue that was not previously contested.

The UCDP terminations dataset records, as precisely as possible, start and end dates for all conflict episodes.[45] The dataset includes information about the outcome of conflict episodes: this can be a peace agreement, a ceasefire, a victory, or—if a conflict falls below the battle-death threshold without a decisive event—"low or no activity" (which in the following discussion we refer to as "other terminations").[46]

All of these termination types can mark the end of a conflict—or merely an interruption of the fighting. Some of the communist insurgencies in East Asia, for example, dropped below the battle-death threshold without an outright victory or a peace settlement but never started up again. In Afghanistan, on the other hand, the conflict halted for a short while due to the victory of the US- and NATO-backed "Northern Alliance" over the Taliban government in 2001. The Taliban have since regrouped and the violence has resumed.

The UCDP/PRIO data allow us to study the duration of armed conflicts, whether as continuous episodes of fighting or in terms of the total number of years that an intermittent dispute results in battle deaths. We can also track patterns in how conflict episodes end and whether or how often they recur. This enables our analysis of persistent conflict to look at both conflicts that last for many years without interruption and conflicts that result in a substantial number of years of warfare spread out over periods of intermittent violent struggle.

This definition includes long-running, uninterrupted conflicts such as the civil war in Colombia, which has been active in each year since 1964, as well as intermittent struggles such as the conflict over the Cabinda territory in Angola, which has broken out in seven episodes of deadly violence since 1989, adding up to nine conflict years in total. In both cases, we have a record of many years of armed clashes, but different patterns of violence.

We use the term "persistent conflict" to include all forms of intrastate conflict that result in more than 25 battle deaths per year over a prolonged time period. The definition includes some conflicts that have seen resolution attempts, but persistent conflicts are not necessarily "intractable";[47] instead, many may persist simply because no real effort has been put into ending them.

Are Conflicts Really Lasting Longer than Before?

In 2003 Paul Collier found evidence that "decade by decade, civil wars have been getting longer."[48] This widely accepted finding appears to be supported by other studies: James Fearon, for example, points out that the average duration of civil wars has almost trebled since the 1960s.[49] The UCDP/PRIO dataset, which uses a slightly different definition of armed conflict, reveals a less consistent trend, but the duration of civil wars still shows an increase over the same period.

Due to the different definitions and datasets, Fearon's numbers are not directly comparable with ours. But we argue that this way of measuring trends in duration represents in any case only one part of the picture. A significant problem arises because figures such as those relied upon by Fearon are affected by a strong upward bias over time. The average duration of ongoing conflicts is skewed upward by the longer-running conflicts or conflict episodes.[50] Short conflicts or conflict episodes will be factored into the average as long as they are active. But once they stop, they cease to be part of the sample and their duration will not affect the average the following year, while the longer-running conflicts keep pushing the average up.

> Understanding what determines the persistence of long-running conflicts is important. Yet these conflicts are clearly not the norm.

Thus, as long as some persistent conflicts remain, the average duration of conflicts in progress will go up in most years. Understanding what determines the persistence of these conflicts is important, but as Roy Licklider observes, long-running conflicts are clearly not the norm but rather outliers.[51] And even though Fearon's measure correctly shows that the world has a significant number of persistent conflicts today, it tells us little about how this compares to other time periods.

Focusing on the most persistent cases does not allow us to analyze whether there are now more or fewer persistent conflicts compared to the past. It also does not tell us enough about whether changes in the ways that conflicts are fought and brought to an end have affected their persistence. These are, however, critical questions for the design and evaluation of policy responses.

A Different Perspective Reveals a Decline in Conflict Duration

To understand whether, at any given time, more or fewer conflicts are becoming persistent, it is useful to look at the average duration of conflicts and conflict episodes that started in the same year or the same time period. Unlike other metrics, this ensures that persistent conflicts are not given more weight than other conflicts.

> To understand whether persistence is increasing, it is useful to look at the duration of conflicts and conflict episodes that started in the same period.

When viewed from this angle, the data show that there is ample reason to doubt that most conflicts are lasting longer than they used to. In fact, the average duration of conflict episodes, sorted by start date, shows a clear downward trend. Episodes starting in the 1970s lasted almost seven years on average, but the average duration dropped to around four years in the 1980s. By the end of that decade, the average duration was around three years and has remained roughly at the same level since.[52] The drop in duration is slightly larger when we count entire conflicts rather than just episodes.[53]

We must be careful, however: measuring trends in duration based on start dates also contains a bias. In this case, it is downward: a conflict episode that started in 1950, for example, could theoretically have lasted 60 years by the year 2009—the most current entry in the dataset—while the maximum duration of an episode starting in 2006 would be four years. The most recent conflicts may only appear to be short at this stage because we cannot look into the future to determine their end dates.

But the sharp decline in the duration of conflict episodes—by more than half—around the mid-1980s is too steep to be wholly the result of this bias. Not only did some long-standing conflicts end during the late 1980s but the proportion of civil conflicts lasting longer than average has declined significantly since the 1980s.

> By the end of the 1980s, the average duration of an episode was around three years and has remained roughly the same since.

Long Periods of Fighting Have Become Less Common

These two different ways of calculating the average duration of civil wars both have their limitations, as shown above. Another way to track how civil war duration has changed over time is to determine how many of the conflicts that started each year eventually exceed a specified length. When applied to uninterrupted episodes of fighting, this measure shows no bias over time, since each episode has the same chance of reaching the threshold. If the proportion of conflict episodes that are longer than the specified length has risen over time, then this clearly indicates an increase in conflict persistence.

Civil war episodes since the end of World War II have lasted on average approximately four years and three months. We therefore applied a threshold of five years to capture conflict episodes that have been longer than average.[54] The results are shown in Figure 6.1.

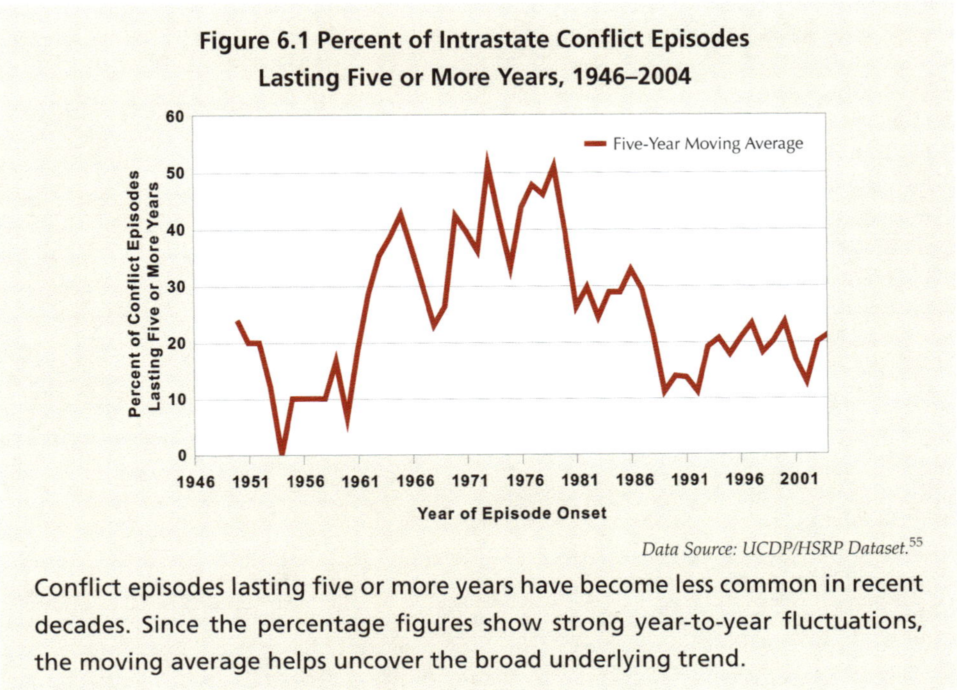

Figure 6.1 Percent of Intrastate Conflict Episodes Lasting Five or More Years, 1946–2004

Data Source: UCDP/HSRP Dataset.[55]

Conflict episodes lasting five or more years have become less common in recent decades. Since the percentage figures show strong year-to-year fluctuations, the moving average helps uncover the broad underlying trend.

The trend line in Figure 6.1 shows that onsets of conflict episodes that lasted five years or more have clearly become less common in recent years. Their share was highest during the 1970s, when almost half of all conflict episodes resulted in five or more years of fighting. This was followed by a decline during the 1980s and, since the 1990s, the share of longer-than-average episodes of conflict has remained lower at approximately 20 percent.[56] In other words, roughly 80 percent of the more recent conflict outbreaks were followed by less than five years of continuous fighting. The fact that this figure is significantly higher than during the preceding decades counters claims that there has been a general increase in conflict duration. Recent conflict episodes appear to be less persistent, not more, than those that started earlier.[57]

The duration of uninterrupted conflict episodes gives just one indication of trends in conflict persistence. As explained above, many conflicts stop and start up again after a short break in the fighting. The downward trend shown in Figure 6.1 is confirmed, however, if we look at the cumulative duration of conflicts—i.e., if we consider all conflicts that resulted in a total of five or more active years that may have been interrupted by a period of inactivity. Application of other thresholds as a way of testing the strength of this conclusion does not significantly alter the trend.[58]

Results drawn from data that include intermittent conflicts may change in the future if more conflicts break out in violence again. Still, the fact that the downward trend in onsets of longer-than-average conflicts and conflict episodes is consistent even when the data are examined in various ways undermines claims that conflicts are generally lasting longer and longer, and counters warnings that persistent conflict is an increasing threat.

> Recent conflict episodes appear to be less persistent, not more, than those that started earlier. Roughly 80 percent lasted less than five years.

Summing Up: Conflict Duration Is Not Generally on the Rise

Our analysis demonstrates that different ways of looking at changes in conflict duration over time reveal different trends in conflict persistence. All of these findings convey important messages.

There is no question that a significant number of persistent conflicts exist today. Twelve—or 18 percent—of the 65 civil conflicts recorded between 2000 and 2009 were active in every single year of that decade. This includes the chronic violence in parts of Ethiopia (Oromiya), in Algeria, in India (Assam and Kashmir), and in Colombia. These persistent conflicts pose major challenges and, as discussed above, they drive up the average duration of conflicts in progress.

These cases are, however, not necessarily representative of overall patterns. Civil wars that have persisted for decades are often difficult to resolve and, obviously, get longer every year. But this does not suggest that conflict persistence in general is a bigger problem than it was during previous periods.

> Conflicts that have persisted for decades are difficult to resolve. This does not suggest that persistence is becoming a bigger problem.

Our analysis shows that the conflict episodes that have started recently tend to be short. The overwhelming majority of episodes of fighting that started since the end of the Cold War have been brief. As we have shown, the proportion of conflict episodes that are shorter than five years increased significantly during the 1980s.

Many of the conflicts active today have multiple episodes, stopping and starting again. We will take a closer look at recurrences in the remainder of the chapter. However, the trend towards shorter duration in recent conflicts discussed above still holds true when we add up the total number of active years spread over a number of episodes. The trend revealed in Figure 6.1 does not, therefore, result simply from the fact that today's conflicts tend to split into many short episodes. More than a third of the conflicts that started since the end of the Cold War have been both short and nonrecurring—in other words, they are far from persistent.

Yet, the tendency of many contemporary conflicts to stop and start again after a short lull in fighting is a reality as well. Approximately half the conflicts that started during the 1990s had more than a single episode. Understanding why conflicts start up again after a halt is therefore crucial for explaining trends in conflict persistence and for the design of policies aimed at peacemaking. The following section takes a closer look at how conflicts end and recur.

Increases in Conflict Recurrence

Conflict relapse has become characteristic of today's civil wars. The UCDP armed conflict termination data clearly demonstrate that a substantial number of today's conflicts are "on-and-off affairs"[59] and that the recurrence rate of violent conflict is higher now than at any time since World War II: 60 percent of the conflict terminations between 2000 and 2004 were followed by renewed violence in less than five years.

Judging solely by the increase in the rate of civil war recurrence, we might be tempted to conclude that there is much cause for alarm. If, however, our major reason for concern about armed conflicts is the death and destruction they cause, then a closer look at the data on conflict recurrence reveals that the trend has some reassuring elements. Most importantly, as we explain below, it is very often the case that the conflicts that recur are relatively small and less deadly, not the ones that are responsible for the majority of battle deaths.

> Though the number of old conflicts erupting into new conflict episodes dropped by one-third from the 1990s to the 2000s, it remained at a very high level.

In 2011 the *WDR* observed that the overwhelming majority of the conflicts currently active are recurrences of violence. In fact, the report finds that "every civil war that began since 2003 was in a country that had a previous civil war."[60]

Figure 6.2 confirms this finding by presenting a similar measure. The number of onsets of new conflicts—i.e., conflicts that have not been recorded before—was lower between 2000 and 2009 than in any other decade in the post-World War II period. Outbreaks of new conflicts peaked in the 1990s, with 46 new conflicts, and dropped to just 13 in the first years of the new millennium, a reduction by more than two-thirds. Although the number of old conflicts erupting into new episodes of violent conflict dropped by about one-third over the same period, this number remained at a very high level. The share of recurrences for the years from 2000 to 2009 exceeded those of the Cold War decades by a factor of roughly two or more. Recurrences of earlier civil wars now make up almost 80 percent of all conflict episode outbreaks.

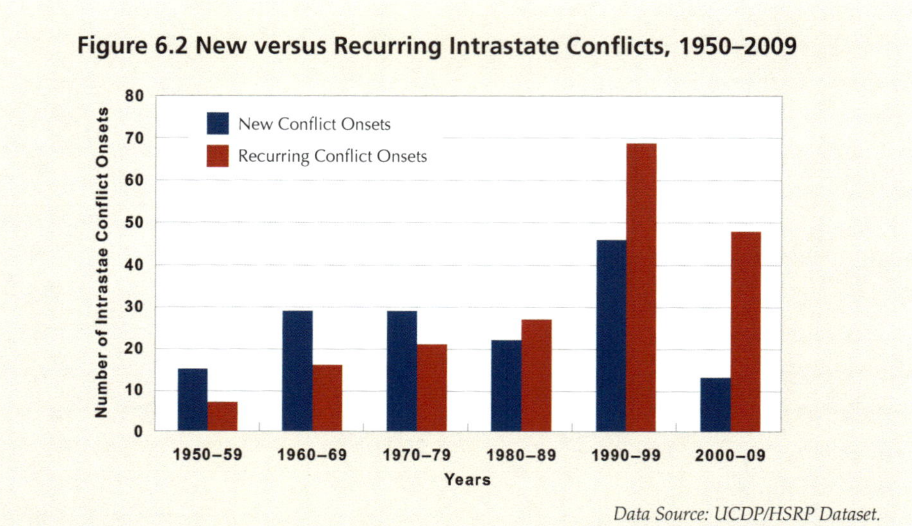

Figure 6.2 New versus Recurring Intrastate Conflicts, 1950–2009

Data Source: UCDP/HSRP Dataset.

Conflicts that recur after a short interruption of the fighting have become very frequent since the end of the Cold War. Yet, encouragingly, the number of new conflict onsets declined sharply after a peak in the 1990s.

Not all of the messages that Figure 6.2 conveys are cause for concern. On the positive side, the drop in the number of new outbreaks of conflict suggests that fewer disputes, whether over territorial autonomy or over who should control government, are turning violent. If instead there was a larger number of new conflicts today, this would certainly be bad news for prevention efforts.

What is more, we have to keep in mind that for a conflict to recur, it first has to stop. The large number of recurring wars must therefore also be seen in the context of the many conflict terminations since the late 1980s. The fact that so many conflicts have terminated is encouraging, but this naturally resulted in more post-conflict settings that always involve a risk of violence recurring.

> The drop in new conflicts suggests that fewer disputes, whether over territory or government, are turning violent.

But the increased number of episodes where violent conflict recurs after a lull remains a concern, because it indicates that terminations of intrastate conflicts have become less stable. The proportion of terminations that are followed by renewed violence in less than five years has shown a substantial and steady increase over the last 40 or so years. Figure 6.3 demonstrates that the rate of recurrence has now reached 60 percent, a more than threefold increase compared to the 1960s.[61] In the first half-decade of the new millennium, the risk of recurrence increased by more than one-third compared to the 1990s.

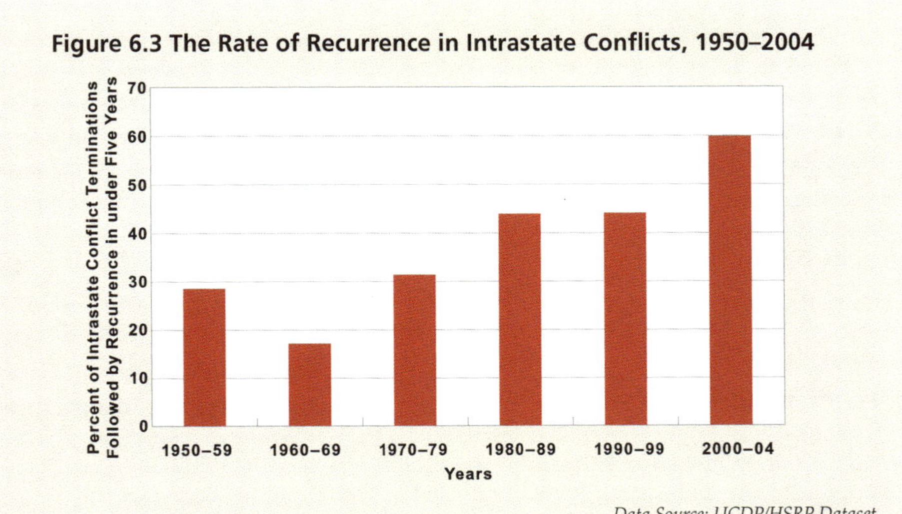

Figure 6.3 The Rate of Recurrence in Intrastate Conflicts, 1950–2004

Data Source: UCDP/HSRP Dataset.

Of the intrastate conflicts that had stopped, the proportion that restarted in under five years has increased significantly since the 1960s. Although this is a concern, the recurring conflicts tend to be less deadly.

Civil Wars Have Become Difficult to Win

Conflict episodes can end in a number of different ways, and some endings are far less stable than others. The prime reason why there is a higher rate of recurrence of violence today is that less stable types of outcomes have become—relatively—much more common. For reasons we explain below, this change is not as big a cause for concern as it may seem.

As mentioned above, the UCDP terminations dataset records whether a conflict episode ends in a victory or a negotiated settlement, which can be a peace agreement or a ceasefire. Conflicts that drop below the 25-deaths activity threshold without a settlement or the defeat of one party fall into the "other" category.[62]

Victories have long been known to be the most stable type of outcome.[63] Table 6.1 shows that between 1950 and 2004, fewer than 20 percent of the conflicts terminated by victories recurred in less than five years. In most cases, victory prevents renewed fighting because the defeated side simply lacks the capability to continue the struggle.

> The reason for the higher rate of recurrence of violence today is that less stable types of outcomes are more common.

By contrast, where hostilities cease as a result of negotiations, both parties often retain their capacity to continue to fight. Given this, and given that the experience of war usually increases suspicion, fear, and mutual antipathy between the parties, it is not surprising that between 1950 and 2004, twice as many ceasefires (38.2 percent) and nearly twice as many peace agreements (32.4 percent) as victories (18.3 percent) were followed by renewed violence within five years.

Table 6.1 also clearly demonstrates that fighting is most likely to recur when a conflict episode ends with neither victory nor negotiated settlement. In most cases where a conflict dies down without a victory or settlement, there is merely a lull in the fighting, followed by renewed violence within a few years.

> In most cases where a conflict dies down without a victory or settlement, there is merely a lull in fighting.

There are cases where conflicts taper off and do not start up again because the rebels quietly give up the fight. This happened, for instance, in Thailand, where the small communist insurgency ended in the 1980s. The rebels were not decisively defeated, nor was there a peace deal, but the conflict has not recurred since.

Yet, this is the exception rather than the rule. Between 1950 and 2004, almost 60 percent of conflict terminations that fell into the "other" category were followed by renewed violence in less than five years. The figure for the early years of the new millennium was nearly 80 percent.

The data presented here show that the risk of conflict recurrence differs considerably for various types of conflict outcomes. But they also demonstrate that the relative frequency of these different outcomes has changed significantly over time. Figure 6.4 displays victories, negotiated settlements, and "other terminations" as a percentage of the total conflict terminations in each decade since 1950. It reveals a major shift over time.

Victories—the type of outcome least likely to be followed by a recurrence of violence—were by far the most common form of conflict termination from the 1950s through the 1970s. But civil wars have become much more difficult to win outright, and victories are becoming very rare.[64] As Figure 6.4 illustrates, approximately only one in 10 of all terminations since 2000 has been a victory by one side over the other.

> Sixty-eight percent of peace agreements and 62 percent of ceasefires recorded in the dataset led to a stable solution of the conflict.

The decline in the number of victories has coincided with a fairly steady increase in negotiated settlements (ceasefires or peace agreements). As Figure 6.4 shows, for each decade of the Cold War period, the share of conflicts ending with a peace agreement or a ceasefire was only 20 percent or less. Since then, however, the share has risen to almost 40 percent.

Table 6.1 shows that in the majority of cases—68 percent for peace agreements and 62 percent for ceasefires—negotiated settlements lead to a stable solution of the conflict. But neither peace agreements nor ceasefires reduce the risk of relapse into violent conflict as much as victories do. That the increase in the number of settlements relative to victories has contributed to a higher overall recurrence rate is therefore no surprise.

Table 6.1 Types of Intrastate Conflict Terminations and Recurrence Rates, 1950–2004

Years	PEACE AGREEMENTS			CEASEFIRES			VICTORIES			OTHER TERMINATIONS			TOTAL TERMINATIONS		
	Total No.	No. Restarted in under 5 Years	% Restarted in under 5 Years	Total No.	No. Restarted in under 5 Years	% Restarted in under 5 Years	Total No.	No. Restarted in under 5 Years	% Restarted in under 5 Years	Total No.	No. Restarted in under 5 Years	% Restarted in under 5 Years	Total No.	No. Restarted in under 5 Years	% Restarted in under 5 Years
1950–59	1	0	0.0	0	0	0.0	14	3	21.4	6	3	50.0	21	6	28.6
1960–69	2	1	50.0	2	0	0.0	18	1	5.6	13	4	30.8	35	6	17.1
1970–79	5	1	20.0	2	0	0.0	18	6	33.3	10	4	40.0	35	11	31.4
1980–89	2	1	50.0	1	0	0.0	18	3	16.7	29	18	62.1	50	22	44.0
1990–99	20	8	40.0	23	9	39.1	21	2	9.5	56	34	60.7	120	53	44.2
2000–04	7	1	14.3	6	4	66.7	4	2	50.0	18	14	77.8	35	21	60.0
Total 1950–2004	37	12	32.4	34	13	38.2	93	17	18.3	132	77	58.3	296	119	40.2

Data Source: UCDP/HSRP Dataset.

Victories were the most stable form of conflict termination for the period 1950–2004, with only 18 percent having restarted in under five years. While peace agreements have a higher rate of conflict recurrence, still only one in three has seen renewed violence within this time threshold. The numbers further suggest that peace agreements have become more stable in the most recent period.

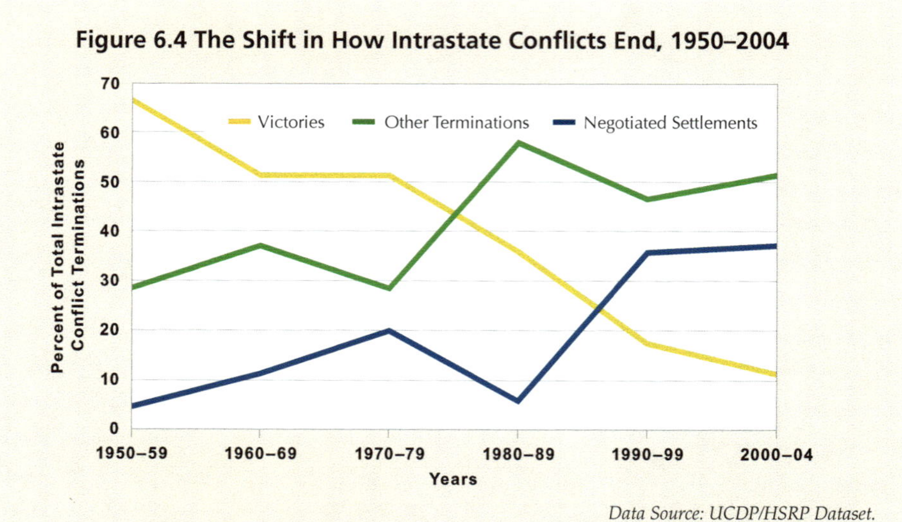

Data Source: UCDP/HSRP Dataset.

The share of intrastate conflicts ending in victories—the most stable termination type—has declined since the end of World War II. This has contributed to the recent elevated recurrence rates in recent years.

Note: Unlike the other line graphs in this section, which show yearly trends, these lines display changes from one decade to the next.

Figure 6.4, however, indicates another major change: unlike during most of the Cold War decades, the majority of today's conflict episodes end without a clear outcome. In the 1980s, "other terminations" surpassed victories as the most common type of outcome. Since then, roughly half of all conflict terminations have been "other terminations," involving neither outright victory nor a ceasefire or peace agreement.

As explained above, these "other terminations" are far more likely to be followed by renewed violence. The change in how most conflicts terminate thus represents the single-most important explanation for today's high rate of recurrent violence. In fact, almost two-thirds of the recurrences since 1990 have been associated with "other" conflict terminations.

The data patterns discussed here clearly demonstrate that the rise in civil war recurrence rates is not because victories or negotiated settlements have become less stable over time. As we point out in the box on pages 178-9, the data seem to suggest instead that peace agreements, at least, have recently become considerably more successful. There is also no clear trend for the stability of victories or for ceasefires.[65] In other words, there is no general increase in recurrence rates of all types of terminations; instead, there is a change in the ways conflict episodes end.

The Least Stable Terminations Occur in the Least Deadly Conflicts

Different types of conflict outcome not only have different risks of recurrence; they are also associated with different levels of lethality. Conflict episodes that end in victory are by far the most deadly. In a sense this is not surprising, since military defeats almost by definition mean large death tolls. By contrast, conflict terminations that fall into the "other" category, making up the majority of all terminations today, have the lowest battle-death tolls. During the two decades since the end of the Cold War in 1989, the civil conflict episodes that terminated with neither victory nor a negotiated settlement had an average annual toll of less than 350 battle deaths. The toll is two times higher for ceasefires, three times higher for conflicts settled through peace agreements, and seven times higher for conflict episodes that ended in victory.

The comparatively small death tolls associated with the termination type that is most prone to conflict relapse suggest a link between low-intensity conflict and high recurrence rates. And there is, as we show below, evidence to support the view that the limited scope of conflicts can favour persistence.

We note that the definitions of conflicts and conflict terminations may partially explain the finding that low-intensity conflicts are more likely to stop and start up again. If a conflict only accounts for a few dozen codable battle deaths and thus hovers just above the threshold of 25 battle deaths a year, not much needs to change for it to be coded as inactive in one year and as starting up again in the next. A high-intensity conflict, on the other hand, killing 1,000 people per year, will require significant changes in the conflict dynamics for the toll to fall below 25 battle deaths.

If the high recurrence rate of low-intensity conflicts were only an artifact of the coding of the data, the finding would be of little value. However, there is evidently more to it. Research based on a new dataset indicates that contemporary conflicts significantly affect only a small fraction of a country's territory.[66] It is often these small conflicts that are also the most persistent conflicts of recent decades.

Thirty-eight percent of the conflicts that recorded three or more episodes over the last two decades had average death tolls of fewer than 100 casualties per year. These include the conflicts in Angola over the territory of Cabinda, the struggle between the government of Eritrea and Islamist rebels based along the Sudanese border, and the conflict over Tripura in India. Only four conflicts with more than two episodes—the conflicts over government power in Pakistan, Somalia, and the Republic of Congo ("Congo-Brazzaville"), as well as the conflict in Sri Lanka—had an average annual death toll of more than 1,000.

> Contemporary intrastate conflicts significantly affect only a small fraction of a country's territory.

Many of the conflicts with the highest number of cumulative years of fighting since 1989 are also of relatively limited scale, both in terms of intensity and geographical scope. India's insurgencies in Assam, Manipur, and Bodoland have each accumulated between 15 and 20 years of conflict but resulted in average annual death tolls lower than 100. There are, of course, a small number of long-lasting conflicts that are also quite deadly, including the civil wars in Afghanistan, Sudan, and Sri Lanka, each of which has claimed more than 1,000 lives per

EVEN FAILED PEACE AGREEMENTS SAVE LIVES

Today a greater share of conflicts is brought to a halt through negotiated settlements than at any time since the end of World War II. But about a third of peace agreements have broken down in less than five years. So, it might seem that peace agreements are an ineffective means of ending civil conflicts.[67] In fact, there is strong evidence that the opposite is true.

There are different forms of negotiated settlements that show a varying risk of conflict recurrence: ceasefires and peace agreements.[68] These settlements differ in the degree to which they address the root causes of the conflict. Unlike ceasefires, peace agreements include concrete steps to resolve the issues at stake between the warring parties.[69] As might be expected, their failure rate is slightly lower, with 32 percent of peace agreements being followed by recurring violence between 1950 and 2004 compared to 38 percent of ceasefires (see Table 6.1).

Even though this is a significant failure rate, most settlements recorded in our dataset succeed in ending the conflict.[70] And, as the last *Human Security Report* points out, there is evidence to suggest that peace agreements became more stable in the new millennium.[71]

When we read that peace agreements have "failed," we might conclude that the peace process is reversed entirely and the affected country relapses into full-scale war with no diminution of deaths. This would be a mistake.

Not everyone goes back to war after a failed settlement. On the contrary, when renewed violence occurs after a peace deal, it sometimes involves rebel groups that did not sign the agreement in the first place. In other cases, only one of several signatories resumes the fighting. The data show that two warring parties who have signed a peace agreement rarely go back to war with each other.[72] Put differently, the recurrence of violence does not always mean that the settlement was a failure since crucial conflict actors usually stick to the agreement despite the presence of spoilers.

A Dramatic, but Little Noticed, Reduction of Violence

That the collapse of an agreement does not always mean complete failure is even more evident when we look at the intensity of the fighting: wars that restart after peace agreements virtually always experience a significant *reduction* in death tolls. In 10 out of the 11 collapsed peace agreements between 1989 and 2004 the annual death toll was lower after the conflict restarted. Peace agreements, in other words, save lives, not only by stopping hostilities, but also by reducing the level of violence if the conflict recurs.

That peace agreements are associated with significant reductions in battle deaths, however, stands in contrast to the work of other authors. In 2010, for example, Harvard University's

Monica Duffy Toft claimed that "the empirical evidence … does not support the normative argument that negotiated settlements save lives."[73] Her definition of "negotiated settlement" is similar to what we refer to here as a peace agreement.

Toft maintains that wars with failed settlements have higher death tolls compared with the average for all recurring conflicts including victories.[74] Yet, her analysis does not permit the conclusion that such higher death tolls are, as she argues, "costs of negotiated settlements."[75] Her comparison tells us only that, in her sample, negotiated settlements occurred in conflicts that are on average more deadly than other recurring conflicts. Nothing in her results suggests that the higher death tolls actually resulted from the peace settlements.[76]

A better way to test how different types of terminations may have an impact on death tolls in conflicts that subsequently recur is to compare the death toll before a conflict stops and after it recurs. As shown in Figure 6.5, the evidence from more recent and fine-grained data than Toft uses clearly suggests that the intensity of the fighting decreases most dramatically when conflicts recur after a peace agreement.[77]

Figure 6.5 Battle-Death Tolls and Termination Types in Recurring Intrastate Conflicts, 1989–2009

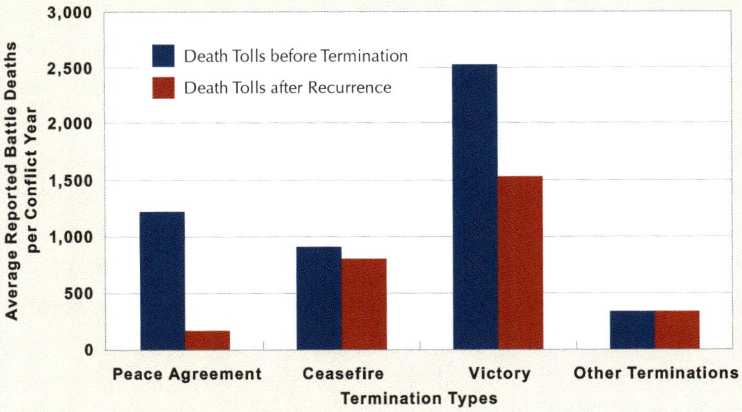

Data Source: UCDP/HSRP Dataset.

Although peace agreements are less stable than victories, they lead to a much greater reduction in battle deaths in recurring conflicts. Ceasefires do little to stem the violence, while conflicts that taper off show no improvement.

As Figure 6.5 demonstrates, the reduction in deadliness associated with peace agreements is very large. The average annual death tolls of civil conflicts drop by more than 80 percent when they recur after a peace agreement. The percentage decline is only half as big for victories, while death tolls for ceasefires and other terminations show little change.

year on average. But aside from these few cases even the more deadly persistent conflicts are usually limited relative to the size of the countries in which they take place. These conflicts typically do not engulf entire nations but are concentrated in smaller areas. Examples are the conflict in Northern Uganda, and in Turkey over Kurdistan.

This raises a question with important policy implications: why are small conflicts so persistent, in terms both of protracted low-level fighting and of high rates of recurrence?

The Persistence of Small Conflicts

We have seen that types of conflict terminations differ markedly in their rates of recurrence, and that the least stable outcomes and some of the longest-running conflicts are associated with very low death tolls. As we show in this section, there is a plausible explanation supported by recent scholarship: the smaller a conflict is, the fewer incentives there are for the parties to end the fighting.

> Guerrilla forces in remote areas are hard to defeat. The government's problem is not defeating them in battle, but locating and engaging them.

Some conflicts are characterized by both persistence and a high intensity of fighting, as in Afghanistan, the Democratic Republic of the Congo (DRC), Somalia, and Sri Lanka. But many of the persistent civil wars active today are limited both in terms of human and material costs and the amount of territory affected by violence, because rebels often choose to base themselves in remote and inaccessible areas.[78]

A number of recent quantitative studies show that small and peripheral insurgencies are more likely to persist. And some of the authors provide support for the argument that strategic considerations in the capital may be one reason for the persistence.[79]

James Fearon has argued that the reason these peripheral cases last a long time "may be that they involve relatively few combatants, pose relatively little threat to the center, and thus stay fairly small. They are difficult to eliminate entirely, and because they tend to be so small, not worth the cost of doing so."[80]

Guerrilla forces in remote areas are extremely hard to defeat. The Philippines Army, for example, possesses military resources that are vastly superior to that of the Communist Party of the Philippines (CPP), an insurgent group mainly active in remote and mountainous areas. But, as in other small, guerrilla-type wars, the government's problem is not so much defeating the rebels in battle, but locating and engaging them.

In other words, while peripheral insurgencies present little real threat, they are nevertheless difficult to put to an end. As a result, governments have few incentives to devote the resources necessary to end the insurgencies, either by military action or by negotiations.

There are additional reasons why state actors might not push forcefully to end low-level insurgencies. A state military organization, for example, may invoke domestic rebellion as a threat to national security in a bid to build its power base, or even to legitimize a coup against the government. Moreover, international actors are less likely to pressure a government to negotiate a settlement where the conflict is small and contained.

It is, of course, difficult for the quantitative studies cited here to determine what motivates the decisions of conflict parties, whether it is a government's indifference or inability that presents obstacles to solving a conflict. But the argument that small-scale conflicts are allowed to persist because they do not significantly hurt the interests of the government side are consistent with findings from the qualitative literature as well. Chester Crocker and colleagues, for example, point out that a state of war can become "a comfort-zone"[81] when there appears to be an acceptable status quo—at least for those in positions of power on both sides.

Explaining Changes in Conflict Persistence

This chapter provides one of the first systematic analyses of trends in conflict persistence. Persistent armed conflict, we argue, can manifest itself in long, uninterrupted periods of fighting, as well as in intermittent conflicts that stop and start again frequently. We have therefore taken a closer look at patterns of conflict duration and recurrence.

First, we noted that the often-cited rise in the average duration of ongoing conflicts, while not untrue, is misleading in that it gives the impression that wars overall are becoming longer and more intractable. There are, of course, significant numbers of decade-long—and longer—conflicts that are still active today. These conflicts, understandably, receive a great deal of attention from researchers, which contributes to the impression that most conflicts are getting longer.

But while long-duration conflicts are a source of obvious concern, and while they inflate the *average* duration of conflicts, they remain the exception, not the rule. In fact, most of the conflicts that have started in recent years have been of short duration.

We point out that the rate at which conflicts restart after a brief calm has increased significantly. Today's high recurrence rate, however, can to a large extent be explained by the trend towards small-scale armed conflict with few violent clashes that are often interrupted by months and years of tranquility.

As noted above, fighting in today's conflicts tends to take place in confined geographic areas. The most persistent of these conflicts also result in low numbers of battle deaths and take place at the periphery of a country. And the data and research discussed above suggest that such conflicts are often allowed to persist precisely because the intensity and scope of the fighting is limited. Paradoxically, the very weakness of rebel groups may help them avoid defeat if it means that they carry out operations in peripheral territories where the violence and destruction they perpetrate do not represent a significant threat to the central government.

> The weakness of rebels may help them avoid defeat if they are not a threat to the government.

A second reason for the higher recurrence rate of conflict episodes today is the increase in the number of negotiated settlements. Since 1990 more conflicts have ended through negotiations than at any other time in the post-World War II era. Because such settlements have a significant risk of relapse into violence, any increase in their share contributes to a higher rate of conflict recurrence. Despite this, as we argue in more detail below, negotiated settlements are almost always the best available outcome for a conflict episode.

The picture we present is more encouraging than most other accounts of trends in conflict persistence. However, this is not to suggest that conflict persistence is a marginal issue. A significant number of persistent conflicts exist today and some of them are highly destructive. Responses to conflict persistence depend on reliable information about trends and what drives them. But just as important as understanding the causes of conflict persistence is trying to account for the positive developments over the last decades.

Why Most Conflicts Today Are Short-Lived

Global changes in the way conflicts are fought and resolved have had a profound impact on patterns of conflict persistence. Since the end of the Cold War, the intensity of armed conflicts has declined dramatically. In many cases, long-standing civil wars came to an end while new conflicts tended to end after only a few years of fighting. As a result, the number of conflicts has declined globally, but as we showed above, the duration of recent conflicts and conflict episodes has also seen a significant drop. The reduction in the intensity of armed conflicts, however, may have contributed to conflict persistence in other cases. As we have argued, some conflicts are able to persist precisely because their intensity is so low that they pose little threat to governments.

For more than four decades following the end of World War II the superpowers and their allies engaged in "proxy" wars by fuelling civil wars in the developing world. This exacerbated death tolls and prolonged the fighting by providing the warring parties with financial, military, ideological, and political support.[82] The end of the Cold War abruptly reduced the external support that had helped sustain both governments and rebel forces. Without it, many long-standing conflicts simply ground to a halt.

> Few of the rebel movements today have much chance of defeating the government.

With fewer sources of external support, the civil wars that started during the 1990s and 2000s became both shorter and less deadly. Few of the rebel movements active today have much chance of defeating the governments they oppose. Indeed, less than 5 percent of terminations in civil wars since 1990 have been insurgent victories.

The reduction of superpower support following the end of the Cold War affected rebel groups but also states.[83] It is often claimed that conflicts persist because weak or "failed" states simply lack the capacity to end them.[84] But they may also persist because governments are much stronger than insurgents, pushing the latter towards the periphery and out of reach of government forces.[85] Where threats to a state are low because rebels are weak, but the challenges of crushing a peripheral insurgency are high, governments may prefer the low-cost option of containing the insurgency, rather than the high-cost route of seeking to defeat it.

The Successes of Peacemaking and Peacebuilding

The end of the Cold War also coincided with an upsurge in peacemaking and peacebuilding missions seeking to bring armed conflicts to an end and to prevent them from starting again. The *Human Security Report 2009/2010* explains how this international activism has helped reduce the number of active civil wars around the world since 1992.[86] But a much-less-remarked-on benefit of these international efforts has been a reduction in conflict duration.

> As peacemaking initiatives have increased, negotiated settlements have become more common. But such settlements have a risk of collapse.

There is strong evidence that the mediation efforts central to post-Cold War peacemaking have shortened the average length of armed conflicts. Patrick Regan and Aysegul Aydin found in 2006 that "diplomatic interventions dramatically reduce the expected duration of a conflict. For example, the expected duration for civil conflicts that have experienced diplomatic interventions is reduced by about 76 percent over conflicts without diplomatic interventions."[87]

Abel Escribà-Folch explains that economic sanctions, which have also increased dramatically in number over the past 20 years, may be much more successful in bringing conflicts to an end than is usually assumed. His models show that sanctions increase the chances of civil war termination or, in other words, shorten the duration of conflicts.[88]

The upsurge in international activism thus provides an additional explanation for the decline in conflict duration since the late 1980s that we have highlighted in this chapter. As internationally supported peacemaking initiatives have increased, negotiated settlements have become more common. But, as we point out above, such settlements have—by their very nature—a considerable risk of collapse.

Today's high rate of conflict recurrence is to some extent related to the increase in negotiated settlements and therefore also to the success of peacemaking, which has helped create more post-conflict settlements, and hence more situations in which conflicts may recur. This raises an important question for policy-makers: does the high recurrence rate of civil wars put into question the success of international efforts to shorten conflicts?

Some observers have argued that because of the high risk of subsequent failure, negotiated settlements artificially prolong the fighting and exacerbate human suffering.[89] By contrast, conflict terminations that result from the decisive military defeat of one of the warring parties are seen as a better outcome because the defeated party often lacks the capability to go back to war.[90] Conflicts that end in the military defeat of one of the warring parties are not immune to recurrence. But, as shown above, only around 18 percent of victories were followed by renewed violence, making it the most stable type of conflict termination.

What then are the advantages of peace agreements as a means of bringing conflicts to an end? The evidence clearly suggests that despite their risk of collapse, negotiated settlements almost always present the best available option to end wars and save lives.

Negotiations may be the only practicable means of ending some conflicts. While victories tend to occur in shorter wars, negotiated settlements are usually needed to bring the longest-running conflicts to an end.[91] Where a conflict is stalemated and victory has become unattainable by either side, the only alternative to a negotiated settlement is continued warfare, perhaps interrupted by short breaks in the fighting. Such "other terminations," as we show above, are even more likely to be followed by renewed violence than negotiated settlements.

> While victories tend to occur in short wars, negotiated settlements are usually needed to end long-running conflicts.

In other words, negotiated settlements do not prevent victories that, according to some scholars, would occur if a conflict was allowed to follow its "natural course."[92] Instead, settlements typically stop those conflicts that are stalemated and unlikely to be resolved through any other means.

In a small number of cases, peace agreements end the fighting even though one side is on the verge of defeat; that is, when victory for the other side is a realistic possibility. These settlements are usually very stable, since they involve a dramatic diminution of the military capacity of one side *and* negotiations that give at least some concessions to the weaker party. The conflict in Angola is a case in point. In 2002 the government struck a deal with the National Union for the Total Independence of Angola (UNITA) after the rebels had been seriously weakened. Since then, UNITA has transformed into a political party and no fighting has recurred in this conflict.

Last but not least, it is seldom recognized how much the costs of conflict are reduced by peace agreements *even when they break down*. The focus on conflict recurrence has drawn attention away from a crucial fact: the analysis in the box on pages 178-9 points to the crucial, but largely unnoticed, finding that even peace agreements that break down almost always lead to a dramatic reduction in battle deaths. Death tolls drop by more than 80 percent on average in conflicts that recur after a peace agreement. This is a greater reduction than for any of the other termination types.

It is true that peace agreements have repeatedly failed to bring about an enduring peace and that this pattern may be repeated in the future. Yet, the evidence presented here clearly shows that peace agreements are often the only available option to raise the chances of peace and decrease casualties in persistent civil conflicts.

Moreover, there are ways to increase the success rate of peace agreements. Reaching and implementing a peace settlement demands a high level of cooperation and trust from the warring parties, yet such sentiments are usually absent in wartime. And, as Barbara Walter has argued, a peace deal usually "offers enormous rewards for cheating and enormous costs for being cheated upon."[93] She argues that this is why security guarantees from outside actors like the United Nations are crucial for reducing the risk of cheating and thus limiting the risk that conflicts will break out again.[94]

UN peacemaking and peacekeeping missions have been shown to be successful at helping to end civil wars and preventing them from restarting.[95] Both effects have the consequence of reducing conflict persistence. But even though peacemaking and peacebuilding efforts have grown rapidly in number since the end of the Cold War, they address only a limited number of conflicts.

The UN tends to deploy peacekeepers to high-intensity conflicts in relatively weak states.[96] Many other conflicts—those on the territories of major powers and major regional actors, as well as small armed struggles—receive little or no direct attention from international actors. This is not likely to change in the future. New research, however, suggests that in these cases, potential improvements in the quality and legitimacy of governance within the conflict-affected state may also reduce the probability of conflicts recurring.[97] There are many fragile and conflict-affected states where there is little prospect of a peace operation being mounted but where the international community may still work with national leaders to help them enhance the quality and legitimacy of their governments.[98]

Nic Dunlop / Panos Pictures. THAILAND.

CHAPTER 7

Non-State Armed Conflict

A number of scholars and reports from international agencies have suggested that there has been a shift in the nature of warfare over the past two decades.[99] According to this thesis, the traditional, state-centric view of armed conflict no longer accurately captures the forms of organized violence taking place today because non-state actors such as rebels, warlords, and communal groups are playing an increasingly important role.

Until recently, however, the only conflicts that were counted in datasets involved states fighting other states or armed non-state groups. This state-based conception of conflict captured much of the armed violence being waged around the world, but it left out an entire class of conflicts. This omission limited the scope of potentially useful quantitative research on armed conflict.

To remedy this, the Human Security Report Project (HSRP) asked the Uppsala Conflict Data Program (UCDP) in 2003 to collect data on *non-state conflicts*, defined by UCDP as those that involve "the use of armed force between two organized armed groups, neither of which is the government of a state, that results in at least 25 battle-related deaths in a year."[100]

Initial data covering 2002 and 2003, presented in the 2005 *Human Security Report*, revealed that although there were more non-state conflicts in these years than state-based conflicts, the death tolls in non-state conflicts were, on average, much lower.

This *Report* analyzes UCDP's non-state data from 1989 to 2009, a period of 21 years, allowing us to trace developments since the end of the Cold War. The data show no real support for claims that non-state conflicts are becoming more widespread than state-based conflicts. The updated information reveals, instead, that non-state conflict numbers do not appear to be increasing overall, although they can fluctuate considerably from year to year.

Conflicts between non-state actors tend to be much shorter than state-based conflicts. And the backdated data confirm our previous finding that these struggles are usually much less deadly than state-based conflicts: reported battle deaths per year from the average non-state conflict between 1989 and 2009 were only about 16 percent of the battle-death toll from the average state-based conflict during the same period. The data also reveal that there are considerable differences in the levels of organization of non-state groups involved in conflicts, and in the geographical concentration of these conflicts. Non-state conflicts and battle deaths have been most numerous in sub-Saharan Africa, followed by Central and South Asia. The other regions of the world have experienced comparatively few non-state conflicts.

What Is Non-State Armed Conflict?

As mentioned above, the UCDP non-state conflict data include only those conflicts that do not involve the government of a state as a party, and that—consistent with its treatment of data from other types of organized violence—result in 25 or more reported battle deaths in a calendar year.

UCDP codes numbers of conflicts and deaths according to clear and consistently applied definitions, thereby reducing the likelihood of double and incoherent counting. There will, however, always be a considerable amount of uncertainty in the battle-death counts. Estimating deaths from armed conflict is difficult as many deaths go unreported, especially in conflicts where international observers, NGOs (nongovernmental organizations), and the media are often absent. Non-state conflicts are particularly prone to undercounting because they tend to erupt spontaneously and do not involve government forces, and draw less attention from journalists, governments, and NGOs than do state-based conflicts. To ensure that the data are comparable over time and across different countries, UCDP includes only those deaths and conflicts that coders are certain occurred.

> Groups have differing levels of organization. Some are highly organized, while in others violence is spontaneous.

Non-state groups involved in conflict have differing levels of organization. Some are highly organized, while in others organization is minimal and violence may be spontaneous. UCDP distinguishes among these non-state groups by categorizing them as either *formally* or *informally* organized. This distinction is discussed in the box, "Comparing Non-State Armed Groups."

Most groups that are involved in non-state conflict are not involved in other types of organized violence. However, about 13 percent have also taken part in state-based conflicts, fighting against national governments, and 10 percent of the groups have perpetrated one-sided violence against civilians (a category of organized violence that we discuss in the next chapter). About 6 percent have been involved in both types of violence. These include, for example, the Liberation Tigers of Tamil Eelam (LTTE) in Sri Lanka and the Ugandan rebel group Lord's Resistance Army (LRA) in Sudan.

COMPARING NON-STATE ARMED GROUPS

Armed groups involved in non-state conflicts can take diverse forms. UCDP codes as *formally organized groups* those military factions or rebel forces that fight under an official name and resemble regular armed forces. Examples are well-organized armed groups such as the Taliban in Afghanistan and, until recently, various factions of the Liberation Tigers of Tamil Eelam (LTTE) in Sri Lanka. Many of these groups are involved in both non-state and state-based conflicts.

At the other end of the spectrum are loosely structured groups that mobilize temporarily along ethnic, clan, religious, national, or tribal lines. Examples include Christians and Muslims in the Philippines in 1993, or the Luo and Kikuyu ethnic groups in Kenya in 2008.[101] UCDP codes these as *informally organized groups*, a category that includes groups involved in what are often called "communal conflicts."

Since 1989 some 60 percent of non-state conflicts have been fought between informally organized groups, while the remaining 40 percent occurred between more organized groups. These two categories of conflicts are an important part of the global picture of organized violence beyond the more familiar state-based conflicts. The information on the different levels of organization provided by the UCDP dataset enable a more nuanced understanding of non-state conflict.

Conflicts between formally organized groups, such as militias and rebel forces, tended to last longer than conflicts between informally organized groups. Less than 20 percent of the conflicts between informally organized groups lasted more than one year, compared with 33 percent of those between formally organized groups.

Among the longest-lasting conflicts were two between formally organized groups: the nine-year fight in Colombia between the United Self-Defense Forces of Colombia (AUC) and the Revolutionary Armed Forces of Colombia (FARC), and the long struggle between Hezbollah and the South Lebanon Army from 1992 to 2000.

It is not surprising that conflicts between formally organized groups last longer. Supplying and training armed groups and sustaining campaigns of violence over a long period require, and perhaps engender, a high degree of organization.

A few conflicts between formally organized groups caused 1,000 or more reported battle deaths in a single year. One such conflict took place in Sudan in the 1990s and caused some 5,000 reported battle deaths. In another example, a single year of fighting in 1996 in Liberia caused some 2,000 reported battle deaths.

Somewhat surprisingly, of the non-state conflicts that caused 1,000 or more reported battle deaths in a single year, the majority have involved informally organized groups. This puzzle deserves further research, as we discuss in Chapter 7.

In rare cases, non-state conflicts cross international borders. Two non-state groups may fight in border areas, or on territory claimed by more than a single country. In 1995, for example, fighting between two rebel forces in Liberia spilled over into neighbouring Côte d'Ivoire. Throughout the 1990s and 2000s, sporadic fighting between rival ethnic groups erupted in an area joining Ethiopia, Sudan, and Kenya. Of the few non-state conflicts that have spanned two or more countries, most have occurred in sub-Saharan Africa, but some have also occurred in other regions.

Global and Regional Trends

In this section we examine global trends in non-state conflicts from 1989 to 2009. During this period, 372 non-state conflicts in the world resulted in some 80,000 reported battle deaths. Numbers of non-state conflicts have fluctuated from year to year, as shown in Figure 7.1, but have not followed the same downward trend as state-based conflicts, which have declined substantially since the end of the Cold War. Because non-state conflicts tend both to erupt and to end quickly, year-to-year fluctuations in conflict numbers do not mean very much when analyzing long-term trends. Overall, there has been no clear upward or downward trend since the end of the Cold War.

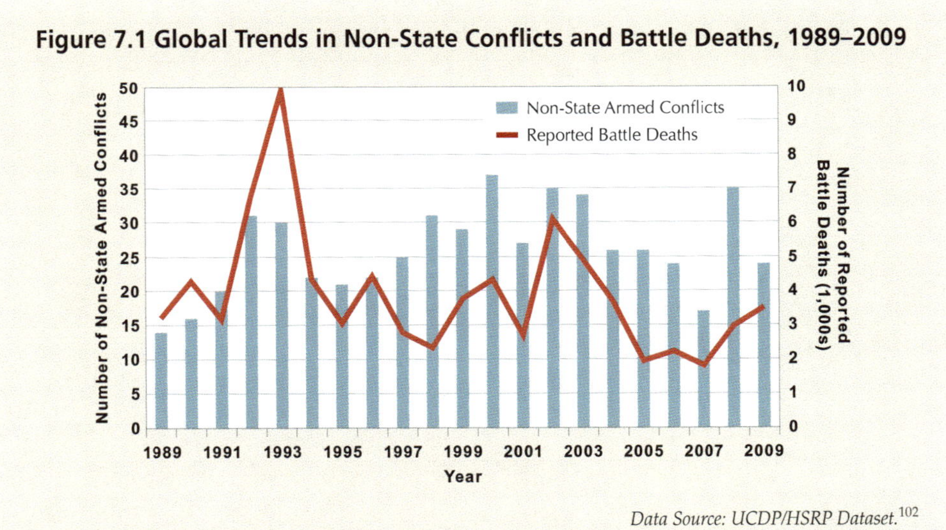

Figure 7.1 Global Trends in Non-State Conflicts and Battle Deaths, 1989–2009

Data Source: UCDP/HSRP Dataset.[102]

After deadly conflicts in the DRC and Sudan caused the spike in 1993, non-state conflicts have become much less deadly. Trends in non-state conflict are largely driven by those in sub-Saharan Africa.

Non-state conflicts, which were recorded as active in 1.5 calendar years on average, tend to be much shorter than the average conflict involving a state.[103] As Figure 7.2 shows, the overwhelming majority of non-state conflicts during the period from 1989 to 2009 were active during only one year; many ended months, weeks, or just days after they began.[104]

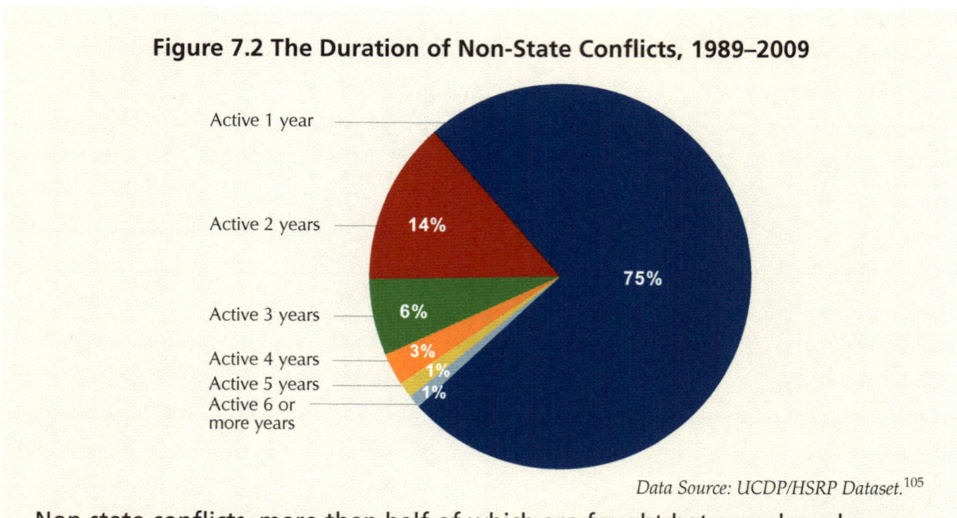

Figure 7.2 The Duration of Non-State Conflicts, 1989–2009

Data Source: UCDP/HSRP Dataset.[105]

Non-state conflicts, more than half of which are fought between loosely organized groups, tend to be short. In the past two decades, the majority lasted up
to a year, while very few were active in three or more years.

The longest-lasting non-state conflict in the dataset was found in Colombia. There, the
two rebel forces, AUC and FARC, fought continuously for nine years from 1997 to 2005. Even
though this conflict lasted an unusually long time, it was not nearly as deadly as most conflicts
involving a state; it resulted in some 200 reported battle deaths per year on average. In the conflict between FARC and the Colombian government, which has lasted almost half a century,
the violence recorded in the dataset between 1989 and 2009 was significantly more deadly. This
state-based conflict led to an average 750 reported battle deaths per year for the 21 years of the
conflict recorded by UCDP—meaning that it was almost four times deadlier than the fighting
between FARC and AUC.

Although the number of non-state conflicts does not show the same post-Cold War decline
as state-based conflicts, there is also no indication that they are becoming more numerous.
And, as Figure 7.1 shows, the annual average death toll has declined in the second half of the
period compared to the first half. The annual average death toll was around 4,400 each year on
average between 1989 and 1999, but dropped by nearly 1,000 deaths in the new millennium.
Moreover, the average non-state conflict tends to be much less deadly than the average conflict
involving states. The average non-state conflict during the period studied, 1989 to 2009, caused
some 150 reported battle deaths per year—much fewer than the 935 deaths per year from the
average state-based conflict in the same period. Conflicts that involve a government are thus,
on average, six times deadlier than conflicts that involve only non-state groups, according
to this measure. Even if we assume that deaths from non-state conflict are less likely to be
reported, the figures show that conflicts that involve a government appear to be many times
deadlier than conflicts that involve only non-state groups.

Eleven of the 372 non-state conflicts during the period studied resulted in 1,000 or more reported battle deaths for at least one of the active years in the conflict. Most of these—nine of the 11—took place in sub-Saharan Africa. The other two were fought in India between 1989 and 1994, and in Burma in the early 1990s. Encouragingly, there have been fewer high-intensity non-state conflicts since the mid-1990s than in the early years covered by the dataset, and none at all since 2005.

The non-state conflict that caused the highest total number of reported battle deaths in the dataset took place in the Democratic Republic of the Congo (DRC). From 1999 to 2003, the Hema and Lendu ethnic groups fought, causing some 6,000 reported battle deaths in total. While the two non-state groups fought one another, the DRC was also involved in a large-scale civil war.

Many countries experiencing non-state conflict between 1989 and 2009 also experienced conflicts in which the state was a warring party—the DRC, above, is an example—even though, as we stated above, most groups that have fought in non-state conflicts were not involved in state-based conflicts. However, non-state conflicts also afflicted a few countries—Brazil, Jamaica, and Canada—that had experienced no state-based conflict since the end of World War II, although in none of these were very high numbers of battle deaths reported. All three of these conflicts involved criminal gangs. In Brazil in 2001, and again in 2004, for example, fighting erupted between rival criminal groups over control of gang territory, causing about 45 reported battle deaths per year on average. In 2001 fighting between supporters of opposing political groups in Jamaica, much of which was related to gang rivalry, caused 116 reported battle deaths in a single year. In Canada turf wars erupted between gangs for a few years in the 1990s, and generated approximately 30 reported battle deaths per year on average. In addition, Ghana, a country without any state-based conflict since 1983, experienced a deadly conflict between ethnic groups in 1994 that resulted in 2,000 reported battle deaths in a single year.

Figure 7.3 shows the trends in non-state conflict in the six regions of the world. Although non-state conflicts took place in every region during 1989–2009, they were most numerous in sub-Saharan Africa, which experienced an average of 18 non-state conflicts per year.

Central and South Asia was the region with the second-highest number of non-state conflicts, but it had just four non-state conflicts each year on average between 1989 and 2009. The Middle East and North Africa averaged fewer than two conflicts each year during the same period, followed by the Americas, with 1.5 conflicts each year on average. The region of East and Southeast Asia and Oceania averaged just over one conflict each year, while Europe, with the fewest each year, has been free of non-state conflict since the mid-1990s.

The difference between sub-Saharan Africa and the rest of the world is also reflected in reported battle-death tolls. Conflicts in sub-Saharan Africa accounted for the majority of the world's battle deaths from non-state conflicts between 1989 and 2009. In 12 of the 21 years in that period—in other words, more than half the time—sub-Saharan Africa had more reported battle deaths than did Central and South Asia in its deadliest year.

FIGURE 7.3

Regional Trends in Non-State Conflicts, 1989–2009

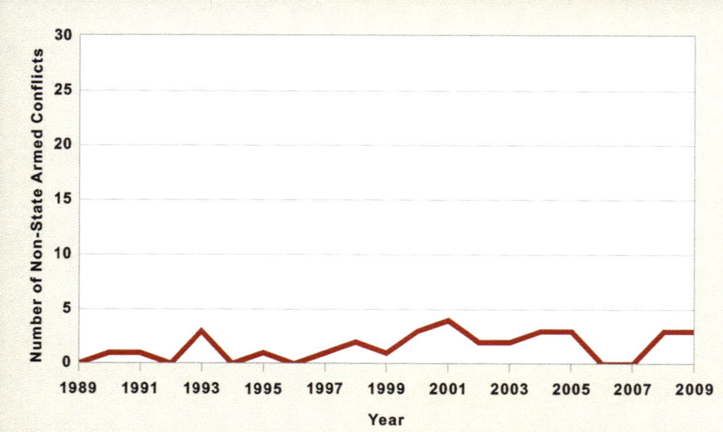

Americas

Non-state conflicts were heavily concentrated in Colombia and Mexico. In the late 1990s to the early 2000s, clashes in Colombia led to increases in conflict activity in the region.

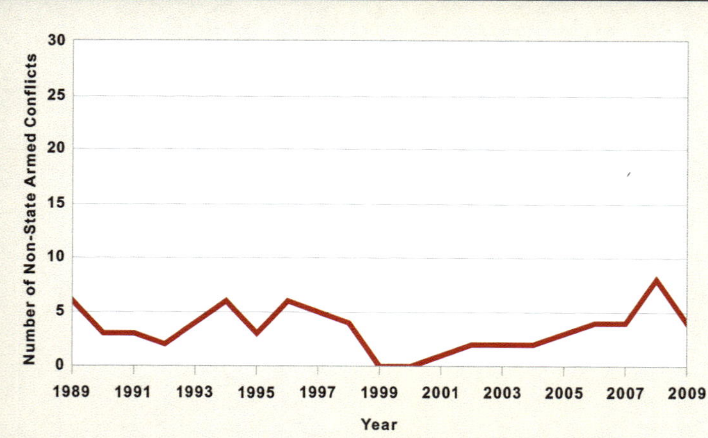

Central and South Asia

This region was one of the few to see an increase in the number of non-state conflicts in the 2000s. The increase was due to the many conflicts erupting in Pakistan and, to a lesser extent, India.

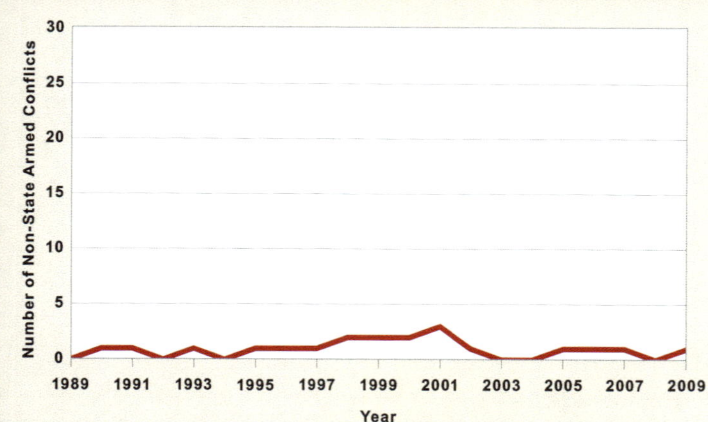

East and Southeast Asia and Oceania

Non-state conflicts and battle deaths in this region were concentrated in Burma and were related to the long-standing, state-based conflicts involving the Burmese government.

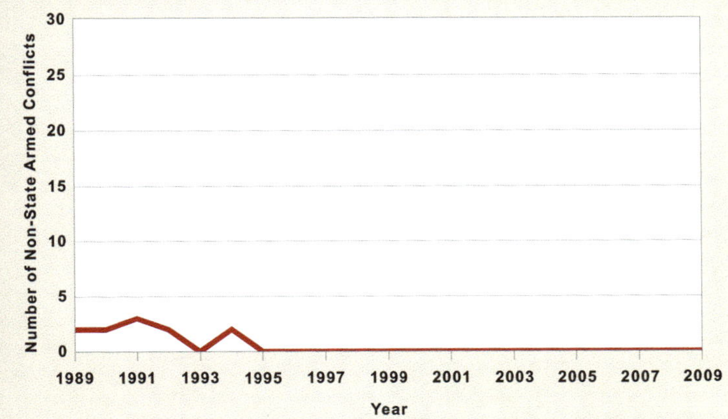

Europe

The few non-state conflicts in Europe took place in the context of post-Cold War wars of independence—for example, the conflict between Azeris and Armenians in the Soviet Union.

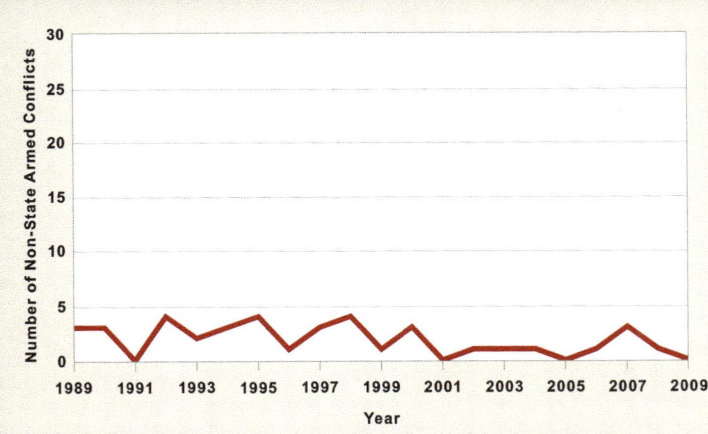

Middle East and North Africa

Non-state conflicts have declined over the years, though they have never been very numerous. In 2008 the only non-state conflict occurred in Lebanon.

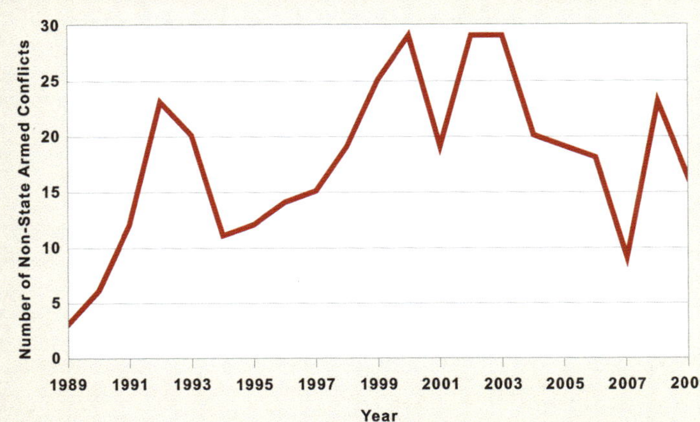

Sub-Saharan Africa

Non-state conflicts in sub-Saharan Africa spiked in the late 1990s and early 2000s due in large part to fighting in Somalia, Nigeria, Ethiopia, and the DRC.

Thus, we turn our focus now to sub-Saharan Africa, and then to Central and South Asia, the two regions that have suffered the highest number of non-state conflicts, as well as the highest number of battle deaths from non-state conflicts.

Sub-Saharan Africa

Figure 7.4 shows trends in non-state conflicts and battle deaths in sub-Saharan Africa between 1989 and 2009. During this period, 271 non-state conflicts in the region resulted in some 60,000 reported battle deaths.

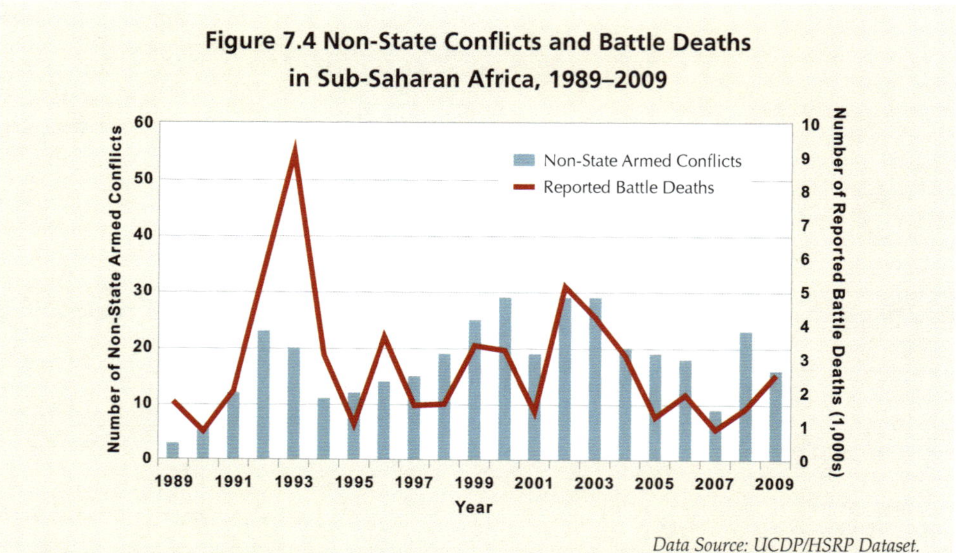

Data Source: UCDP/HSRP Dataset.

Deadly conflicts in Sudan, the DRC, and Nigeria caused the dramatic peak in battle deaths in 1993. Non-state conflicts in the region were on average deadlier from 1989 to 1999 than in the new millennium.

Within sub-Saharan Africa, most of the non-state conflicts were concentrated in three sub-regions: the Great Lakes, the Horn of Africa (defined here to include Sudan), and West Africa.

Somalia, Nigeria, Sudan, and Ethiopia experienced the most non-state conflicts of any countries in the world, while Sudan, the DRC, Somalia, and Nigeria experienced the highest numbers of reported battle deaths.[106] Sudan alone, with less than 1 percent of the world's population,[107] has experienced nearly a fifth of all reported global battle deaths attributable to non-state conflicts. Many of the conflicts in Sudan were caused or exacerbated by its government's deliberate strategy of weakening opposition groups by pitting them against one another.[108]

> Between 1989 and 2009, non-state conflicts in sub-Saharan Africa resulted in some 60,000 battle deaths.

Central and South Asia

Central and South Asia had the second-highest number of non-state conflicts during 1989–2009. In this region, 44 non-state conflicts caused some 8,000 reported battle deaths, as shown in Figure 7.5.

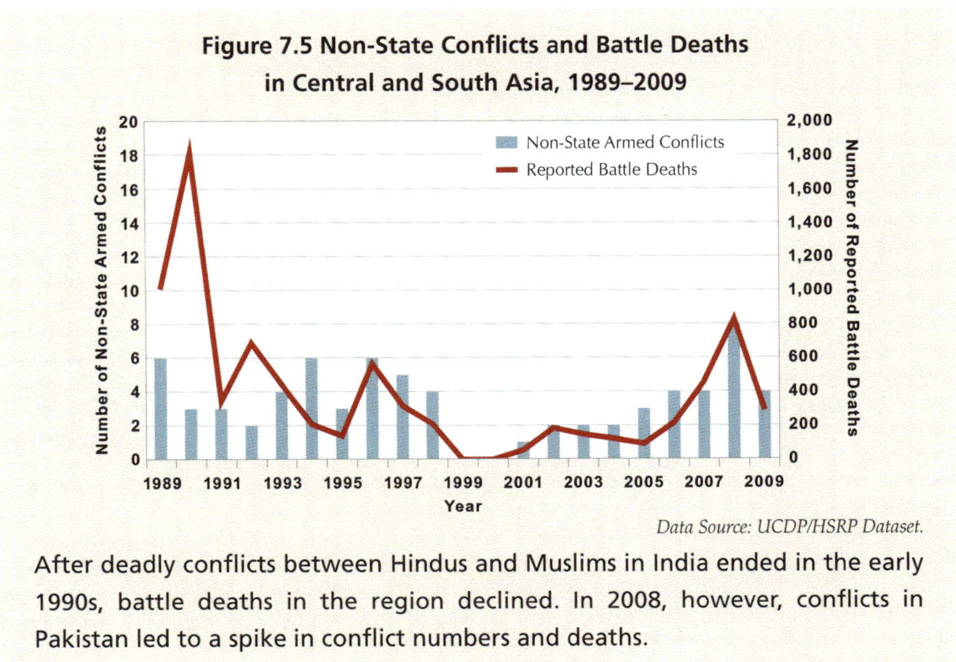

Data Source: UCDP/HSRP Dataset.

After deadly conflicts between Hindus and Muslims in India ended in the early 1990s, battle deaths in the region declined. In 2008, however, conflicts in Pakistan led to a spike in conflict numbers and deaths.

Over the period 1989–2004, Afghanistan recorded the highest number of non-state conflicts in the region—with a total of 21 different conflicts. Since then, most have been in Pakistan, which was the location for all four non-state conflicts in the region in 2009. Several of these involved conflicts between the Pakistan Taliban movement and tribal armies in northwest Pakistan that had turned pro-government.

The deadliest year in the region for non-state conflicts during this period was 1990. Most non-state conflicts in Central and South Asia have killed relatively few people, but a single conflict—between Hindus and Muslims in India—was active every year from 1989 to 1994 and resulted in some 3,000 reported battle deaths. In 1990, the deadliest year of that conflict, fighting caused nearly 2,000 reported battle deaths, or 95 percent of the total in Central and South Asia in that year.

New Directions in Conflict Research

UCDP's backdated non-state dataset for the years 1989–2009 creates opportunities for new research on conflicts between armed groups. In addition, UCDP has also geo-referenced the data on non-state conflicts, as well as on state-based conflicts and one-sided violence, in a new dataset. The data provide information on the location of deaths from non-state conflict and other forms of organized violence, a first version of which was released in December 2011 and covers sub-Saharan Africa. This section reviews some of the first studies to use the expanded non-state conflict data and the geo-referenced data on non-state conflicts, and suggests directions for future research.

The backdated and geo-referenced non-state datasets create new ways for researchers to test claims about factors that increase the risk of organized violence.[109] This can be illustrated by the debate over the relationship between environmental factors and the onset of armed conflict.

> Since non-state conflicts tend to be localized and occur over land or other resources, they may be influenced by environmental changes.

Policy-makers and researchers devoted considerable attention to an argument made in 1994 by Robert Kaplan, and by others, that future wars would arise over environmental and resource disputes.[110] However, there was little clear research-based evidence demonstrating how environmental degradation and resource scarcity would affect the risk of armed conflict.[111] Since then, numerous studies have investigated the effect of environmental factors, focusing exclusively on state-based conflicts, but the results have been mixed.[112] Now, it is possible to investigate correlations of environmental stresses with localized violence—such as non-state conflict—using UCDP's geo-referenced data. Since non-state conflicts tend to be very localized and often occur over land rights or other resources, they may be more influenced by changes in the environment.[113]

Early findings from such research appear to support Kaplan's argument that there is an association between environmental degradation and violent conflict. A 2011 study by Eric Melander and Ralph Sundberg found, for example, that acute soil degradation in areas of extreme population density in sub-Saharan Africa was strongly correlated with an increased risk of onset of non-state conflicts.[114]

Similarly, in 2007 Ole Magnus Theisen and Kristian Brandsegg examined the association between localized changes in rainfall and conflicts arising in the same locations. They found that changing levels of precipitation were associated with a higher risk of non-state conflicts.[115]

The geo-referenced data on non-state conflicts also allow researchers a new perspective on the impact of inequality on the risk of organized violence. Previous research has used national-level datasets to examine correlations between grievances—those associated with economic inequality, but also ethnic and religious divisions, and political repression[116]—and the outbreak of state-based conflicts.[117] Some of the most-cited earlier studies, including those by James Fearon and David Laitin, as well as Paul Collier and Anke Hoeffler, had failed to find any relationship between grievances and the outbreak of state-based conflict.[118]

Again, the non-state data allow for new insights. In 2011 Hanne Fjelde and Gudrun Østby examined the impact of economic inequality between regions on the risk of non-state conflict in sub-Saharan Africa using UCDP's geo-referenced data on non-state conflicts and

Demographic Health Survey (DHS) data on subnational socio-economic welfare.[119] They found that unequal access to economic benefits increased the likelihood that local groups would use violence against other groups. Rather than fighting the government—an approach requiring resources that these marginalized groups likely do not have—groups within these marginalized regions instead fight more privileged local groups for benefits.

Political instability can also increase the risk of non-state conflict. In a 2011 paper, Joakim Kreutz and Kristine Eck show that during major regime transitions, it becomes more difficult to regulate the behaviour of groups.[120] In a cross-national study, they found that regime transitions not only decrease the ability and willingness of the state to constrain violence between groups, but they also erode the legitimacy of in-group policing mechanisms. Moreover, this risk is more pronounced when the government in the previous period was authoritarian, led by an unconstrained executive, or dominated by a single ethnic group.

Much of the research thus far has focused on how non-state conflicts begin. How non-state conflicts terminate is not well understood and has been little examined. Part of the reason is that such conflicts usually end quickly, they are small, and there is little involvement by national or international peacemaking interventions.

> Some of the deadliest non-state conflicts were fought between communal groups.

Another understudied area of non-state conflicts concerns a counterintuitive result that involves informally organized groups. Such groups generally lack the resources needed to fight effectively over long periods of time and are not permanently armed. Yet, some of the deadliest non-state conflicts between 1989 and 2009 were those fought between informally organized communal groups.

Although research on non-state conflicts is still new, use of UCDP's backdated non-state dataset and geo-referenced data have provided us with deeper insight into the distinct phenomenon of non-state conflict. As we point out above, non-state conflicts are much less destructive than their state-based counterparts. Nevertheless, the data that allow us to study this form of organized violence also contribute significantly to our understanding of issues left unclear by previous national-level research on state-based conflicts.

CHAPTER 8

Deadly Assaults on Civilians

Since its inception, the *Human Security Report* has sought to present a comprehensive picture of trends in organized violence around the world. *One-sided violence*—the targeting of civilians with deadly force—is an important part of this picture. Yet, until recently, it has been largely under studied compared to other forms of organized violence.

Prior to 2005, global data on one-sided violence were limited. This permitted a number of mistaken beliefs to flourish unchallenged, including the widely accepted claim that civilians have been increasingly targeted in contemporary wars.

The Human Security Report Project (HSRP) commissioned the Uppsala Conflict Data Program (UCDP) to create a dataset on one-sided violence. The first findings were published in the 2005 *Human Security Report*.

Using an updated version of the dataset, this chapter reviews the global and regional trends in one-sided violence over the past 21 years, and some recent research findings. The

> The conventional wisdom suggesting that civilians are increasingly being targeted in today's wars is simply incorrect.

data indicate that in 2009 the number of deadly campaigns against civilians was the lowest recorded since 1989—the earliest year for which UCDP has data. The conventional wisdom that civilians are increasingly being targeted in today's wars is simply incorrect.

The data also reveal that between 1989 and 2009 most campaigns and deaths from one-sided violence were concentrated in sub-Saharan Africa. Since the early 2000s, however, the incidence of one-sided violence in this region has declined. The Central and South Asia region has seen the second-highest number of campaigns against civilians—and fatalities—but here too there has been a decline in recent years. The remaining regions have suffered comparatively fewer campaigns of one-sided violence.

This chapter also reviews the burgeoning research literature on organized violence against civilians that uses the new dataset to explore a range of issues related to one-sided violence.

What Is One-Sided Violence?

UCDP defines *one-sided violence* as the organized use of armed force directed at civilians by a government or a formally organized group that results in at least 25 reported deaths in a calendar year.[121] Unlike civilians who die in the crossfire of armed conflict—and whose deaths are counted as battle-related deaths—victims of one-sided violence are the direct, rather than the inadvertent, victims of an attack.

"One-sided violence" is a relatively neutral term, and has thus far avoided the sort of controversy that swirls around the concepts of "terrorism" and "genocide"—both of which also focus on the killing of civilians. It is also in some ways a more inclusive category than either genocide or terrorism. First, it includes both large-scale massacres and small-scale campaigns that meet the fatality threshold of 25 reported deaths in a calendar year. The term "genocide," on the other hand, generally applies to large-scale killings.

Second, one-sided violence can be perpetrated by either a government or a formally organized non-state group. There is disagreement about whether the term "terrorism" applies in cases where the government intentionally kills civilians. Most terrorism analysts argue that *terrorism* is the intentional use of violence against civilians for political ends by non-state groups, and argue that where governments intentionally kill civilians this may well be a war crime, but it is not terrorism.

Third, according to the standard definition, *genocide* has the goal of destroying, in whole or in part, a national, ethnic, or religious group.[122] The definition of one-sided violence does not involve identifying the target of violence—other than the fact that it is civilians.

One-sided violence is a broader category than terrorism and genocide in some ways, yet it is narrower in one important respect: targets of one-sided violence must be unarmed civilians. In the literature there is no consensus with respect to whether victims of terrorism or genocide must be either civilian or unarmed.

"Collateral Damage" versus One-Sided Fatalities

As pointed out, civilians can become victims of organized violence outside of wars. Within the context of armed conflicts, however, there are two analytically distinct circumstances in which civilians can be killed. The first is when they are caught "in the crossfire" of combat—i.e., when they become the unintended victims of either gunfire, or exploding bombs or improvised explosive devices (IEDs). Such deaths are often euphemistically referred to as "collateral damage." The second circumstance involves the targeting of civilians by government or nongovernment forces that often takes place during wars but sometimes also in peacetime. This is one-sided violence.

Although battle-related civilian deaths and one-sided violence both result in the death of noncombatants, they are conceptually different. The former is in effect an inevitable consequence of fighting; the latter is the result of tactical choices by combatants to target civilians.

> Around 16 percent of campaigns recorded in the dataset occurred in countries that did not experience civil conflict in the same year.

There are several reasons for treating deaths from the targeting of civilians separately from deaths of civilians caught in the crossfire. First, one-sided violence constitutes a crime under international law, whereas military engagements that inadvertently cause civilian casualties are not considered unlawful. The policy responses to situations in which civilian targeting is a war tactic differ from those in which civilians are accidentally caught in the crossfire of conflict.

Second, campaigns of one-sided violence may occur outside of war settings. Around 16 percent of campaigns of one-sided violence recorded in the dataset occurred in countries that did not experience civil conflict in the same year. One prominent example is the deadly assault on civilians by Chinese government forces in the Tiananmen Square massacre in 1989. These deaths would not be counted by data-gatherers for standard battle-death datasets because there was no combat. The victims did not, indeed could not, fight back.

Third, the level of one-sided violence varies substantially from conflict to conflict. Some conflicts see significant levels of one-sided violence; the most severe recent example, the Rwandan genocide in 1994, took place while the country was in the midst of a civil war. Yet, in other conflicts—for example, the intrastate conflict in Yemen in 1994—no instances of civilian targeting were recorded. The use of one-sided violence also differs among conflict actors. A 2011 study by Madelyn Hsiao-Rei Hicks and colleagues found that while 11 percent of non-state conflict actors targeted civilians as their "sole form of lethal behaviour in conflict," 61 percent completely refrained from using one-sided violence.[123]

In other words, the large-scale killing of civilians is not part of every armed conflict, nor does it play a role in every warring party's strategy. But the variation in the use of one-sided violence can be studied only if the phenomenon is treated separately from collateral damage.

Even though there is a clear advantage in analyzing the two types of civilian fatalities separately, it is often difficult to clearly identify one-sided violence when it occurs. This is why there is a higher degree of uncertainty with respect to one-sided violence fatality numbers than is the case with data on battle deaths. The fact that killing civilians—unlike killing combatants—is universally proscribed means that governments and non-state armed groups are often reluctant to claim responsibility for acts of one-sided violence that they may perpetrate. Plus, the distinction between one-sided violence and collateral damage, while clear in theory, is often difficult to make in practice for those coding the data.

Research on One-Sided Violence

The recent availability of data on one-sided violence has already led to a small, but growing, number of analytic studies that are increasing our understanding of this phenomenon.

The study by Hicks and colleagues looks at the degree to which conflict parties resort to targeting civilians.[124] Their finding—that most warring groups in conflict between 2002 and 2007 did not target civilians—shows that, notwithstanding claims to the contrary targeting civilians is not a widely employed tactic.[125] Between 2002 and 2007, only 39 percent of conflict parties carried out some degree of one-sided violence.

Another stream of research looks at the drivers of one-sided violence. In 2009 Chyanda Querido, for example, examined cases of one-sided violence in the context of armed conflict and found that where countries in conflict possessed natural resources, such as easily lootable diamonds and onshore oil reserves, there was an increased probability that the government would carry out mass killings of civilians.[126]

In 2007 Lisa Hultman and Kristine Eck of Uppsala University found that regime type is associated with the risk of one-sided violence.[127] Autocratic regimes are associated with increased risks of one-sided violence perpetrated by government forces in wartime. However, somewhat surprisingly, there is a higher risk of one-sided violence in democracies than semi-democracies, although in the former case the perpetrators tend to be rebel groups rather than government forces.

In 2010 Reed Wood studied the relationship between a rebel group's strength and its tendency to perpetrate one-sided violence.[128] He found that weak rebel groups that lack the capacity to provide benefits to the civilian population are unlikely to receive voluntary support. In such situations, rebels use violence to coerce support from civilians because the latter are unwilling to provide it voluntarily.

> Recent research found that peace operations in a conflict setting can unintentionally increase attacks on civilians by non-state groups.

Other research has analyzed some potential negative effects of efforts to support the resolution of armed conflict on one-sided violence. In 2010 Lisa Hultman looked at the effect of a peacekeeping presence in ongoing conflicts on the incidence of one-sided violence.[129] She found that peace operations in an ongoing conflict setting can unintentionally increase the level of one-sided violence perpetrated by non-state groups. For example, warring parties facing an intervention might anticipate a settlement to the conflict and therefore target civilians as a "last-minute strategy" to gain territory.[130]

In 2010 Margit Bussmann and Gerald Schneider examined whether various "protection of civilians" mechanisms are effective in restraining parties in civil war from targeting civilians.[131] Their analysis reveals that the presence of a neutral actor, such as the International Committee of the Red Cross (ICRC), deters some government groups from targeting civilians, but fails to deter rebel troops.

Global and Regional Trends in One-Sided Violence

Figure 8.1 below shows the trend in campaigns of one-sided violence between 1989 and 2009. Although state-based conflict numbers declined in the post-Cold War period, one-sided violence campaigns increased unevenly until 2004 then started to decline. And, as the figure shows, the number of campaigns in 2009 was the lowest recorded between 1989 and 2009.

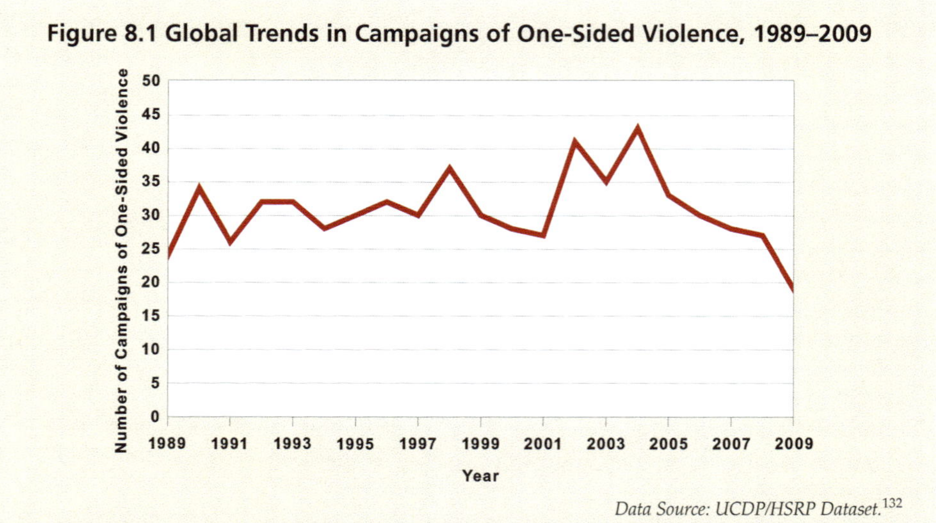

Data Source: UCDP/HSRP Dataset.[132]

Campaigns of one-sided violence peaked in the early 2000s, with the largest increase seen in the DRC. In 2009 four of 19 campaigns took place in the DRC, though all regions except Europe were affected.

While there has been a clear decline in the number of campaigns of one-sided violence since 2003 and 2004, there has been no comparable decline in the number of *fatalities* caused by assaults on civilians. Figure 8.2 shows the global trends in deaths from one-sided violence between 1989 and 2009. Deaths from one-sided violence in 2009 increased by over 60 percent compared to the record low in 2008, but remained much lower than during the mid-1990s.

As noted earlier, deaths from one-sided violence are extremely difficult to estimate, which means that we should treat absolute numbers of estimated deaths in any particular year with due caution. There are obvious reasons why both governments and non-state groups might deny intentionally killing civilians, not least being that—unlike killing in combat—one-sided violence is a grave violation of international law. But there are also cases—Bosnia, for example—where one-sided violence estimates have been grossly overestimated.[133]

> Deaths from one-sided violence in 2009 increased by over 60 percent, but remained much lower than during the mid-1990s.

Data Source: UCDP/HSRP Dataset.

The Rwandan genocide in 1994, which killed some 500,000 civilians, overshadows other deadly campaigns. The truncated graph shows that 1996 was also a deadly year largely due to one campaign in the DRC that killed at least 27,000.

Note: The total in 1994 is 504,084 deaths, some 500,000 of which are attributed to the genocide in Rwanda.

UCDP's estimates of one-sided violence are revised as new information becomes available. For example, the version of the data presented in this *Report* contains a major revision to the death toll from deadly assaults on civilians in the Democratic Republic of the Congo (DRC). Previous estimates had indicated that the rebel group Alliance of Democratic Forces for the Liberation of Congo-Zaire (AFDL) killed around 6,000 civilians in 1996. New evidence, however, has increased that figure to at least 27,000.[134]

In the deadliest years in the dataset—1994 and 1996—the overwhelming majority of the fatalities recorded in each year were generated by just one campaign in that year. In 1994 the genocide in Rwanda caused 99 percent of the deaths from one-sided violence in that year. The AFDL's campaign in the DRC caused 84 percent of the global one-sided death toll in 1996.

The tendency for a few campaigns to be responsible for the majority of the yearly death tolls also helps explain the uptick in fatalities from 2008 to 2009. Although there were 19 campaigns of one-sided violence in 2009, just two campaigns—again in the DRC—were responsible for half the global death toll that year. Most of the campaigns in 2009 were not very deadly by comparison; indeed, if we exclude these two campaigns, the average death toll for each campaign in 2009 was just over 150.

Despite the increase between 2008 and 2009, deaths from one-sided violence have declined substantially since the mid-1990s. The trend remains the same even if we exclude the huge and unprecedented death toll from Rwanda. Absent Rwanda, the average death toll from one-sided violence per year declined by half in the new millennium compared to the period 1989–1999.

When it comes to determining which type of actor—government or non-state group—has been the deadliest perpetrator of one-sided violence, there is no clear-cut answer. Between 1989 and 2009, governments were responsible for 83 percent of global deaths from one-sided violence. However, this result is predominantly driven by one-sided violence campaigns in the first half of the period considered. One prominent campaign, as we discuss below, is the Rwandan genocide in 1994, in which (according to UCDP's "best estimate") some 500,000 civilians were killed at the hands of the government.[135] Indeed, the data show that the share of one-sided violence deaths perpetrated by non-state actors has clearly grown over time. This trend,

In the 2000s, non-state groups were responsible for 70 percent of deaths from one-sided violence.

highlighted in our last *Report*,[136] continues to be supported by the updated data: between 1989 and 1999, non-state groups were responsible for 12 percent of the deaths. In the new millennium, however, they were responsible for 70 percent of the deaths—a remarkable shift.

Regional Trends

The percentage of campaigns and fatalities due to one-sided violence varies substantially between regions. Figure 8.3 shows the proportion of campaigns of one-sided violence for each region. Just under half of all recorded campaigns took place in sub-Saharan Africa. Central and South Asia was second with just under a quarter of the total campaigns, followed by the Middle East and North Africa with 12 percent.

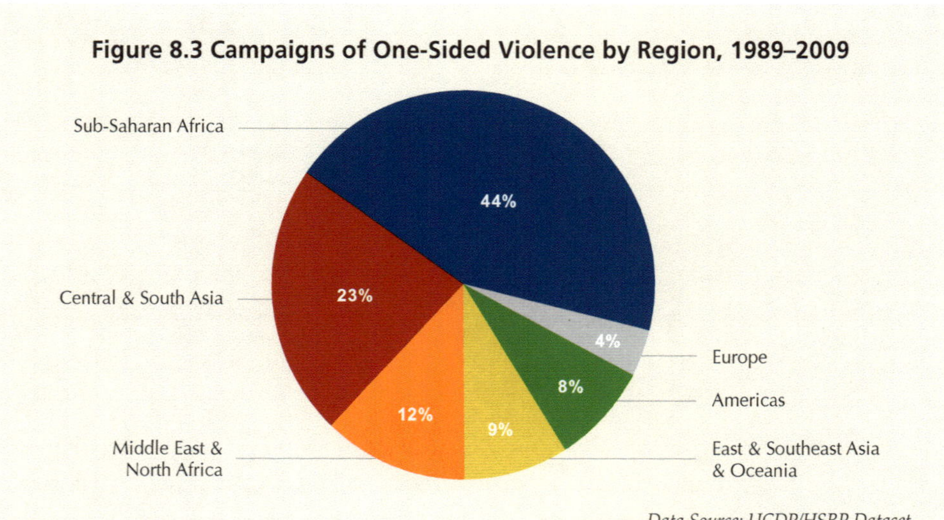

Data Source: UCDP/HSRP Dataset.

More attacks on civilians were recorded in sub-Saharan Africa than in any other region. However, no region was free of one-sided violence. Now peaceful, Europe saw campaigns well into the start of the new millennium.

The divergence between sub-Saharan Africa and the rest of the regions is even more marked when we look at fatalities. Figure 8.4 shows the proportion of deaths due to one-sided violence that occurred in each region.[137] Sub-Saharan Africa accounted for 90 percent of the total number of fatalities from one-sided violence between 1989 and 2009. By contrast, the region accounted for just under half of all battle deaths from state-based conflict in the same period.

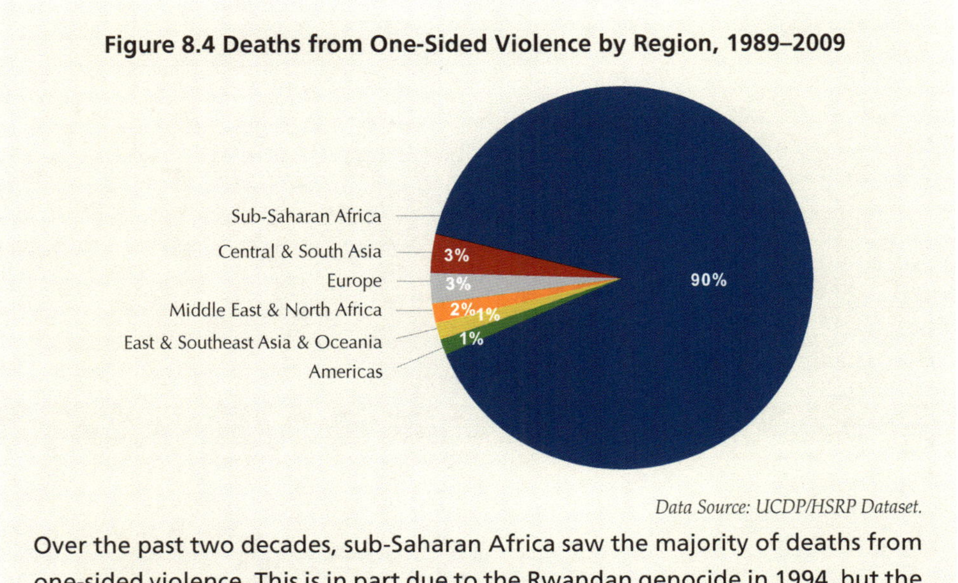

Figure 8.4 Deaths from One-Sided Violence by Region, 1989–2009

Data Source: UCDP/HSRP Dataset.

Over the past two decades, sub-Saharan Africa saw the majority of deaths from one-sided violence. This is in part due to the Rwandan genocide in 1994, but the result holds even if we exclude that lethal campaign.

The regional differences can also be seen in the trends over time. Figure 8.5 shows the trends in one-sided violence campaigns and deaths between 1989 and 2009 for each region.

In almost every year the death toll was higher in sub-Saharan Africa than in any other region. Because sub-Saharan Africa had such a large share of total civilian deaths, its trend tends to drive the worldwide trend.

For example, the global peaks in the death tolls in 1994 and 1996 were due to one-sided violence campaigns in Rwanda and the DRC, respectively. Campaigns in sub-Saharan Africa were also responsible for the recent global increase in deaths due to one-sided violence between 2008 and 2009. The Lord's Resistance Army (LRA) and Democratic Forces for the Liberation of Rwanda (FDLR), both active in the DRC, perpetrated the deadliest campaigns of one-sided violence in 2009.

Governments in sub-Saharan Africa were responsible for the overwhelming majority— 88 percent—of deaths in the region. However, as was the case at the global level, this was primarily a result of the staggering death toll in a single case—the Rwandan genocide. If Rwanda is excluded from the analysis, government actors were responsible for just over a third of civilian fatalities.

FIGURE 8.5

Regional Trends in One-Sided Violence Campaigns and Deaths, 1989–2009

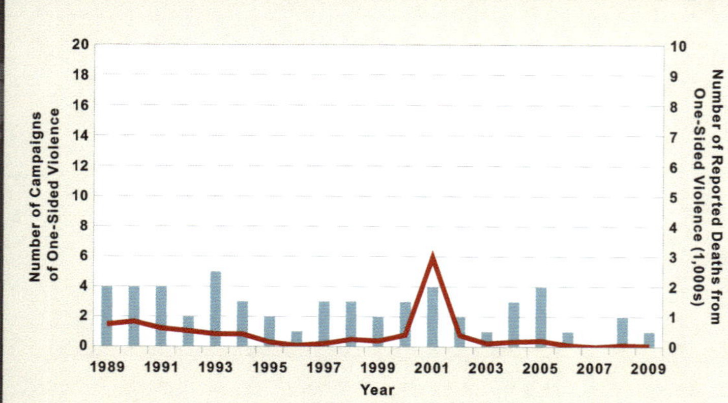

Americas

Few campaigns were recorded in this region and they were generally not very deadly. One exception was in 2001, when the events of 9/11 caused 89 percent of the deaths that year.

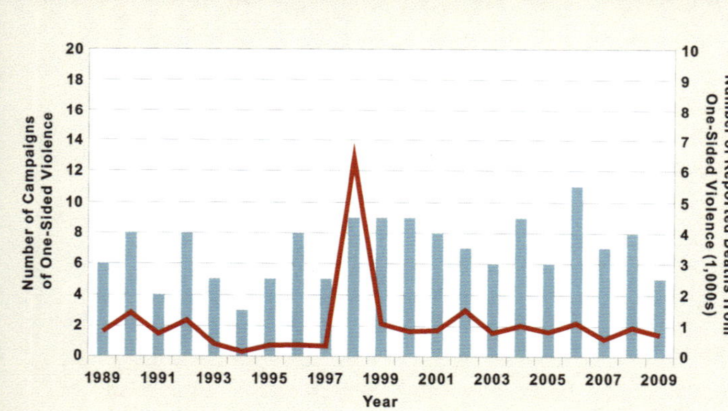

Central and South Asia

A single campaign in Afghanistan perpetrated by the Taliban government accounted for almost the entire death toll in 1998. Campaigns in this region otherwise caused relatively few deaths.

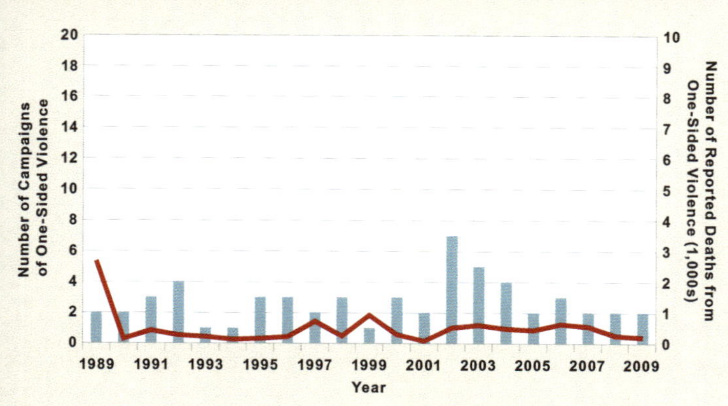

East and Southeast Asia and Oceania

The events at Tiananmen Square in China caused a spike in deaths in 1989, while attacks on civilians in Indonesia and the Philippines increased the number of campaigns in 2002.

Data Source: UCDP/HSRP Dataset.

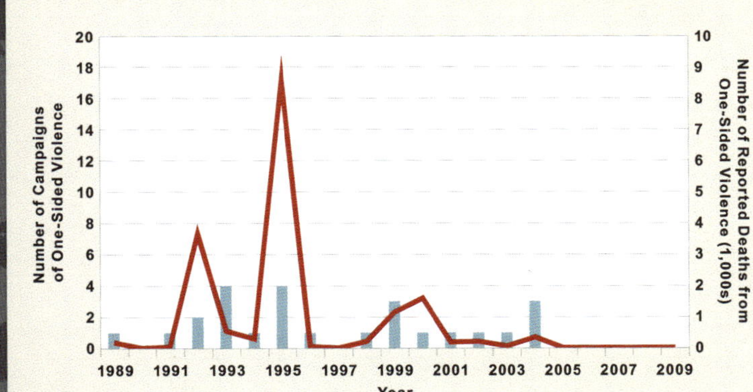

Europe

The deadliest campaigns occurred early in the post-Cold War period. The attacks on civilians in Bosnia-Herzegovina caused deaths to peak in 1992 and 1995.

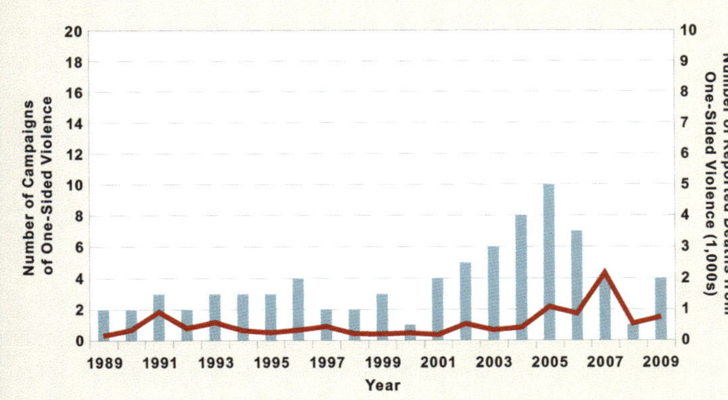

Middle East and North Africa

In 2004 and 2005 targeted attacks on civilians in Iraq were the primary cause of the spikes in campaigns in this region, as well as the sole cause of the spike in deaths in 2007.

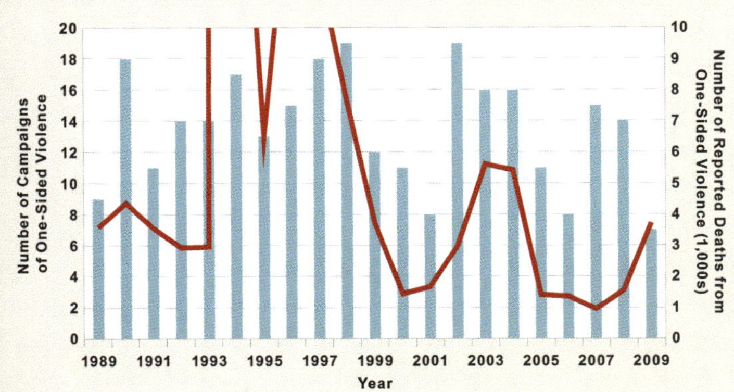

Sub-Saharan Africa

Deadly campaigns in Rwanda in 1994 and in the DRC in 1996 caused deaths to peak (exceeding the axis limit here). Attacks on civilians in the region have been much less deadly since.

Death tolls in sub-Saharan Africa as a proportion of the global tolls have been much lower in recent years compared to the 1990s. The region suffered 93 percent of the global total fatalities between 1989 and 1999, but less than half the total between 2000 and 2009.

The region has also witnessed a decline in the number of campaigns of one-sided violence. Indeed, much of the global decline in campaign numbers since the mid-2000s can be attributed to the decline in sub-Saharan Africa.

Although sub-Saharan Africa stands out for having the highest number of campaigns of, and fatalities from, one-sided violence, no region was free of deadly assaults against civilians between 1989 and 2009.

Central and South Asia had the second-highest number of deadly assaults against civilians. The number of campaigns of one-sided violence in this region fluctuated from year to year between 1989 and 2009. In 2006 the region saw a slight increase due in part to new campaigns in India.

In 1998 deaths due to one-sided violence in the region spiked sharply. A campaign by the Taliban, which controlled the Afghan government at the time, resulted in nearly 6,000 civilian deaths. Since then, estimated annual death tolls in the region have varied between 500 and 1,500.

The Middle East and North Africa saw just 12 percent of the global campaigns and less than 2 percent of global fatalities. However, it is one of three regions—including Central and Southeast Asia, and East and Southeast Asia and Oceania—to have had more campaigns of one-sided violence in the new millennium than during the 1990s. In the Middle East and North Africa, the total number of campaigns in the 2000s was 85 percent higher than in the previous decade—a much larger increase than the ones seen in the other two regions.

Since the mid-2000s, however, the Middle East and North Africa has seen a downward trend in the number of campaigns. The number has decreased 60 percent from the peak year in 2005, while deaths have declined 65 percent since the peak year in 2007. As a consequence of the so-called Arab Spring, there may well be a considerable increase in both campaign and fatality numbers in 2011. At the time of writing, these data are still being collated.

> Since the mid-2000s, the Middle East and North Africa has seen a decline in the number of campaigns.

The most active perpetrator in the Middle East and North Africa was the government of Iraq, which committed one-sided violence against civilians in 11 of the 21 years covered by the data. Its activity spanned two countries, Iraq and Kuwait—though in Kuwait there were only two campaigns, in the context of the Gulf War in the early 1990s. In Iraq, however, the government perpetrated one-sided violence every year between 1991 and 1996, then again in 1999, and then every year from 2005 to 2007.

The East and Southeast Asia and Oceania region saw comparatively few campaigns of one-sided violence. The deadliest perpetrator in the region was the government of China.

During the Tiananmen Square massacre of 1989, government forces killed some 2,600 people, accounting for 27 percent of all one-sided violence in the region between 1989 and 2009. It is, however, difficult to obtain accurate information on one-sided violence in China and other countries with tightly controlled media. The death toll, in fact, may well be much higher than that which UCDP records.

In 2002 East and Southeast Asia and Oceania suffered the highest number of campaigns of one-sided violence in any year covered by the data. In Myanmar and the Philippines, deadly campaigns of violence against civilians were associated with state-based armed conflicts that were being waged at the same time. In Indonesia the majority of the deaths that year can be attributed to the bombings in Bali, which killed over 200 people. Although the number of campaigns in the region began to decline in 2003, the number of fatalities did not significantly decline again until 2008 and 2009.

Like East and Southeast Asia and Oceania, the Americas region has accounted for only a small proportion of the total campaigns of one-sided violence, and most killed fewer than 100 civilians a year.

The deadliest campaign in the region took place in 2001 in the United States. The deaths associated with the events on 11 September accounted for 45 percent of the global total deaths due to one-sided violence that year.

> The perpetrators of the highest number of campaigns in the Americas were FARC and AUC. The campaigns are connected to the war in Colombia.

The perpetrators of the highest number of campaigns of one-sided violence in the Americas were Revolutionary Armed Forces of Colombia (FARC) and United Self-Defense Forces of Colombia (AUC) non-state armed groups in Colombia. FARC perpetrated one-sided violence every year in the dataset from 1994, except 2007, while AUC killed civilians each year from 1997 through 2005, with the exception of 2003. These campaigns are connected to the ongoing drug-fuelled civil war in the country. AUC has also fought another rival group, the National Liberation Army (ELN), and FARC has long been fighting against the government of Colombia.

Europe saw the fewest campaigns of one-sided violence. But the campaigns that occurred in the region tended to be deadly, though the high deaths tolls may have reflected more complete reporting than may have occurred in some other regions. In fact, after sub-Saharan Africa, Europe saw the highest number of campaigns causing 1,000 or more deaths a year. This was primarily a result of the one-sided violence in Bosnia and Herzegovina and in the Caucasus region of Russia.

Campaigns in Bosnia and Herzegovina caused an estimated 40 percent of the global death toll from one-sided violence in 1992, and 53 percent in 1995. The Russian government's deadly assaults against civilians in Chechnya caused the spike in deaths seen at the start of the millennium.

PART II

APPENDIX

Estimating Battle Deaths: A Challenging Exercise[138]

There are currently two datasets that provide estimates of the number of worldwide battle deaths—i.e., combat-related deaths—that occur in state-based armed conflicts.[139] (*State-based armed conflicts* are those in which at least one of the warring parties is the government of a state.) Battle deaths include not only combatants but also civilians caught in the crossfire—deaths that are often referred to as *collateral damage*.

The Uppsala Conflict Data Program (UCDP) has battle-death data for the period from 1989 to 2010 and the dataset is updated annually. The Peace Research Institute Oslo (PRIO), on the other hand, currently has data from 1946 to 2008. This dataset is updated periodically.

The trends in battle deaths described by the two datasets are quite similar, as Figure A.1 shows, although the PRIO "best estimates" of worldwide battle deaths are higher than those of UCDP—several times higher in some years. (This can be seen more clearly in Figure A.2, below.) As Figure A.1 demonstrates, there has been a clear long-term, but highly uneven, decline in battle deaths since 1946.

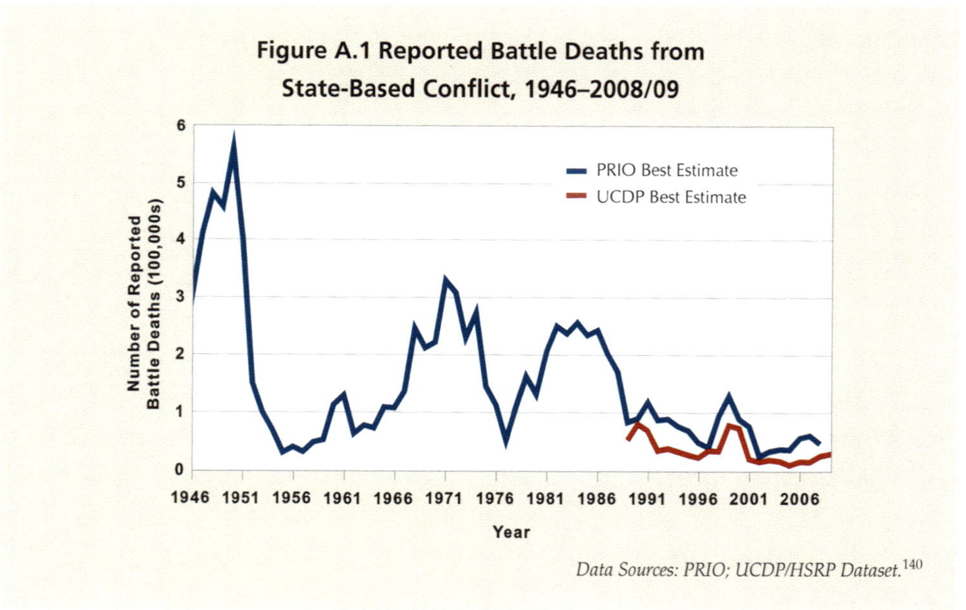

Data Sources: PRIO; UCDP/HSRP Dataset.[140]

The methods used by UCDP and PRIO are similar, but to understand why PRIO's best estimates are mostly greater than those of UCDP, we need to know how each dataset is compiled.

The Datasets

The PRIO dataset was originally created to determine if there were any long-term trends in the deadliness of armed conflict in the post-World War II era. The starting point for the coding of battle deaths was the list of armed conflicts from 1946 contained in the UCDP/PRIO Armed Conflict Dataset.[141] The coding was undertaken by Bethany Lacina.

The first iteration of the dataset was released in 2005 and covered the period 1946–2002.[142] The dataset has been updated twice, in 2006 and 2009, and the latest version covers the period 1946–2008. As of 12 March 2012, no final decision had been made on the next update.

UCDP, unlike PRIO, collects data on three types of organized violence. In 2005 data from all three new UCDP datasets were published for the first time in the *Human Security Report*. In addition to the battle-death data for state-based conflicts, UCDP introduced two new datasets—one on non-state battle deaths, and one on deaths from one-sided violence. Subsequently, each dataset has been updated annually—currently to 2010. Moreover, all three UCDP datasets have now been backdated to 1989.

Both the PRIO and UCDP provide "low," "high," and "best" estimates of fatality numbers for each year.[143]

Summary Estimates versus Incident Counting

PRIO and UCDP both use a wide range of sources in compiling their estimates. But there is one major difference between their approaches—one that helps explain why PRIO's estimates are generally higher than those of UCDP.

The UCDP dataset is compiled primarily by counting the annual total of combat-related fatalities (national and global) from reports of fatalities in individual violent incidents (battles, clashes, etc.) in each state-based conflict being waged around the world. To do this, UCDP uses a variety of sources, including news reports and on-the-ground reports from human rights organizations, local NGOs (nongovernmental organizations), etc.

This approach not only provides very detailed information about particular violent events but also gives UCDP researchers considerable confidence that they have a reliable estimate of the *minimum* number of battle deaths in a conflict. But since it is highly unlikely that all battle deaths will be recorded—particularly in conflicts where outside observers are banned from war zones—this methodology will almost certainly underestimate the actual number of battle deaths.[144]

By contrast, the PRIO dataset relies heavily on *summary estimates*—i.e., expert assessments of overall fatalities. There is no reason to assume that summary estimates will systematically undercount battle deaths as does UCDP's incident-based estimation method.[145]

In producing estimates of battle deaths for the early decades of the post-war era, PRIO researchers had no choice but to rely on summary reports of war deaths—which were typically estimates of how many people had been killed over the course of an entire conflict.[146] During these early decades, there was nothing remotely like the Factiva database, with its 35,000-plus news sources, that among other sources has enabled UCDP to undertake electronic searches for reports of individuals killed in battle.

Second, as noted earlier, UCDP data coders disaggregate deaths from organized violence into several categories. This means, for example, that UCDP will not count fatalities from intentional one-sided violence against civilians in its battle-death category, since these fatalities are collected in a separate dataset. However, the summary estimates of war deaths on which PRIO relies may well include the intentional killing of civilians along with battle deaths, because their sources do not always distinguish between the two types of violence.[147] Where PRIO battle-death tolls include civilian deaths that UCDP counts separately, the effect will again be to increase the PRIO toll relative to that of UCDP.[148]

Third, UCDP's stringent coding rules mean that violent deaths will not be recorded as battle deaths unless the identity of the perpetrators is known. But of course it is sometimes not possible to identify the perpetrators. Where this is the case, UCDP does not record the fatalities. This helps explain why UCDP's battle-death counts in Iraq are lower than the battle-death counts of other sources, and is yet another reason why PRIO's best-estimate battle-death tolls are higher on average than UCDP's.[149]

Fourth, another difference between the two datasets arises from the fact that UCDP updates its data annually. UCDP researchers may well find, and include, important new sources of data for early conflict periods that were not available at the time to PRIO researchers. The PRIO dataset cannot include these data until its next periodic update.

These four differences account for most of the variation between PRIO and UCDP battle-death estimates.[150]

Conclusion

Although the differences in battle-death counts between the two datasets are often considerable, the overall trends track each other reasonably closely as Figure A.2 indicates. Both datasets show a clear, though very uneven, decline in battle deaths over the past two decades, the period in which the two datasets overlap. If different data collection methodologies generate data that follow similar trends, then we can be reasonably confident that the trends are real.

This is important because the most prominent—and most contested[151]—finding that has emerged from more than six decades of PRIO battle-death data is that there has been a long-term, but uneven, secular decline in deadliness of warfare around the world.[152]

Notwithstanding their differences—and in part because of them—the two datasets are clearly complementary. Only the PRIO dataset has trend data in battle deaths for the first four decades of the post-World War II era, but only UCDP provides updates and revisions every year. This means that UCDP's data are usually more up to date than PRIO's and thus of particular interest to policy-makers. Plus, UCDP provides separate, but compatible, datasets on violent deaths from one-sided violence and non-state conflicts. Because of their incident-based method of data collection, UCDP is not only able to differentiate between distinct types of organized violence but the data can also provide more detailed information on where and when the deaths occurred.

As pointed out below, a primary objective of the PRIO dataset is to provide data on long-term historical trends in the number of battle deaths, while the UCDP dataset focuses on recent time periods and allows for more detailed and disaggregated analysis of violent events. Users must take this into account when choosing the appropriate dataset for a specific research question.

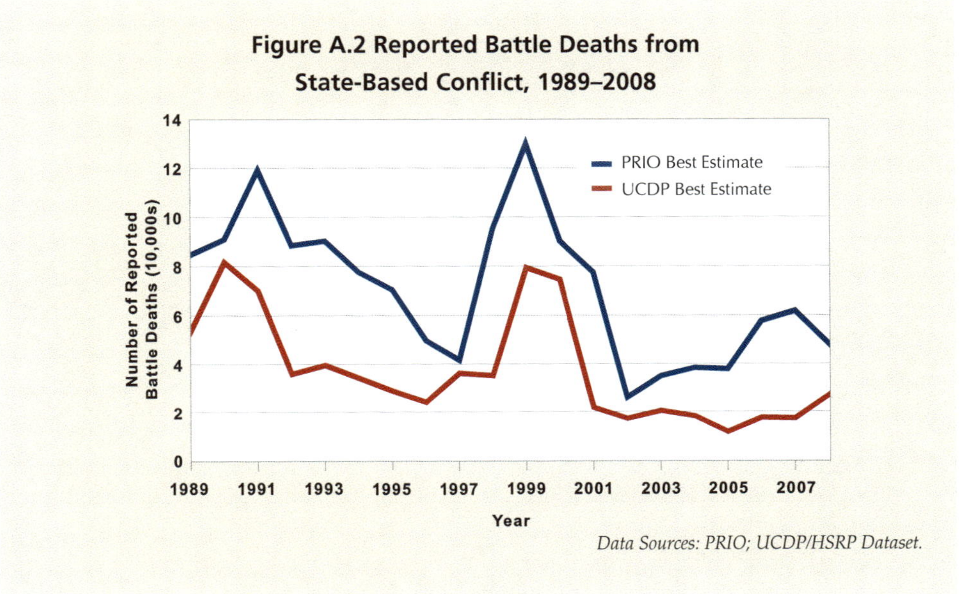

Policy-makers and other researchers can be confident that UCDP's data accurately reflect the minimum number of battle deaths that occur in each conflict each year, but its overall estimates are likely to undercount the true extent of the death toll for reasons spelled out above—and by UCDP itself.

PRIO's data, on the other hand, not only cover six-plus decades of conflict but will tend to provide higher, and often more realistic, estimates of overall death tolls than UCDP's battle-death counts, precisely because PRIO's methodology is not affected by the factors that tend to reduce battle-death estimates in the UCDP dataset. But it is also possible that PRIO's estimates, which are based in large part on judgments about the accuracy of sources, rather than on counting reports of deaths in individual incidents, will overestimate the extent of battle deaths in some cases. It is highly improbable that this would happen with the UCDP estimates.

We should also be clear that these datasets are not intended—nor are they suitable—for the sort of painstaking in-depth investigations of human rights violations and deaths from organized violence that Benetech's Human Rights Data Analysis Group (HRDAG) undertakes—often for truth and reconciliation commissions in post-conflict settings.[153]

However, HRDAG's intensive investigations often take multiple years to complete. They are essentially one-off exercises and are carried out only in a minority of war-affected countries in each year. As such, they cannot be used for mapping global *trends* in organized violence on an ongoing basis.

For researchers and policy-makers interested in understanding trends in death tolls from organized violence and what drives them, and in determining the impact of violence-reduction strategies, there are no substitutes for the trend data revealed by the PRIO and UCDP battle-death datasets. The datasets serve different but complementary purposes.

PART II

ENDNOTES

C H A P T E R   5

1   For the purpose of this chapter, the US, the UK, France, and Russia (USSR) are considered major powers. In some conflicts, such as in Iraq and in Afghanistan, the government may receive support from both major powers and other countries—the latter rarely involved in more than a minor combat role. Where this is the case the conflict is still treated as a civil war with military involvement by a major power.

2   Uppsala Conflict Data Program (UCDP), Uppsala University, Uppsala, Sweden/Centre for the Study of Civil War, International Peace Research Institute Oslo (PRIO), Armed Conflict Dataset v.4-2010, http://www.pcr.uu.se/research/ucdp/datasets/ucdp_prio_armed_conflict_dataset/ (accessed 14 March 2012).

3   This *Report*, like previous editions, uses battle-death data from two datasets. For the long-term trend from 1946 to 2008, we rely on the dataset compiled by the International Peace Research Institute (PRIO). Data from the Uppsala Conflict Data Program (UCDP) are now available from 1989 and are updated annually. The overall trends for the period where the two datasets overlap—the post-Cold War period—are very similar. There are, however, differences in absolute death tolls between the two datasets that reflect the different approaches to estimating battle deaths. UCDP's methodology, which requires much more detail in order to code battle deaths, tends to report lower battle-death tolls. The number of battle deaths reported by either UCDP or PRIO for any individual conflict should therefore be treated with caution, but the trend is reliable (see Appendix for more details).

4   We consider the post-Cold War period to start in 1989.

5   Each *conflict* year represents a calendar year in which a conflict was ongoing. Most calendar years involve more than one conflict year because more than one conflict was being fought during that year.

6   The long-term trend remains the same steep decline shown in Figure 10.4 of the last *Human Security Report*, however the numbers are different. The last *Human Security Report* used PRIO data for 1946–2001 and UCDP data for 2002–2008. Figure 5.2 in this *Report* only uses PRIO data and ends in 2008, the last year of the dataset. UCDP data, which cover the period 1989–2009, are graphed separately.

The Human Security Report Project (HSRP) has also changed how it calculates best estimates for the PRIO dataset in cases where PRIO has not provided a best estimate. In the past, HSRP calculated the straight average. HSRP now uses the geometric mean to calculate best estimates. This reduces the upward bias when there is a substantial difference between the high and low battle-death estimates.

7   Centre for the Study of Civil War, International Peace Research Institute Oslo (PRIO), Battle Deaths Dataset 3.0, http://www.prio.no/CSCW/Datasets/Armed-Conflict/Battle-Deaths/The-Battle-Deaths-Dataset-version-30/ (accessed 14 March 2012), updated from Bethany Lacina and Nils Petter Gleditsch, "Monitoring Trends in Global Combat: A New Dataset of Battle Deaths," *European Journal of Population* 21, no. 2–3 (2005): doi: 10.1007/s10680-005-6851-6.

8   This last conflict was also associated with significant levels of *one-sided violence*—deaths due to targeted attacks on civilians by government forces or by formally organized non-state armed groups. See Chapter 8 of this *Report* for more analysis of this type of organized violence.

9   HSRP, *Human Security Report 2009/2010: The Causes of Peace and the Shrinking Costs of War* (New York: Oxford University Press, 2011), 160.

10   The battle-death data graphed here are similar to, but not exactly the same as, those shown in Figure 10.4 of the last *Human Security Report*. The last *Human Security Report* used PRIO data for 1946–2001, and UCDP data for 2002–2008. Figure 5.4 only uses UCDP data, which are now available for the period 1989–2009. PRIO data are graphed separately.

11   Uppsala Conflict Data Program (UCDP), Uppsala University, Uppsala, Sweden/ Human Security Report Project, School for International Studies, Simon Fraser University, Vancouver, Canada.

12   While no one doubts that the war-related death toll in the DRC was very high, the last *Human Security Report* demonstrated that the much-cited estimated 5.4 million death toll is a substantial overestimate. Nor is the claim that the war in the DRC is the world's deadliest conflict since the end of World War II correct. Deaths from organized violence— both in total numbers and per population—were many times higher during the Korean War, for example. See HSRP, *Human Security Report 2009/2010*, 121.

13   Some intrastate conflicts are internationalized in only some of the years of the conflict. Following the coding of the UCDP dataset, the term *internationalized intrastate conflict* in this chapter refers only to conflict years (see endnote 5) with external military intervention. When comparing internationalized intrastate conflicts with other types of conflicts, we check the robustness of our findings by comparing all civil conflicts that have ever had foreign military involvement with those that have never had such an involvement.

With both definitions, UCDP data for 1989–2009 show internationalized intrastate conflicts as just over twice as deadly as other intrastate conflicts. PRIO data from 1946 to 2008 confirm this with the latter definition. When considering conflict years, PRIO data show internationalized intrastate conflicts as nearly four times as deadly on average as other intrastate conflicts.

14   The definition of internationalized intrastate conflict excludes solely indirect military assistance, such as the provision of arms. Internationalized intrastate conflicts, however, include some cases in which fighting occurs outside the territory of the disputed government. The rebel group may be fighting the forces of more than one government but has only stated its intention to target one, so all related deaths are considered part of that conflict, and the forces of the other governments are considered to be fighting on behalf of the targeted government. These cases include the fighting in Sudan, the Central African Republic, and the DRC involving the Lord's Resistance Army (LRA), which is in conflict with Uganda; the fighting in the DRC involving the Democratic Forces for the Liberation of Rwanda (FDLR), which is in conflict with Rwanda; plus, the fighting in Afghanistan, Pakistan, Saudi Arabia, Somalia, and Yemen involving al-Qaida, which UCDP codes as conflict with the US.

15   Most peacekeeping missions start when a peace process is already significantly advanced. Peace agreements tend to be in place before the UN deploys a peacekeeping mission, which is then mandated to support that peace. This role is quite different from military operations intended to secure victory for one side of the conflict.

16   Bethany Lacina, "Explaining the Severity of Civil Wars," *Journal of Conflict Resolution* 50, no. 2 (2006): 285–287, doi: 10.1177/0022002705284828 (accessed 13 August 2012).

17   Kristine Eck, "From Armed Conflict to War: Ethnic Mobilization and Conflict Intensification," *International Studies Quarterly* 53, no. 2 (2009): 380, doi: 10.1111/j.1468-2478.2009.00538.x (accessed 13 August 2012).

18   Patrick M. Regan, "Third-Party Interventions and the Duration of Intrastate Conflicts," *Journal of Conflict Resolution* 46, no. 1 (2002): 57, doi: 10.1177/0022002702046001004 (accessed 13 August 2012).

19   See, for example, Paul Collier, Anke Hoeffler, and Måns Söderbom, "On the Duration of Civil War," *Journal of Peace Research* 41, no. 3 (2004): 253–273. doi:10.1177/0022343304043769.

20   See Regan, "Third-Party Interventions," 55–73.

21   See, for example, Dylan Balch-Lindsey and Andrew J. Enterline, "Killing Time: The World Politics of Civil War Duration, 1820–1992," *International Studies Quarterly* 44, no. 4 (2000): 615–642. Ibrahim A. Elbadawi and Nicholas Sambanis, "External Interventions and the Duration of Civil Wars" (unpublished manuscript, World Bank, March 2000), http://www-wds.worldbank.org/external/default/WDSContentServer/IW3P/IB/2000/09/30/000094946_00091405494827/additional/122522322_20041117154546.pdf; Regan, "Third-Party Interventions," 55–73.

22   David E. Cunningham, "Blocking Resolution: How External States Can Prolong Civil Wars," *Journal of Peace Research* 47, no. 2 (2010): 124–125, doi: 10.1177/0022343309353488 (accessed 13 August 2012).

23 The US also supported the National Union for the Total Independence of Angola (UNITA) but not with armed forces on the ground.

24 Cunningham, "Blocking Resolution," 116–117.

25 Therese Pettersson, "Pillars of Strength: External Support to Warring Parties," in *States in Armed Conflict 2010*, edited by Therese Pettersson and Lotta Themner (Uppsala: Uppsala University, 2011), 51.

26 Bethany Lacina, "Explaining the Severity of Civil Wars," 285.

27 Ibid., 286.

28 Andrea Kathryn Talentino, whose definition is broader than the one we use here for internationalized intrastate conflict, also finds an increase in intervention following the end of the Cold War: "[o]f all post-Cold War [conflicts], 71 percent saw some form of intervention, compared to 59 percent during the Cold War." Andrea Kathryn Talentino, *Military Intervention after the Cold War: The Evolution of Theory and Practice* (Athens: Ohio University Press, 2005), 26.

29 These data include interstate conflicts. However, because interstate conflicts have been very rare in the new millennium, the recent surge in conflicts with external troop support is almost entirely in internationalized intrastate conflicts. See Pettersson, "Pillars of Strength," 49, 57.

30 The number of internationalized intrastate conflicts is significantly lower than the number of intrastate conflicts in every year. This in large part explains why the trend in Figure 5.2 is more uneven than that of the intrastate conflicts.

31 Although China may also come to mind as a major power, we do not include it in this list, as China has not been involved in any internationalized intrastate conflicts since 1989.

32 As we showed in our last *Report*, France, the UK, the US, and Russia (USSR) have each been involved in more international conflicts—which include interstate as well as internationalized intrastate—since the end of World War II than any other state. HSRP, *Human Security Report 2009/2010*, 165.

33 In some cases, the conflict may involve both major and other powers, such as in the Kosovo conflict in 1999, fought between the Serbian military and US-supported Kosovo rebel force, with additional military forces from other NATO countries. For the purpose of this discussion, we consider these conflicts to be civil wars with external military support by a major power.

34 Ann Hironaka, *Neverending Wars: The International Community, Weak States, and the Perpetuation of Civil War* (Cambridge, MA: Harvard University Press, 2008), 155.

35 HSRP, *Human Security Report 2009/2010*.

CHAPTER 6

36   An extended version of the arguments made in this chapter has appeared in Sebastian Merz, "Less Conflict, More Peace? Understanding Trends in Conflict Persistence," in *Conflict, Security & Development* 12, no. 3 (2012): 201–226. doi:10.1080/14678802.2012.703532.

37   Fen Osler Hampson, Chester A. Crocker, and Pamela Aall, "If the World's Getting More Peaceful, Why Are We Still in Danger?" *Globe and Mail*, 20 October 2005, A25.

38   James D. Fearon, "Why Do Some Civil Wars Last So Much Longer than Others?" *Journal of Peace Research* 41, no. 3 (2004): 275–301, 275, doi: 10.1177/0022343304043770 (accessed 13 August 2012).

39   Paul Collier, *Breaking the Conflict Trap: Civil War and Development Policy*, ed. World Bank, A World Bank policy research report (Washington, DC: World Bank; Oxford University Press, 2003), 99–100; Ann Hironaka, *Neverending wars: The International Community, Weak States, and the Perpetuation of Civil War* (Cambridge, MA: Harvard University Press, 2005), 4.

40   The World Bank, *World Development Report 2011: Conflict, Security, and Development* (Washington, DC: The International Bank for Reconstruction and Development/The World Bank, 2011), 57.

41   Unlike in other chapters of this *Report*, the term *conflict* will in this chapter refer only to intrastate conflicts. This includes *internationalized intrastate* conflicts where foreign troops are involved on at least one side. The category of intrastate conflict also includes a number of bloody coups d'etat. Note that because coups are very short and occurred most frequently during the Cold War years, the inclusion of some of these coups makes conflicts that occurred prior to 1989 appear shorter than if all coups were excluded. Even so, the data show that Cold War-era conflicts have tended to last longer than more recent conflicts.

42   Paul Collier, Anke Hoeffler, and Måns Söderbom, "On the Duration of Civil War," *Journal of Peace Research* 41, no. 3 (2004); 253–273, 257. doi: 10.1177/0022343304043769; Fearon, "Why Do Some Civil Wars Last So Much Longer than Others?" 278–279.

43   At the core of UCDP/PRIO's definition of *conflict* is the "contested incompatibility" between the warring parties, which could be over the control of government power or over control of a specific territory. According to this definition, there can be only one conflict over government in a country, which means that in a few cases, episodes of fighting involving unrelated rebel groups are coded as part of the same conflict, even if those episodes occurred many years apart. Such cases are relatively rare, but we have checked our findings that refer to the duration of entire conflicts by using alternate definitions of conflicts. For this, we coded as a new conflict over government any cases where the conflict had been inactive for 10 or more years and the rebel side had changed completely. The result was not appreciably different.

44   As a consequence of this coding rule, the coding of terminations lags one year behind all other conflict data; in other words, the data presented in this *Report* include conflict outbreaks through 2009 and conflict terminations through 2008.

45   The start date of a conflict episode is the first day when a conflict (for the first time, or for the first time after at least a year of nonactivity) reaches the threshold of 25 battle deaths in a year; the end date is the last day of fighting before a full calendar year of inactivity. See Joakim Kreutz, *UCDP Conflict Termination Dataset Codebook*, Version 2010-1, http://www.pcr.uu.se/digitalAssets/55/55056_UCDP_Conflict_Termination_Dataset_v_2010-1.pdf (accessed 27 May 2011).

46   We simplify the termination types from the UCDP dataset, using just four categories: peace agreements, ceasefires (which we sometimes discuss together as *negotiated settlements*), victories, and "other." UCDP differentiates between two types of ceasefires, which we count in a single category here, and also has two categories without specific outcome events that we combine in the category "other terminations" here. See Kreutz, UCDP *Conflict Termination Dataset Codebook*.

47   Crocker and colleagues use the term "intractable" specifically for conflicts that resist resolution. See Chester A. Crocker, Fen O. Hampson, and Pamela R. Aall, eds., *Grasping the Nettle: Analyzing Cases of Intractable Conflict* (Washington, DC: United States Institute of Peace Press, 2005), 5.

48   Collier, *Breaking the Conflict Trap*, 4, see also 82–83.

49   Fearon, "Why Do Some Civil Wars Last So Much Longer than Others?" 276 (Figure 1).

50   Fearon does not distinguish between conflicts and conflict episodes. He considers a war terminated if there is "either a military victory, wholesale demobilization, or truce or peace agreement followed by at least two years of peace." See ibid., 279.

51   Roy Licklider, "Comparative Studies of Long Wars," in *Grasping the Nettle: Analyzing Cases of Intractable Conflict*, ed. Chester A. Crocker, Fen O. Hampson, and Pamela R. Aall (Washington, DC: United States Institute of Peace Press, 2005), 42.

52   When using the median value, which is less vulnerable to distortion by outliers, the rate of decline is almost two-thirds, from 3.5 years in the 1970s to just over 1 year during the 1980s, and has remained at that level.

53   Using the duration of entire conflicts rather than conflict episodes shows the average duration halved between the 1970s and the 1980s. Because conflicts may restart any time in the future, however, choosing total conflict duration aggravates the problem of truncated data.

54   The percentage of onsets of civil wars and international conflicts followed by 10 years of fighting—that is, the most persistent conflicts—dropped significantly after the 1970s, as we reported in the *Human Security Report 2009/2010*.

55 Uppsala Conflict Data Program (UCDP), Uppsala University, Uppsala, Sweden/ Human Security Report Project, School for International Studies, Simon Fraser University, Vancouver, Canada.

56 The graph ends in 2004 to make sure that all conflict episodes in the sample had an equal chance of reaching the five-year threshold.

57 The total number of civil war episodes of five years or more dropped during the 1980s, spiked in the 1990s, and declined again in the early 2000s. In other words, there is no consistent decline in the absolute number of longer-than-average conflict episodes when the length threshold is five years. This, however, must be seen in the context of an extraordinary increase in the total number of conflict onsets during the 1990s: twice as many civil wars broke out during the 1990s as in any other post-World War II decade. The trend displayed in Figure 6.1 shows that longer episodes increased to a much lesser extent, which means that long conflict episodes as a percentage of all conflict episodes shrank.

58 The overall trend is the same if we apply a 10-year threshold to the conflict-episode duration data. Almost one in three episodes starting in the 1970s lasted for 10 years or more. In the 1990s it was only roughly one in 11. If we do an analysis similar to Figure 6.1, but using conflict rather than episode duration, the trend is confirmed both with a five-year and a 10-year threshold (using conflict duration, however, again confronts the truncated-data problem described above).

59 Joakim Kreutz, "How and When Armed Conflicts End: Introducing the UCDP Conflict Termination dataset," *Journal of Peace Research* 47, no. 2 (2010): 244, doi: 10.1177/0022343309353108 (accessed 13 August 2012).

60 World Bank, *World Development Report 2011*, 58. The *WDR* cites UCDP/PRIO data and thus its results are comparable with the data presented here.

61 In our figures, we only include conflict terminations through 2004 and consider them recurred when renewed violence is recorded within five years. This is to ensure that all terminations have the same amount of time to recur, making sure that figures are comparable across time.

62 We simplify the termination types from the UCDP dataset (see endnote 46). The difference between ceasefires and peace agreements is explained in more detail in the box on pages 178–9.

63 Roy Licklider, "The Consequences of Negotiated Settlements in Civil Wars, 1945–1993," *The American Political Science Review* 89, no. 3 (1995): 681–690. The well-established finding that victories tend to be stable outcomes (not followed by another episode of violence) is not undermined by the fact that between 2000 and 2004, as shown in Table 6.1, victories have shown an exceptionally high recurrence rate of 50 percent, because the 50 percent figure is based on only four cases.

64 Page Fortna, "Where Have All the Victories Gone? Peacekeeping and War Outcomes" (prepared for presentation at the annual meetings of the American Political Science Association, Toronto, ON, 2009), http://papers.ssrn.com/sol3/papers.cfm?abstract_id=1450558 (accessed 5 December 2011).

65 The high failure rate of victories in the 2000s is based on a very small number of cases: two of the four victories counted between 2000 and 2004 broke down. Similarly, only very few ceasefires were recorded in civil conflicts before 1990, which may have been due in part to under-reporting. The small number of cases makes it difficult to discern reliable trends, because the results are influenced heavily by only a handful of observations.

66 Raleigh and colleagues analyze a sample of new geo-referenced data on conflicts between 1997 and 2010, and find that, on average, repeated fighting takes place in only 15 percent of the territory. See Clionadh Raleigh, Andrew Linke, Håvard Hegre, and Joakim Karlsen, "Introducing ACLED: An Armed Conflict Location and Event Dataset: Special Data Feature," *Journal of Peace Research* 47, no. 5 (2010): 651–660.

67 Several scholars have questioned the effectiveness of peace agreements and other settlements. Luttwak, "Give War a Chance," 36–44; Robert Wagner, "The Causes of Peace," in *Stopping the Killing: How Wars End*, ed. Roy Licklider (New York, New York University Press, 1995), 235–268; Monica D. Toft, "Ending Civil Wars: A Case for Rebel Victory?" *International Security* 34, no. 4 (2010), 20, doi: 10.1162/isec.2010.34.4.7 (accessed 4 April 2012).

68 As pointed out in endnote 46, the Uppsala Conflict Data Program (UCDP) differentiates between two types of ceasefires, which we count in a single category here.

69 Kreutz, *UCDP Conflict Termination Dataset Codebook*, 2–3, http://www.pcr.uu.se/digitalAssets/55/55056_UCDP_Conflict_Termination_Dataset_v_2010-1.pdf (accessed 27 May 2011).

70 Note that the dataset records only terminations followed by at least one calendar year in which the conflict does not reach the threshold of 25 battle deaths.

71 As Table 6.1 in this *Report* shows, the most recent recurrence rate for the years 2000–2004 is significantly lower than the 40 percent figure of the turbulent 1990s. Because two peace agreements signed since 2004 (not included in Table 6.1) have already failed, the preliminary recurrence rate for the new millennium currently stands at some 20 percent, but this figure will be subject to change as new data become available.

72 D. Nilsson, "Partial Peace: Rebel Groups Inside and Outside of Civil War Settlements," *Journal of Peace Research* 45, no. 4 (2008): 479–495, doi: 10.1177/0022343308091357 (accessed 4 April 2012). At this (dyadic) level of analysis, the failure rate of peace agreements in intrastate conflicts between 1950 and 2004 is a mere 10 percent.

73 Toft, "Ending Civil Wars: A Case for Rebel Victory?" 20.

74   Ibid., 20. See also the discussion of these findings in Toft, *Securing the Peace*, 61–62. Note that Toft's findings are based on a total of five failed peace agreements. In two out of these cases more than 10 years lie between termination and recurrence.

75   Toft, *Securing the Peace*, 62.

76   In fact, the reverse is very likely the case. Toft's finding appears to be driven by death tolls *before* a settlement. It is much more plausible that the willingness of the conflict parties to settle their dispute through negotiations was influenced by the high intensity of protracted fighting—a so-called hurting stalemate—rather than the other way around.

77   In Figure 6.5 we focus on the period 1989–2009 for which we have updated battle-death data and a larger number of observations than Toft's sample that covers the years 1940–2003. Terminations are included through 2004 to make sure that all terminations had an equal chance of reaching the five-year recurrence threshold; battle deaths are included through 2009. The patterns remain the same if the analysis is extended to the entire post-World War II period.

78   Fearon, "Why Do Some Civil Wars Last So Much Longer than Others?" 283; Karl R. de Rouen and David Sobek, "The Dynamics of Civil War Duration and Outcome," *Journal of Peace Research* 41, no. 3 (2004): 303–320, 307, doi: 10.1177/0022343304043771 (accessed 13 August 2012).

79   Halvard Buhaug, Scott Gates, and Päivi Lujala, "Geography, Rebel Capability, and the Duration of Civil Conflict," *Journal of Conflict Resolution* 53, no. 4 (2009): 544–569. doi: 10.1177/0022002709336457; Daron Acemoglu, Andrea Vindigni, and Davide Ticchi, "Persistence of Civil Wars," *Journal of the European Economic Association 8*, nos. 2–3 (2010): 664–676, doi: 10.1111/j.1542-4774.2010.tb00536.x (accessed 13 August 2012).

80   Fearon, "Why Do Some Civil Wars Last So Much Longer than Others?" 289.

81   Chester A. Crocker, Fen O. Hampson, and Pamela R. Aall, "Introduction: Mapping the Nettlefield," in *Grasping the Nettle: Analyzing Cases of Intractable Conflict*, ed. Chester A. Crocker, Fen O. Hampson, and Pamela R. Aall (Washington, DC: United States Institute of Peace Press, 2005), 6–7.

82   Bethany Lacina and Nils P. Gleditsch, "Monitoring Trends in Global Combat: A New Dataset of Battle Deaths," *European Journal of Population* 21, no. 2–3 (2005): 145–166, doi: 10.1007/s10680-005-6851-6 (accessed 13 August 2012); Hironaka, *Neverending Wars*, 124–125.

83   Stathis N. Kalyvas and Laia Balcells, "International System and Technologies of Rebellion: How the End of the Cold War Shaped Internal Conflict," *American Political Science Review* 104, no. 3 (2010): 415–429, http://stathis.research.yale.edu/documents/Kalyvas_Balcells_APSR.pdf (accessed 21 September 2011).

84   Hironaka, *Neverending Wars*, 151; Karen Ballentine and Jake Sherman, *The Political Economy of Armed Conflict: Beyond Greed and Grievance* (Boulder, CO: Lynne Rienner Publishers, 2003), 9.

85   Rouen and Sobek, "The Dynamics of Civil War Duration and Outcome."

86   HSRP, *Human Security Report 2009/2010: The Causes of Peace and the Shrinking Costs of War* (New York: Oxford University Press, 2011).

87   Patrick M. Regan and Aysegul Aydin, "Diplomacy and Other Forms of Intervention in Civil Wars," *Journal of Conflict Resolution* 50, no. 5 (2006): 748–749, doi: 10.1177/0022002706291579 (accessed 13 August 2012).

88   A. Escribà-Folch, "Economic sanctions and the duration of civil conflicts," *Journal of Peace Research* 47, no. 2 (2010), 129–141, doi: 10.1177/0022343309356489 (accessed 13 August 2012); HSRP, *Human Security Report 2009/2010*, 74.

89   Edward N. Luttwak, "Give War a Chance," *Foreign Affairs* 78, no. 4 (1999): 36–44, http:// digilib.bc.edu/reserves/sc094/finn/sc09436.pdf (accessed 18 November 2011).

90   Ibid.

91   Kreutz, "How and when armed conflicts end," 246.

92   Luttwak, "Give War a Chance," 36. In the *Human Security Brief 2006*, we provide a more detailed critique of this argument. See Human Security Centre, *Human Security Brief 2006* (Vancouver, BC: Liu Institute for Global Issues, University of British Columbia, 2006), 22, http://hsrgroup.org/human-security-reports/2006/text.aspx.

93   Barbara F. Walter, *Committing to Peace: The Successful Settlement of Civil Wars* (Princeton: Princeton University Press, 2002), 161.

94   Ibid., 90. For a different view on security guarantees, see Monica Duffy Toft, *Securing the Peace: The Durable Settlement of Civil Wars* (Princeton: Princeton University Press, 2010), 30–32.

95   Virginia P. Fortna, *Does Peacekeeping Work? Shaping Belligerents' Choices after Civil War* (Princeton: Princeton University Press, 2008). For a more in-depth discussion of the effect of peacekeeping and peacebuilding missions on the risk of recurring violence, see HSRP, *Human Security Report 2009/2010*, Chapter 4.

96   Michael Gilligan and Stephen Stedman, "Where Do the Peacekeepers Go?" *International Studies Review* 5, no. 4 (2003): 37–54.

97   James D. Fearon, "Governance and Civil War Onset: World Development Report 2011 Background Paper," http://wdr2011.worldbank.org/sites/default/files/pdfs/WDR%20 Background%20Paper_Fearon_0.pdf (accessed 9 August 2012).

98   Indeed, this is one of the objectives of the New Deal for Engagement in Fragile States agreement—an initiative of the International Dialogue on Peacebuilding and Statebuilding—that was concluded at the Fourth High Level Forum on Aid Effectiveness at Busan, South Korea, on 1 December 2011.

CHAPTER 7

99 For more discussion about the shift in armed conflict, see Mary Kaldor, *New & Old Wars: Organized Violence in a Global Era*, 2nd ed. (Cambridge [England]; Malden, MA: Polity Press,2006); Jacob Bercovitch and Richard Jackson, *Conflict Resolution in the Twenty-First Century: Principles, Methods, and Approaches* (Ann Arbor, MI: University of Michigan Press, 2009); Martin van Creveld, "The Transformation of War Revisited," *Small Wars & Insurgencies* 13, no. 2 (2002): 3–15. doi: 10.1080/09592310208559177 (accessed 13 August 2012); *World Bank, World Development Report 2011: Conflict, Security, and Development* (Washington, DC: International Bank for Reconstruction and Development/World Bank, 2011), 53, http://wdr2011.worldbank.org/fulltext (accessed 13 December 2011).

100 Kristine Eck, Joakim Kreutz, and Ralph Sundberg, "Introducing the UCDP Non-State Conflict Dataset,"Uppsala University, 2010, unpublished manuscript.

101 UCDP codes broad categories of identification, such as Christian and Muslim, by country; an example would be Christians versus Muslims in Nigeria. A global conflict between Christians and Muslims, by contrast, would not be coded in this dataset. See Ralph Sundberg, *Non-State Conflict Dataset Codebook v 2.3-2010* (Uppsala, Sweden: Uppsala University, Department of Peace and Conflict Research, 2009), 3.

102 Uppsala Conflict Data Program (UCDP), Uppsala University, Uppsala, Sweden/Human Security Report Project, School for International Studies, Simon Fraser University, Vancouver, Canada.

103 State-based conflicts, on the other hand, were recorded as active for 6.4 years on average. Note these figures are not directly comparable to figures provided in Chapter 6. Here we consider the cumulative number of calendar years a conflict was active, whereas in Chapter 6 we consider the number of consecutive years in a conflict episode, using more precise coding for start and end dates.

104 Therése Pettersson, "Non-State Conflicts 1989–2008—Global and Regional Patterns," in *States in Armed Conflict 2009*, Research Report 92, ed. Therése Pettersson and Lotta Themnér (Uppsala, Sweden: Uppsala University, Department of Peace and Conflict Research, 2010), 187. One reason that non-state conflicts have generally been short is that the majority of them are fought between groups that are less organized for combat than state actors. Few such groups have the resources to sustain long periods of fighting.

105 In the measure of duration used here we count the number of years in which a non-state conflict was active. The conflict does not need to be active for the entire 365 days of a given year to be considered"active"in that year.

106 In the relatively rare case of a failed state with no effective government (the situation in Somalia is a case in point), UCDP codes fighting between rebel groups and militias over government power as non-state conflicts.This will result in a higher number of non-state conflicts being coded than if one of the warring parties was holding government power.

107 World Bank,"World Development Indicators 2010,"(Washington, DC: International Bank for Reconstruction and Development/World Bank, 2010), http://data.worldbank.org/sites/default/files/wdi-final.pdf (accessed 5 April 2012).

108 Pettersson,"Non-State Conflicts 1989–2008,"195.

109 Recent research identifying such factors can be found in papers such as Håvard Hegre and Nicholas Sambanis, "Sensitivity Analysis of Empirical Results on Civil War Onset," *Journal of Conflict Resolution* 50, no. 3 (August 2006): 508–535. doi: 10.1177/0022002706289303; and Jeffrey Dixon, "What Causes Civil Wars? Integrating Quantitative Research Findings," *International Studies Review* 11, no.4 (December 2009):707–735. doi: 10.1111/j.1468-2486.2009.00892.x.

110 Robert Kaplan, "The Coming Anarchy: How Scarcity, Crime, Overpopulation, Tribalism, and Disease are Rapidly Destroying the Social Fabric of Our Planet," *The Atlantic*, February 1994, http://www.theatlantic.com/magazine/archive/1994/02/the-coming-anarchy/4670/?single_page=true (accessed 9 November 2011).

111 See N. P. Gleditsch, "Armed Conflict and the Environment: A Critique of the Literature," *Journal of Peace Research* 35, no. 3 (1998): 381–400, doi: 10.1177/0022343398035003007 (accessed 8 November 2011).

112 Halvard Buhaug, Nils P. Gleditsch, and Ole M. Theisen, "Implications of Climate Change for Armed Conflict," in *Social Dimensions of Climate Change: Equity and Vulnerability in a Warming World*, ed. Robin Mearns and Andrew Norton (Washington, DC: World Bank, 2010), 89–93.

113 Eric Melander and Ralph Sundberg, for example, describe non-state conflict as a "form of violence that carries a much lower cost of initiation than interstate and intrastate wars, and that is known to be much more localized in its geographic scope, and thus can be expected to be more sensitive to local conditions"; Melander and Sundberg, "Climate Change, Environmental Stress, and Violent Conflict," 8 November 2011, unpublished manuscript, 4.

114 Ibid.

115 Ole M. Theisen and Kristian B. Brandsegg, "The Environment and Non-State Conflicts," (paper presented at the 48th Annual Convention of the International Studies Association, Chicago, 2007), http://www.svt.ntnu.no/iss/fagkonferanse2007/intern/papers/Ole.Magnus. Theisen@svt.ntnu.noThe%20Environment%20and%20Non-State%20Conflicts.doc (accessed 9 November 2011).

116 For more on the debate, see HSRP, *Human Security Report 2009/2010: The Causes of Peace and the Shrinking Costs of War* (New York: Oxford University Press, 2011), 68.

117 Paul Collier and Anke Hoeffler, "Greed and Grievance in Civil War," *Oxford Economic Papers* 56, no. 4 (2004): 563–595, doi: 10.1093/oep/gpf064, (accessed 8 November 2011).

118 Collier and Hoeffler, "Greed and Grievance in Civil War"; James Fearon and David Laitin, "Ethnicity, Insurgency, and Civil War," *American Political Science Review* 97, no. 1 (2003): 75–90, doi: 10.1017/S0003055403000534 (accessed 8 November 2011).

119 Hanne Fjelde and Gudrun Østby, "Economic Inequality and Inter-group Conflicts in Sub-Saharan Africa, 1990–2008," last modified 10 November 2011, unpublished manuscript.

120 Joakim Kreutz and Kristine Eck, "Regime Transition and Communal Violence," 8 November 2011, unpublished manuscript.

CHAPTER 8

121 Joakim Kreutz, *One-Sided Violence Codebook v 1.3* (Uppsala, Sweden: Uppsala University, Department of Peace and Conflict Research, 2008), 2, http://www.pcr.uu.se/digitalAssets/55/55080_UCDP_One-sided_violence_Dataset_Codebook_v1.3.pdf (accessed 18 January 2012).

122 United Nations General Assembly, "Convention on the Prevention and Punishment of the Crime of Genocide," http://www.hrweb.org/legal/genocide.html (accessed 28 November 2011).

123 Madelyn H.-R. Hicks et al., "Global Comparison of Warring Groups in 2002–2007: Fatalities from Targeting Civilians vs. Fighting Battles," *PLoS ONE 6*, no. 9 (2011): 1–14, 2, doi: 10.1371/journal.pone.0023976 (accessed 13 April 2012).

124 Ibid.

125 Mary Kaldor, *New & Old Wars: Organized Violence in a Global Era*, 2nd ed. (Cambridge [England]; Malden, MA: Polity Press, 2006). See also our discussion of these claims in Chapter 3 of this *Report*.

126 Chyanda M. Querido, "State-Sponsored Mass Killing in African Wars—Greed or Grievance?" *International Advances in Economic Research* 15, no. 3 (2009): 351–361, doi: 10.1007/s11294-009-9207-x (accessed 13 April 2012).

127 Kristine Eck and Lisa Hultman, "One-Sided Violence against Civilians in War: Insights from New Fatality Data," *Journal of Peace Research* 44, no. 2 (2007): 233–246, doi: 10.1177/0022343307075124 (accessed 13 April 2012).

128 Reed M. Wood, "Rebel Capability and Strategic Violence against Civilians," *Journal of Peace Research* 47, no. 5 (2010): 601–614, doi: 10.1177/0022343310376473.

129 Lisa Hultman, "Keeping Peace or Spurring Violence? Unintended Effects of Peace Operations on Violence against Civilians," *Civil Wars* 12, nos. 1–2 (2010): 29–46, doi: 10.1080/13698249.2010.484897 (accessed 13 April 2012).

130 Ibid., 30.

131 Margit Bussmann and Gerald Schneider, "A Porous Humanitarian Shield: The Laws of War, the Red Cross, and the Killing of Civilians," September 2010, unpublished manuscript, http://147.142.190.246/joomla/peio/files2011/papers/Bussmann,%20Schneider%20 27.09.2010.pdf (accessed 8 September 2011).

132 Uppsala Conflict Data Program (UCDP), Uppsala University, Uppsala, Sweden/ Human Security Report Project, School for International Studies, Simon Fraser University, Vancouver, Canada.

133 Lara J. Nettelfield, "Research and Repercussions of Death Tolls," in *Sex, Drugs, and Body Counts: The Politics of Numbers in Global Crime and Conflict*, ed. Peter Andreas and Kelly M. Greenhill (New York: Cornell University Press, 2010), 159–188.

134 The adjustments to the death toll were made based on new evidence from the UN *Mapping Report*, which was published in 2010. See Office of the High Commissioner for Human Rights, "DRC: Mapping Human Rights Violations 1993–2003," August 2010, http://www.ohchr.org/Documents/Countries/ZR/DRC_MAPPING_REPORT_FINAL_ EN.pdf (accessed 21 November 2011).

135   UCDP's high estimate for the Rwandan genocide in 1994 is around 800,000, while the low estimate is approximately 150,000.

136   HSRP, *Human Security Report 2009/2010: The Causes of Peace and the Shrinking Costs of War* (New York: Oxford University Press, 2011), 182.

137   The percentage of deaths that occurred in sub-Saharan Africa includes the Rwandan genocide. However, excluding deaths in Rwanda, the region still accounts for 61 percent of global deaths from one-sided violence.

APPENDIX

138   The discussion about the differences between the Peace Research Institute Oslo (PRIO) and Uppsala University's Conflict Data Program (UCDP) datasets on battle deaths from state-based armed conflict was initiated by Gerdis Wischnath and Nils Petter Gleditsch, with subsequent input from UCDP and the Human Security Report Project (HSRP). This overview, prepared by HSRP, reflects the views of all three institutions.

139   State-based conflicts from 1946 to 2010 are recorded in the now widely used UCDP/PRIO Armed Conflict Dataset.

140   Centre for the Study of Civil War, International Peace Research Institute Oslo, (PRIO), Battle Deaths Dataset 3.0, http://www.prio.no/CSCW/Datasets/Armed-Conflict/Battle-Deaths/The-Battle-Deaths-Dataset-version-30/ (accessed 14 March 2012), updated from Bethany Lacina and Nils Petter Gleditsch, "Monitoring Trends in Global Combat: A New Dataset of Battle Deaths," European Journal of Population 21, no. 2–3 (2005): doi: 10.1007/s10680-005-6851-6; Uppsala Conflict Data Program (UCDP), Uppsala University, Uppsala, Sweden/ Human Security Report Project, School for International Studies, Simon Fraser University, Vancouver, Canada.

141   See Nils Petter Gleditsch, Peter Wallensteen, Mikael Eriksson, Margareta Sollenberg, and Håvard Strand, "Armed Conflict 1946–2001: A New Dataset," *Journal of Peace Research* 39, no. 5 (2002): 615–637. doi: 10.1177/0022343302039005007, and the two websites, http://www.pcr.uu.se/research/ucdp/datasets/ucdp_prio_armed_conflict_dataset/ and http://www.prio.no/CSCW/Datasets/Armed-Conflict/UCDP-PRIO/ (accessed 27 April 2012).

142   Bethany Lacina and Nils Petter Gleditsch, "Monitoring Trends in Global Combat: A New Dataset of Battle Deaths," *European Journal of Population* 21, no. 2–3 (2005): 145–166. doi: 10.1007/s10680-005-6851-6. One version of the PRIO dataset has data going as far back as 1900. See Bethany Lacina, Nils Petter Gleditsch, and Bruce Russet, "The Declining Risk of Death in Battle," *International Studies Quarterly* 50, no. 3 (2006): 673–680. doi: 10.1111/j.1468-2478.2006.00419.x. The replication data are found at http://www.prio.no/cscw/datasets (accessed 27 April 2012).

143   More information on the coding of the low, high, and best estimates for each dataset can be found by consulting the respective PRIO and UCDP codebooks, available on the websites cited above.

144   For a description of UCDP's data collection methodology, see UCDP, "How are UCDP datacollected?" http://www.pcr.uu.se/research/ucdp/faq/#How_are_UCDP_data_collected_ (accessed 27 April 2012).

145   Summary estimations of battle deaths may be based in part on body-count data from the warring parties. Typically, both sides will tend to minimize their own casualties and maximize those of their enemies. Reliance on such data is not likely to lead to any systematic upward or downward bias, however.

146   To produce annual battle-death estimates in these cases, PRIO had little choice but to divide estimates for the entire period of the war by the number of years it had lasted. The researchers recognized, of course, that in reality, the probability that each year of conflict would have the same number of battle deaths was low. This is another cause of the difference between PRIO's annual estimates and UCDP's—the latter are always based on incident data of reported battle deaths.

147   They may also include some *non-state* conflict deaths—fighting between rival militias, for example, which would be counted separately by Uppsala.

148   Conflicts that are likely to include a high level of one-sided violence are noted in the documentation for the PRIO dataset.

149   This is an even greater problem with estimating deaths from one-sided violence, since few armed groups are likely to boast about killing civilians.

150   There are additional technical issues that we do not elaborate on here. Most notably, PRIO researchers do not publish best estimates for conflict years where they lack reliable information based on their set of sources. Using an average of high and low estimates to replace the missing best estimates as we do in Figure A.2 exaggerates the differences between PRIO and UCDP. Note also that the PRIO and UCDP battle-death data currently available are based on different versions of the UCDP/PRIO Armed Conflict Dataset, which means that some conflict years are coded in one, but not the other, battle-death dataset.

151   See Ziad Obermeyer, Christopher J. L. Murray, and Emmanuela Gakidou, "Fifty Years of Violent War Deaths from Vietnam to Bosnia: Analysis of Data from the World Health Survey Programme," *British Medical Journal* 336, no. 7659 (2008): 1482. doi: 10.1136/bmj.a137. See rebuttal by Michael Spagat, Andrew Mack, Tara Cooper, and Joakim Kreutz, "Estimating War Deaths: An Arena of Contestation," *Journal of Conflict Resolution* 53, no. 6 (2009): 934–950. doi: 10.1177/0022002709346253. See also Meredith R. Sarkees, Frank W. Wayman, and J. David Singer, "Inter-State, Intra-State, and Extra-State Wars: A Comprehensive Look at Their Distribution over Time, 1816-1997," *International Studies Quarterly* 47, no. 1 (2003): 49–70. See rebuttal by Bethany Lacina, Nils Petter Gleditsch, and Bruce Russett, "The Declining Risk of Death in Battle," *International Studies Quarterly* 50, no. 3 (2006): 673–680. doi: 10.1111/j.1468-2478.2006.00419.x. See also Anita Gohdes and Megan Price, "First Things First: Assessing Data Quality before Model Quality," *Journal of Conflict Resolution*, forthcoming (a response by Bethany Lacina, Nils Petter Gleditsch, and Bruce Russett will be published in the same issue).

152 See Steven Pinker, *The Better Angels of Our Nature* (New York: Viking, 2011); Joshua Goldstein, *Winning the War on War: The Decline of Armed Conflict Worldwide* (New York: Dutton, 2011); and *HSRP, Human Security Report 2009/2010: The Causes of Peace and the Shrinking Costs of War* (New York: Oxford University Press, 2011).

153 See HRDAG, "Projects," http://www.hrdag.org/about/projects.shtml (accessed 30 April 2012).